A SHORT

HISTORY OF THE HEBREWS

TO THE ROMAN PERIOD

Quum iustitia et dilectio quae erat erga Deum cessisset in oblivionem et exstincta esset in Aegypto, necessario Deus, propter multam suam erga homines benevolentiam, semetipsum ostendebat per vocem, et eduxit de Aegypto populum in virtute, uti rursus fieret homo discipulus et sectator Dei.

IREN. IV. 16. 3.

A SHORT

HISTORY OF THE HEBREWS

TO THE ROMAN PERIOD

BY

R. L. OTTLEY,

RECTOR OF WINTERBOURNE BASSETT, WILTSHIRE,
SOMETIME STUDENT OF CHRIST CHURCH AND
FELLOW OF MAGDALEN COLLEGE, OXFORD.

WITH MAPS

CAMBRIDGE:

AT THE UNIVERSITY PRESS.

1901

CAMBRIDGE UNIVERSITY PRESS
Cambridge, New York, Melbourne, Madrid, Cape Town,
Singapore, São Paulo, Delhi, Mexico City

Cambridge University Press
The Edinburgh Building, Cambridge CB2 8RU, UK

Published in the United States of America by Cambridge University Press, New York

www.cambridge.org
Information on this title: www.cambridge.org/9781107639850

© Cambridge University Press 1901

First published 1901
First paperback edition 2013

A catalogue record for this publication is available from the British Library

ISBN 978-1-107-63985-0 Paperback

PREFACE.

THE present "Short History" is an attempt to furnish teachers or students of the Old Testament with a sketch of the actual course of Hebrew history, somewhat more consistent with the present state of our knowledge than the textbooks now in use. The book presupposes, and is intended to encourage, a careful and intelligent study of the text of the Bible. With a brief outline of the history in his hands, a thoughtful student is probably best left to himself. In regard to many points of detail, he must freely use his own judgment, and the broad lessons, moral and religious, of the history, may be trusted to impress themselves on his mind without the aid of a manual.

I have not thought it desirable to distract the reader's attention either by minute discussion of critical problems, or by special reference to points of Old Testament theology. For practical purposes, the study of Hebrew *religion* may be well kept distinct from that of Hebrew *history*. With regard to questions of historical criticism, there is one period of obvious difficulty, namely, that which is covered by Chapters II. and III. It has seemed best, in dealing with the patriarchal and nomadic stages in Israel's history, to follow the plan of Kittel[1], so far as to give an outline of the Hebrew tradition, with a few introductory remarks, touching upon the peculiar nature of the narrative, and a brief concluding summary of what may be called its historical substance. In spite of the industry and research which well-known writers have devoted to this period, the results of archaeology cannot be fairly said to have corroborated the actual incidents recorded in Genesis and Exodus ; and it is

[1] In his *History of the Hebrews.*

hard to say which is the greater mistake :—to maintain, in face of the analogy presented by the early history of other nations, that the vivid narratives of the Pentateuch are literally, and in all their details, true to fact; or to assert that if they are not in the strict sense historical, they are therefore destitute of moral and spiritual value.

New discoveries may yet throw light on the substance of these narratives; but in the mean time, it seems our wisest plan to accept the ancient tradition for what it is worth, and not to devote disproportionate space to elaborate speculation as to the precise course of primitive Hebrew history, or to minute descriptions of the atmosphere and circumstances in which the patriarchs may be supposed to have lived. Whatever archaeology may still have to teach us, it is well to recognize the fact that the patriarchal period is described to us in narratives which were compiled in their present form about a thousand years later than the events they describe, and of which therefore, as Prof. G. A. Smith truly observes, "it is simply impossible for us at this time of day to establish the accuracy[1]."

I have generally employed the divine name JEHOVAH in preference to JAHVEH or YAHWE, as that form occurs in the Revised Version (Isai. xii. 2), from which all biblical quotations are taken. A list of books is given which includes those most accessible to ordinary readers.

R. L. O.

June, 1901.

---

[1] *The Preaching of the Old Testament to the Age*, p. 37. See the same writer's weighty discussion of this topic in *Modern Criticism and the Preaching of the O.T.* (Yale Lectures), Lect. III. Prof. G. A. Smith fairly sums up the state of the case in the following sentences : " While archaeology has richly illustrated the main outlines of the Book of Genesis from Abraham to Joseph, it has not one whit of proof to offer for the personal existence or characters of the Patriarchs themselves............This is the whole change archaeology has wrought: it has given us a background and an atmosphere for the stories of Genesis; it is unable to recall or to certify their heroes."

CONTENTS.

MAPS.

CORRIGENDA.

P. 85 note, [2] omitted.

Pp. 100 and 149, **for** *The Lord* **read** *The LORD*.

P. 166, l. 16, **for** 'were' **read** 'was.'

P. 179 note, **for** 'Ebion-Gezer' **read** 'Ezion-Geber.'

P. 262 (foot), **for** 164 **read** 165.

CHAPTER I.

EARLY NARRATIVES OF GENESIS.

THE history of the Hebrew race differs in one important respect from that of all other ancient nations. It is the story of a people which believed that it had been entrusted with a religious mission to the world. Strictly speaking indeed Israel's national history cannot be said to begin before the period of the exodus from Egypt, but the Hebrew historians could never forget that they belonged to a race chosen by Almighty God to proclaim His Name to all the nations of the earth. Accordingly they took pains to collect and to preserve with scrupulous care, not merely the popular narratives which described the supposed ancestry of the Hebrew people, but even those current traditions of the Semitic tribes which dealt with the origin of man and of the universe itself. The Old Testament accordingly begins with an account of the Creation, which is followed in due order by narratives describing the antediluvian world, the catastrophe of the Deluge, the formation and gradual dispersion of the primitive races of mankind. With the history of Abraham and his reputed descendants opens the record of Israel's own eventful career.

Corresponding to the unique character and vocation of

Israel is the special peculiarity of the Book in which the greater part of its history is related.   The Old Testament forms a library of national literature, containing a large amount of material which is not all of equal value or importance for the purposes of a modern historian.   The historical books were gradually compiled by a series of writers who regarded the rise and progress of the Hebrew race almost exclusively from a religious point of view.   It was not their aim to give a full and complete account of past events; nor did they attempt to harmonize strictly the various documents which they employed in the construction of their narrative.   Their object was simply to trace the chequered career of a divinely chosen and divinely guided people; to describe with such knowledge as they could command, its origin, its special vocation, its early migrations, its separation from other nations, its varied fortunes and achievements, its oft-repeated failures to rise to the height of its ideal calling, its sins and the chastisements which they provoked.   We may in fact describe the Old Testament history most correctly as the record of God's providential dealings with the people of His choice: in other words, as a 'Sacred History,' which, while it provides the historian with valuable material for his purpose, needs to be interpreted, supplemented, and in some cases corrected by evidence derived from other sources.

This brings us to the question, What original authorities do we possess for the history of the Hebrew people?   The Old Testament itself of course is of primary importance.   According to the arrangement of the Jewish Canon it consists of three portions, which were gradually arranged in their present shape, and were successively ranked as 'canonical Scripture' some time between the beginning of the fifth and the close of the third century, B.C.   The Law (*Torah*) comprises the five books of the Pentateuch.   This division of the Old Testament, sometimes called 'The book of the Law,' carries back the history of the Hebrews to its remote origins and brings it down to the close of the wanderings in the wilderness of Paran. The Pentateuch also contains various codes of legislation, which evidently belong to widely different periods or stages in the development of the nation. A large proportion of this legal matter is arranged in the form of an historical narrative, describing in detail the special circumstances under which the various enactments were supposed to have been originally framed.

The Prophets (*Nebîîm*) form the most important source from which our knowledge of Israel's history is derived. The name 'former prophets' was in fact applied by the Jews to four *historical* books: those of Joshua, Judges, Samuel, and Kings. The title 'latter prophets' includes the writings of Isaiah, Jeremiah, Ezekiel, and the twelve minor prophets (these last forming in the Jewish Canon a single book). The prophetical literature contains a considerable amount of actual history, but it is chiefly important in so far as it bears undesigned testimony to the moral and religious condition of the Hebrews during the particular epochs when the various prophets lived, taught, and wrote. These writings lay bare those currents of national thought and feeling which issued in the public actions, measures, or lines of policy adopted by Israel's kings or statesmen. They throw a vivid light upon the dangers, external or internal, which threatened Israel's welfare at different periods between the eighth and the third centuries, B.C.

The Writings (Heb. *Kethûbhîm*, Gk. *Hagiographa*), which form the third and last section of the Old Testament Canon, were probably collected at a comparatively late stage in Jewish history. For the most part they describe or illustrate the religious condition of the Jews, and their habits of thought and life, at a time subsequent to the return from Babylon (536 B.C.). They throw

but little light on earlier periods of Hebrew history.   Only a
few of the books can be described as historical works (e.g.
Chronicles, Ezra and Nehemiah, which were originally combined in a single book).   Others, such as Esther and Ruth,
seem to be historical only in form, and may be regarded as
'studies' of certain incidents or epochs of Jewish history,
written from a religious point of view and intended to convey
a particular moral.   None of these books however, considering
their peculiar character and the date of their composition, can
be safely employed as independent or complete sources of
information.

   Such, briefly described, is the nature and scope of the
historical documents contained in the Old Testament.   But
the evidence derived from this source does not
stand alone.   During the nineteenth century the
research of many scholars in various fields of
investigation has accumulated a mass of information which has shed a vivid light upon the course of Israel's
history, and upon the gradual growth of its religious customs
and ideas.   It is indeed a remarkable fact that Israel itself
supplies practically little or nothing that supplements or eluci-
dates the biblical narratives,—no inscriptions, no tombs, no
monuments[1].   But in Assyria, Babylon, Phoenicia, Egypt and
elsewhere, tablets, monuments and hieroglyphic inscriptions
have been discovered which illustrate to a remarkable extent
the primitive beliefs of the Semitic race, the incidents of
Hebrew history, the relations of Israel to the neighbouring
peoples, and other similar matters.   It is not too much to say
that recent discoveries have in a great measure revolutionized
the study of the Old Testament.   They have in many ways
vindicated both the honesty and the accuracy of the Hebrew

ii. Evidence of archaeology, inscriptions, etc.

---

[1] The inscription found in the tunnel of Siloam throws some light on
the topography of Jerusalem, but otherwise is of little historical interest.
For a description see Sayce, *Fresh Light from the Ancient Monuments*,
ch. iv.

historians; but at the same time they have enabled us to understand and fairly appreciate the necessary limitations under which they worked. We now perceive that the inspiration which we justly attribute to the Old Testament writers did not protect them from occasional errors and inaccuracies, nor did it hinder them from freely using their own judgment in the selection and arrangement of their materials. But although their manner of writing history was in general the same as that of other oriental historians, a careful and reverent study of their work makes it evident that they were in a true sense 'inspired': they were endowed with a God-given insight which led them to read history in the light of the divine purpose, and guided them to discern the true moral significance of the events which they recorded.

The historical books close with an account of the work of Nehemiah (*c.* 430 B.C.). For information respecting the subsequent period we have to depend for the most part on extra-canonical authorities.   iii. Later authorities.
The writings of Josephus and a few allusions in classical literature help us to some extent: but it must be admitted that comparatively little is recorded of Jewish history during the period of nearly 300 years between the death of Nehemiah and the age of the Maccabees. The first and second books of Maccabees are fairly trustworthy for the period which they cover, and there are various apocryphal and pseudepigraphic writings[1] which contain information bearing upon the history, and the characteristic beliefs, of post-exilic Judaism. Speaking broadly, however, the age of Hebrew history of which we are most easily enabled to form an accurate idea, is the eighth century, B.C., the period, that is, during which Amos, Hosea, Micah, and Isaiah fulfilled their ministry in Israel and Judah. The writings of these great prophets help us to estimate the real importance of the events summarily recorded in the

---

[1] *e.g.* some portions of the *Sibylline Oracles*, the *Fourth Book of Esdras*, the *Psalms of Solomon*, the *Book of Enoch*, etc.

historical books; they are amply illustrated by the evidence of contemporary monuments, and they enable us to understand the inner condition of the Hebrew people during what was perhaps the most critical epoch of its entire history.

The early chapters of the book of Genesis are concerned
The narra-
tives of
Genesis i.—xi. with ages even more remote. They contain extracts selected from the ancient folk-lore of the Semitic race, relating to the creation of the world, and the origin of the various races of mankind. The aim and purport of these simple narratives is clearly religious. Indeed the first eleven chapters of Genesis may be regarded as a kind of preface to the Old Testament, teaching in a poetic form those fundamental truths of religion and human nature which the Hebrew writers believed to lie behind the history of their own race, and to explain its peculiar calling and promised destiny.

The history opens with two accounts of the Creation of the world, the first (contained in Gen. i. 1—ii. 4 *a*)
The story
of Creation. apparently belonging to a document which forms the groundwork not merely of Genesis, but of the first six books of the Old Testament (the 'Hexateuch'). Owing to certain internal characteristics, this document is generally known as the 'Priestly writing' or 'Priests' Code,' and from its preference for the name *'Elôhim* (God) rather than *Jahveh* (LORD), its author is sometimes called the Elohist. The document is generally regarded as being of much later origin than the other Pentateuchal sources. There are two points worthy of special notice in connection with this narrative. First, it is not primarily intended to convey instruction upon points of physical science, but rather to inculcate certain religious lessons. It is quite beside the mark to enquire
(i) Its reli-
gious purpose. curiously into the relation of the biblical cosmogony to the ascertained facts of modern science. The important point is that Israel's sacred book begins with a *religious* account of the origins

both of the universe and of mankind,—an account which
is designed to render the whole subsequent story credible
and intelligible. For the history of Israel, it must be remembered, is a history of redemption : the underlying interest of
the whole Old Testament is the fact that it points from the
first to the accomplishment of a divine purpose of salvation[1].
That Almighty God, the God who specially revealed Himself
to the Jewish people, called the universe into being ; that He
existed before it and is distinct from it ; that all created nature
depends immediately upon His sustaining power at each stage
of its upward development ; that all things which owe their
existence to Him are essentially *good* ; finally, that there is
an 'ascent of life' in nature—i.e. a certain fixed order and
gradation in the appearance of different forms of life—these
primary truths are conveyed in the form of a simple and
singularly impressive narrative of the cosmogony which was
originally common to perhaps the greater part of the Semitic
race.

The second point calling for remark is that the Hebrew
account of creation is apparently adapted from
an ancient legend, which, in the form of an
epic poem, had been current in Babylonia
(ii) Its
Babylonian
origin.
from a very remote period[2]. The legend was in all probability cherished among the Hebrew clans and transmitted
to posterity. A careful comparison of the Assyro-Babylonian
story of creation with the narrative of Gen. chh. i. and ii.
reveals certain striking points of similarity between the two

---

[1] Cp. John iv. 22 'salvation is of the Jews.'

[2] Portions of this remarkable poem, inscribed on mutilated tablets of
clay which were excavated at Kouyunjik, were discovered and deciphered
by the eminent Assyriologist, George Smith. A popular account of them
is given by Prof. Sayce, *Fresh Light from the Ancient Monuments*, and by
Prof. Ryle, *The Early Narratives of Genesis*. See also the essay by Dr
Driver on ' Hebrew Authority' in *Authority and Archaeology, sacred and
profane*, pp. 9 foll.

accounts which conclusively prove their interdependence. In each case the drama of creation is represented as taking place in seven acts or stages; the same word in a slightly different form is used to denote the primaeval chaos, and speaking generally the same order is observed in describing the successive epochs of the Creation. But the points of contrast are not less remarkable. The Babylonian legend contains certain mythological elements which are clearly derived from a rude and primitive polytheism. It represents the Creation as the outcome of a conflict between two orders of deities, whereas the Hebrew narrative is in every respect consistent with the teachings of a strict monotheism. While the main outlines of the original story are retained, the fantastic creation-myth of the Semites is recast, and entirely purged of all those puerile and immoral details that might be inconsistent with the doctrines of a pure and spiritual faith. Speaking generally "where the Assyrian or Babylonian poet saw the action of deified forces of nature, the Hebrew writer sees only the will of the supreme God[1]." Indeed the very keynote of the Old Testament is contained in the master-thought which inspires the narrative, —that of the omnipotence and perfect goodness of the God whom Israel had learned to worship. And it is noticeable that the spiritual view of nature which pervades the story became habitual to devout Israelites. It reappears in such passages as Job xxxviii. and in many of the Psalms (especially perhaps Pss. civ., cxlvii., cxlviii.).

In Gen. ii. 4 *b*—25 we find a second account of the

Second narrative of Creation.

Creation evidently derived from a different source and introduced, so far as we can judge, with a widely different motive and purpose. The author of this passage holds chiefly in view the origin of *man*; he describes his first dwelling-place and his relation to other orders of created being. Internal evidence shows that the

[1] Sayce, *The Higher Criticism and the Monuments*, p. 71.

narrative belongs to a document which has been skilfully interwoven with the 'Priestly' writing, and is sometimes described as 'Prophetical', inasmuch as it seems to embody those ethical and religious ideas of which the prophets of Israel were the great exponents. The most striking point of contrast between the 'Priestly' and 'Prophetical' narratives of creation is a variation in the divine name. In Gen. i. 1— ii. 4 *a* the title of God is *'Elôhim*; in Gen. ii. 4 *b* foll., the characteristic name is *Jahveh 'Elôhim*[1]. Scholars have noted other differences between the two accounts, clearly pointing to two distinct traditions: e.g. the absence in the second narrative of any reference to successive 'days' of creation, and the appearance of man on the earth while it is yet unclothed with verdure. Not to dwell further on details, however, it may suffice to remark that the compilers of Genesis have here placed in juxtaposition two divergent accounts of the cosmogony, and the whole passage (Gen. i. 1—ii. 25) supplies the first example of those 'double narratives' of the same event which so frequently recur in the history, and which modern critical analysis of the Hebrew text has enabled us to distinguish. It is noticeable that the compilers make little or no attempt to harmonize conflicting statements. They are only anxious to preserve each tradition, so far as possible, in its integrity. They doubtless regard each as conveying some elements of sacred teaching, which it is important to preserve[2].

It is doubtful how far the 'Prophetical' account of man's earliest abode is connected with kindred Babylonian legends. A distinguished modern scholar has maintained that the site of Paradise can be recognized in a certain district of Mesopotamia,

---

[1] The usual symbol employed to denote the 'Prophetical' writer is 'J'; the 'Priestly' writer is generally referred to as 'P.'

[2] On the way in which the Hebrew writers employ the ordinary methods of Oriental historians see Kirkpatrick, *The Divine Library of the O.T.* p. 14. Cp. Sanday, *The Oracles of God*, pp. 27, 28.

but the identification of the spot is only a matter of interest
in so far as it strengthens the presumption that the Babylonian
epic of Creation also included a description of the Temptation
and Fall of man, which the Hebrews inherited from the race
to which they belonged and eventually incorporated, in some
purified form, among their sacred writings.

The interest of the passage, Gen. ii. 4 *b*—iii., 24 lies chiefly
in its teaching as regards man's nature and
destiny, the entrance of sin into the world and
its culmination in a divinely-inflicted judgment.
The story of the Fall (iii. 1—24) is an attempt to solve a
problem which from the earliest ages has perplexed and
baffled human thought—the problem of *evil*, its origin and
meaning. The account in Genesis is perhaps intended to
teach the true character and consequences rather than the
origin of sin. Certain great spiritual truths lie on the surface
of the narrative: that man, while akin to the lower orders of
creation in bodily structure, is yet capable of dominion over
them in virtue of his spiritual endowments; that his original state
as a being made 'in the image of God' though rudimentary,
was yet good and fair; that his upward development was
marred and perverted by the subtle intrusion of sin; that
the process of man's recovery involves painful antagonism to
evil. Thus the narrative, in spite of its poetical and childlike
form, gives expression to moral facts which certainly find their
verification in human experience. It prepares the way for the
idea and promise of Redemption which runs like a golden
thread through the history of the Chosen People, and which
culminates in the conception of a coming Messiah. The verse
Gen. iii. 15 is from this point of view sometimes called the
Protevangelium, inasmuch as it contains the germ of all subsequent Messianic prediction:

I will put enmity between thee and the woman, and between
thy seed and her seed: it shall bruise thy head, and thou shalt
bruise his heel.

> Story of the
> Fall. Its pur-
> pose.

The passage implies that the true destiny of man is victory in the inevitable conflict with evil. It contains only a vague hint respecting the manner and conditions of that victory; but the narrative strikes at the outset of redemptive history the note of promise and of hope.

The book of Genesis, having started from the fact of man's alienation from God through sin, proceeds to describe in broad outline the condition of mankind in the earliest ages. The narrative is very The primaeval world. fragmentary and seems to *presuppose* many circumstances of importance: for instance, the gradual rise of agriculture and pastoral pursuits, the practice of sacrificial worship (perhaps implied in Gen. iv. 4, 5), and the primitive custom of blood-revenge (iv. 14). It takes for granted a rapid growth of population after the expulsion of the first pair from Paradise (Gen. v. 4). In the main, however, the evident intention of the compiler is to illustrate the rapid development and fatal culmination of human sin. The disobedience of Adam and Eve is swiftly followed by the fratricidal deed of Cain (iv. 8)— a crime which was traditionally supposed to account for the curse that seemed to rest upon nomadic life—its restless wandering in the deserts and its jealous retention of the custom of blood-revenge. *Cain, we read, went out from the presence of the Lord and dwelt in the land of Nod* ('wandering') *on the east of Eden.* At the same time *the Lord appointed a sign* or tribal mark *for Cain* to protect him from the vindictiveness of other nomad tribes[1].

The story of Cain's banishment is followed by an enumeration of his descendants to the seventh generation. This passage (Gen. iv. 16 foll.) seems to be based on another tradition of Cain's history, The Cainites, Gen. iv. 16—24.

---

[1] If Cain was the ancestor or eponymous hero of the Kenites, as Dr Cheyne suggests (*Encyclopaedia Biblica*, vol. i. p. 621), the *sign* may mean the fact that Cain and his tribe were worshippers of Jahveh, and therefore had a claim on His protection.

representing him not as a homeless fugitive, but as the earliest builder of a city, and the founder of primitive civilization.   In connection with Lamech, Cain's descendant in the sixth gene- ration, we find the first mention of *polygamy.*   The three sons of Lamech, Jabal, Jubal and Tubal-Cain, are represented as founders of the fine and useful arts—the care of cattle, music, and the working in metals.   Hebrew folk-lore in this particular resembled that of many other nations, among whom the origin of the necessary crafts and chief conveniences of life is traced to legendary personages, divine or semi-divine.   Similar traditions existed among the Phoenicians, and have left their traces in early Teutonic literature, while the mythology of Greece supplies a parallel instance in the familiar story of Prometheus[1].   It is noteworthy that in this case also, popular legends are carefully purged of all polytheistic elements ; while on the other hand the strictly religious intention of the narrative appears in such a portrait as that of Lamech, in whom the moral character and tendencies of the Cainite race are sup- posed to be fully manifested.   Lamech's enigmatical address to his wives (iv. 23, 24) is apparently inserted with the design of illustrating by an example the temper of lawless violence and self-reliance which sin had engendered.   The fortunes of Cain's descendants are not traced any further; they had no permanent place in the story of redemption.

The descendants of Seth to the tenth generation are enumerated in Gen. v.   Six of the names in this list
The Seth- ites. Gen. v.   are closely similar in sound and form to those of the Cainites—a fact which suggests the infer- ence that the genealogies of Cain and Seth represent two distinct versions of one original 'culture-legend[2].'   The numbers seven and ten evidently constitute an artificial basis of genea- logical classification, and the analogy afforded by the prehistoric

[1] Cp. Aesch. *Prom. Vinct.* 436—506; Hes. *Theog.* 365 f.
[2] *i.e.* a legend describing the origins of civilization and the discovery of the most important arts and occupations.

myths of other races points to the conclusion that the names comprised in these two lists are those of legendary heroes to whom the origins of civilization, science and art, were popularly ascribed. The Hebrew writer however depicts these dim primaeval figures as mere men, and he employs the two narratives 'Priestly' and 'Prophetical' in such a way as to assign to the Cainites the invention of secular arts, while the Sethites are regarded as the founders of religious worship (Gen. iv. 26) and therefore as the direct ancestors of Israel. In Enoch, the seventh from Seth, the godliness of the Sethites finds its highest expression and reward: *Enoch walked with God, and he was not, for God took* or *received him* (Gen. v. 24; cp. Ps. xlix. 15, Heb.). The last-mentioned of the Sethite series, Noah, is represented, like Lamech, as the father of three sons, Shem, Ham and Japheth, who became the reputed ancestors of the three main races known to the ancient Hebrews.

One other point calls for passing notice : viz. the enormously long duration of life ascribed to the men of the 'ante-diluvian' age. Suffice it to say that it is quite unnecessary to insist upon the literal accuracy of the figures. The compiler of the different genealogies seems to have held some precise notions as to the length of the period that intervened between the Creation and the Deluge, on which all his calculations are based[1]. A parallel account of primaeval longevity is found in the folk-lore of other nations, who likewise assumed that prehistoric man enjoyed a longer span of life than his degenerate posterity[2].

The span of life.

---

[1] Probably the author of the "Priestly" document accepted the ordinary Jewish tradition that the interval between the Creation of the world and the expected advent of the Messiah was to be 4000 years. Of this period two-thirds (1656 years between the Creation and the Flood, and 1010 years between the Flood and the Exodus: total 2666) were supposed to have already elapsed at the time of the Exodus.

[2] Josephus, *Antiq.* i. 3 § 9, mentions the existence of similar traditions

In the Old Testament story, as in classical legendary lore, the duration of life is gradually contracted until it reaches a normal limit. No one has ever succeeded in basing upon the figures of Gen. v. any satisfactory system of biblical chronology[1]. In fact, speaking generally, we have every reason to believe that the early legends of Hebrew literature exhibit the same general features as those of other peoples. The primitive myths of the Semitic race were not discarded. They served to supply the popular imagination with a rude but intelligible picture of primitive antiquity, while at the same time they supplied a foundation on which religious truths and lessons could be easily based.

The sixth chapter of Genesis opens with a passage taken from the 'Prophetical' narrative, describing the wide-spread wickedness and corruption which drew down upon mankind the judgment of the Deluge. It preserves dim reminiscences of unnatural marriages, and of the existence of *mighty men of old* or *giants* (*Nephīlīm*). The *sons of God* mentioned in vi. 2 are most probably to be regarded as angelic or semi-divine beings whose union with the daughters of men was believed to account, if not for the actual origin of evil, at least for the appearance of a generation renowned, like the Titans of Greek mythology, for their monstrous and lawless wickedness. We even find in a later book of the Old Testament an allusion to this primaeval race of giants (Num. xiii. 33). The religious purpose however of the passage Gen. vi. 1—8 is to furnish a suitable introduction to the narrative of the Deluge which ensues.

The ante-diluvian world, Gen. vi.

'both among the Greeks and barbarians': he mentions as authorities Manetho, Berosus, Hestiaeus, Hesiod, Hecataeus and others.

[1] It is important to notice that the numbers in Gen. v. vary considerably in the Hebrew text, the Samaritan version, and the Septuagint. See the subject fully discussed in Hastings' *Dictionary of the Bible*, art. 'Chronology, O.T.'

A tradition of the Deluge is common to many races. Similar legends were current among the Greeks, Persians, Indians, Mexicans and other nations: but the Hebrew story is most closely parallel to

The Deluge, Gen. vii., viii.

a Babylonian version which was discovered in 1872[1] and which evidently forms part of an entire epic-cycle dealing with the origins of the human race. The Babylonian story may, for aught we know, be based on actual reminiscences of some devastating inundation which at an early period overwhelmed the region occupied by the primitive Semites; in any case it may be safely reckoned to be the real source of the biblical narrative. The 'Deluge-story' in Genesis, however, has been obviously constructed by the fusion of two somewhat inconsistent narratives[2]: an earlier and simpler 'Prophetical' tradition being interwoven with the more elaborate and precise 'Priestly' account. As in the case of the Creation-story the Hebrew compilers make but little effort to reconcile discrepancies in the two accounts. Their purpose is didactic and religious. Accordingly the Babylonian tradition is purified from its heathenish elements. The Flood is depicted as a necessary judgment upon sin, and the story is so told as to illustrate certain laws and methods of divine action, whether displayed in the chastisement of the wicked or in the salvation of the righteous. The favour of God crowns and rewards the obedient faith of man. Noah, we are told, *walked with God*, i.e. pleased Him[3]. As a reward of his faith and obedience he and his household are saved from destruction and with him,

---

[1] It was discovered by George Smith among the remains of the library of Asur-bani-pal at Kouyunjik, and translated by him in his *Chaldaean Genesis* (ch. xvi.).   See Ryle, *Early Narratives of Genesis*, p. 104; Driver in *op. cit.*, p. 22 foll.

[2] They differ in several important points, particularly in their account of the *duration* of the Flood.   Characteristic of P. are the precise details as to the structure and dimensions of the ark (Gen. vi. 14—16, etc.).

[3] Gen. vi. 9, LXX. τῷ θεῷ εὐηρέστησε Νῶε.   Cp. Heb. xi. 7; 1 Pet. iii. 20.

after the Deluge, is established the first of those 'covenants' between God and man which are so often alluded to in different parts of Scripture.   The covenant with Noah has

The covenant with Noah, Gen. ix. 1—17.

its appointed sign, the rainbow[1]; it is also accompanied by a gracious promise on God's part, conditional upon the observance of certain moral precepts by man.   In the two enactments mentioned in Gen. ix. 4—6 the compiler's apparent intention is to explain the origin of two fundamental customs of the East: (1) abstention from the use of blood in the eating of flesh, and (2) the forfeiture of the manslayer's life.   But it is worthy of remark that he represents the Noachic covenant as universal in its scope, embracing the whole human race and not merely the descendants of Shem.   In the same way the promise on God's part is one that concerns mankind and the whole creation.   It has been naturally supposed that the account dates from a period when Israel was in frequent contact with the heathen, and when Gentiles were occasionally seeking admission within the pale of Judaism[2].

The three sons of Noah are particularly mentioned as the ancestors of all the races of mankind known to the compilers of Gen. i.—xi.   To their detailed account of the forefathers of Israel is accordingly prefixed a brief catalogue of the other

---

[1] In Gen. ix. 13 the words 'I do set' seem to imply not an act of creation but a divine appointment.   There seems to be no parallel to this incident in the Babylonian Deluge-story.   On the ideas of other nations respecting the rainbow, see Dillmann, *Commentary on Genesis*, ch. ix. 17. The 'Priestly' compiler, in tracing the supposed origin of Israel's peculiar rites and institutions, takes occasion to give an account of the popular belief concerning the rainbow.   From the earliest times it was regarded by the Hebrews as a symbol of the everlasting mercy of God.   Cp. Isai. liv. 9, Apoc. iv. 3.

[2] 'This covenant was a law for mankind (Is. xxiv. 5), and in later times abstinence from blood was imposed on proselytes, and even on Gentiles in the early Church (Acts xv. 29).'   Davidson in Hastings' *DB*, vol. I. p. 513.

nations of the ancient world. Speaking roughly, SHEM appears
in this catalogue as the ancestor of Abraham and
his descendants ; HAM, whose impious conduct   The sons of
brought upon himself a curse instead of the   Noah.
paternal blessing, is the typical father of the despised
Canaanites[1]; while JAPHETH is the reputed ancestor of the
nations inhabiting the zone north of the Semitic world. The
tradition that *Noah began to be a husbandman and planted a
vineyard* (ix. 20) may possibly be derived from some other
source than that which connected his name with the Deluge : a
source which perhaps represented Noah as the original inventor
of the art of husbandry. Of the three sons of Noah, Canaan
is placed in subjection to his two brethren, who are both
solemnly blessed by their father, but Shem more richly than
Japheth. Noah is described as invoking a benediction not
upon Shem himself but upon *Jahveh the God of Shem* (ix. 26),
as if to intimate that the special privilege of Shem's descendants would consist in their knowledge and worship of the true
God. The fortunes of Japheth are made dependent on the
close and peaceful association of his posterity with the elect
race of Shem. Thus the oracle of Noah may be not inaccu-
rately described as "a Messianic forecast," in so far as it hints
at the universality of the. divine purpose of grace towards
Israel, and anticipates the benediction afterwards pronounced
upon Abraham (Gen. xii. 2, 3) and his descendants.

The ethnographical table of ch. x. traces to the sons of
Noah the origin of the other nations of the   Ethno-
ancient world. Characteristic of the biblical   graphy of
writers is the view that mankind forms a unity,   Gen. x.

---

[1] According to Gen. ix. 25, 26, Canaan was the son of Noah himself.
The traditional curse upon Canaan was probably recorded on account of
the shameless sensuality and idolatry which made the Canaanites such
dangerous neighbours to the later Israelites. Cp. Lev. xviii. 24 f., xx. 23 ;
Deut. xii. 30, 31. Their degraded condition is accordingly traced to an
ancestral curse provoked by the unfilial deed of their forefather.

and that Israel is only one of many peoples embraced in the
purpose of God, though specially chosen to be the channel of
grace and blessing to the rest.   The ethnology of this passage
is cast in genealogical form, but the names are rarely those of
individuals.   Such plural names as 'Kittim,' 'Ludim' evidently
denote tribes or communities.   Again, some names that might
have been looked for in such a list are absent: e.g. Edom,
Ammon, and Moab, races whose origin was traditionally
associated with a later stage in Israel's history.   The particular legend that connected the foundation of Nineveh with
a primaeval hero called Nimrod (x. 11) seems to rest on
a historical basis[1]; but speaking generally the table consists
of a somewhat artificial classification of the nations arranged
in order according to their geographical situation.

1.   Among the descendants of Japheth, *Gomer* (the 'Cim-
merians' of the Greek historians) may be a comprehensive
name for the tribes bordering on the Black Sea; *Magog* is
explained by some ancient writers to mean the Scythians,
by others the inhabitants of northern and eastern Armenia;
Madai are probably the Medes; in *Tubal* and *Meshech* may be
recognized the Tibareni and Moschi mentioned by Herodotus[2];
Tiras seems to be the title of an ancient Pelasgian tribe; *the
sons of Javan* (Ionia) include the most southerly of the northern
races; *Elishah* may represent the inhabitants of Sicily and
lower Italy, or possibly those of Illyria; *Tarshish* is Tartessus
in Spain; *Kittim* are the inhabitants of Cyprus; *Rodanim*
(probably the correct reading in x. 4) are the Rhodians.

2.   The descendants of Ham mentioned in the table are
Cush or *Kash*, a name given in later times to the district south
of Egypt; *Mizraim* are the two Mazors, i.e. Egypt, upper and

---

[1] See Dillmann *in loc.*; Ryle, *Early Narratives*, etc. p. 127.

[2] On the question whether Gomer, Madai, Tubal and Meshech are to
be identified with the *Gimirrai, Madâ, Tabali* and *Musku* of the Assyrian
inscriptions, see Dillmann on *Gen.* x., and Driver in *op. cit.*, p. 28.

lower; *Phut* is probably to be identified with some district of lower Egypt. The fact that *Canaan* is mentioned among the descendants of Ham indicates that the Israelites, by whom the Canaanites were eventually dispossessed, regarded them as an alien race[1]. *Sidon* ('fishers' town') was reputed to be the most ancient of the Canaanitish cities. *Heth*, the Hittite race, whose principal seat from very early times was the district lying north-west of Phoenicia, is loosely described as a 'son' of Canaan. In the same way *Mizraim* is regarded as the father of the *Ludim*[2], the *Lehabim* (Libyans), the *Pathrusim* (inhabitants of upper Egypt) and the *Caphtorim* (probably here used to designate the Philistines). It is noteworthy that *Cush* is reputed to be not only the ancestor of the nomadic tribes which occupied various parts of Arabia and north-eastern Africa, but also the forefather of the legendary hero who was popularly supposed to have founded the mighty empires of Western Asia. *Cush* we are told *begat Nimrod*[3]. The dominions of Nimrod were believed to have extended northwards from Babylonia and its cities *Babel, Erech, Accad, Calneh*, into Assyria. Recent research has Nimrod, Gen. x. 8 foll. indeed confirmed the fact that Assyria owed her civilization to Babylon, and so far the statement that Nimrod built Nineveh, with the suburban places[4] which formed a part of the great city, may have historical foundation: but there is some reason to suppose that 'Nimrod' is a mythical figure, and

[1] As a geographical term 'Canaan' (lit. 'the lowlands') was ultimately extended so as to include the whole of Western Palestine.

[2] Probably a people of lower Egypt, or *possibly* the Lydians, mentioned here because Lydian mercenaries aided Psammitichus, king of Egypt (663—610), in throwing off the yoke of Assyria. They became in fact a standing part of the Egyptian army.

[3] Gen. x. 8. Schrader and others consider that the mention of Nimrod is due to a confusion between *Kush* and a Babylonian tribe called *Kassi*, to which Nimrod may have belonged.

[4] Gen. x. 11, 12, *Rehoboth 'Ir* : literally 'open spaces' or 'squares of the city.'

that the name is really another form of 'Merodach,' the reputed king and patron deity of the city of Babylon.

3. The sons of Shem (x. 21 foll.) include the remaining populations of the geographical zone that lay nearest to the Israelites. Five different branches of the 'Semitic' race are enumerated. *Elam* ('high') was a mountainous region in Eastern Babylonia, the seat of an ancient monarchy which was at one time a formidable foe of Assyria. *Asshur* is of course Assyria. *Arphaxad* seems to signify Chaldaea[1], *Aram* includes the greater portion of Mesopotamia and Syria. *Lud* remains as yet unidentified, but certainly denotes a Semitic people. The list of Shem's posterity also includes various Arabian and Aramaean tribes, the identity of which is at present uncertain[2].

The posterity of Shem.

In the story of the building of Babel may be recognized a primitive attempt to account for that distinction of races and languages which was doubtless a matter of perplexity to the ancients. That the legend originated thus seems evident from the fact that the point of the narrative lies in the supposed meaning of the word *Babel.* In the language of Babylonia the name Babylon (Bab-Ilu) actually means 'Gate of God': but the close resemblance of the word to the Hebrew verb *balbel* ('confound' or 'mix together') suggested the notion of a primaeval confusion of tongues. The narrative is abruptly introduced by the words *they journeyed east* (xi. 2), which point to its being a fragment of some more detailed tradition, based on reminiscences of a real historical incident. In prehistoric as in later times, the vast plain of Shinar was inhabited by a strange medley of races[3]. On the other hand Babylon was supposed to be one of the most ancient cities of the East. Its gigantic

The story of Babel, Gen. xi.

[1] See *Encycl. Biblica*, s.v.

[2] The name *Eber* (Gen. x. 24, xi. 15) seems to represent a supposed eponymous ancestor of the Hebrews.

[3] Jer. li. 44.

towers, some of which may have been left unfinished or may have fallen gradually into disrepair, naturally suggested to the primitive Semites the notion that the great city had a mysterious and immensely remote origin. One slight touch in the story, the plural verb employed in xi. 7 *Let us go down*, is an indication that the legend was derived from a non-Israelitish and probably polytheistic source. We may believe that it was adapted by the compilers of Genesis to the purpose of conveying religious instruction. Underlying the narrative we can discern the Hebrew conception of sin as consisting in self-assertion and rebellion against God. The story also reflects the conviction that the separation of races is an evil, due to a primaeval curse which in the Messianic age is destined to be reversed[1].

This naive legend, like others we have had occasion to notice, evidently belongs to an age in which there prevailed on the one hand a powerful spirit of curiosity as regards the origin of things, and on the other, a very simple and childlike conception of the divine nature. Conclusion. Hebrew historians employed such legends with perfect freedom, nor did they hesitate to adapt or alter them in any way that might bring them into closer conformity with the spirit of their religion. Narratives of this class are not so much a substitute for real history as the usual form which it assumes in early stages of human culture. What a historian has said of the primitive Greek peoples is applicable to the ancient Semites, and indeed to all other races known to us. "These myths or current stories constituted the entire intellectual stock of the age to which they belonged…They furnished aliment to the curiosity, and solution to the vague doubts and aspirations of the age; they explained the origins of those customs and standing peculiarities with which men were familiar[2]." Hebrew folk-lore however differs from that of the

---

[1] Cp. Deut. xxviii. 49, Jer. v. 15.

[2] G. Grote, *Hist. of Greece*, vol. i., ch. xvi. *init.*

heathen races in its rationality, its dignified sobriety, and its almost entire freedom from immoral or irreligious elements. The study of comparative history, while it has clearly demonstrated the close connection which subsists between the early narratives of Genesis and the primitive myths of other Oriental peoples, has enabled us to discern in the former that controlling guidance and selecting action of the Holy Spirit of God which we commonly call 'Inspiration.'

The partial recapitulation and continuation of Shem's genealogy in ch. xi. 10 foll. forms a transition from the history of primaeval mankind to that of the chosen people. It leads us into the sphere of the tradition peculiar to the Hebrews. With the mention of Terah, the story of the Patriarchal age may be said to begin.

CHAPTER II.

THE STORY OF THE PATRIARCHS.

Gen. xii.—l.

IN approaching the Old Testament account of the Patriarchal age it is necessary to form some idea of its essential character and to estimate the degree of historical value that may be claimed for it. It

Introductory.

must be carefully borne in mind that the earliest period of Israel's development is rightly described as *prehistoric.* This period corresponds with what is usually called the 'heroic age' in Greek history, and the narratives relating to it are analogous in many respects to the folk-lore of other ancient nations. The story in Genesis in fact rather resembles an epic poem than history in the modern sense of the term. It deals with obscure incidents of early tribal history, of which we can scarcely hope to acquire exact or definite knowledge ; and since the primitive narratives were probably committed to writing in their present form at an interval of several centuries after the events recorded, we cannot expect to find in them a contemporaneous picture of patriarchal life. It can scarcely be doubted that the sacred writers occasionally depict under the form of personal or family incidents, events which are manifestly ordinary episodes of *tribal* life ; and they follow the common practice of ancient historians in idealizing to some extent the forefathers and founders of the Hebrew race, ascribing to them both the moral characteristics which marked their descendants, and the institution of such peculiar practices or customs as were familiar in a later age.

Accordingly, although many of the patriarchal narratives may well contain a historical kernel, we only do justice to these life-like and beautiful tales when we remember that those who recorded them were less concerned with the question of their literal truth than with the religious lessons that might be based upon them. Like the early historians of other ancient peoples, the compilers of the book of Genesis were dominated by certain religious ideas and convictions, in comparison with which the accurate knowledge of facts seemed relatively unimportant. They were far more deeply interested in the providential dealings of Almighty God, and in the methods by which He had chosen to reveal His will and purpose, than in the exact course of events in a remote past. In fact they employed the ancestral legends and oral traditions of their race—a race singularly gifted with imaginative power and religious fervour—as apt vehicles of spiritual teaching; and to treat these picturesque stories as if they were strictly historical in the modern sense of the term, is to misconceive not only the intention and aim of the writers, but also the very nature and characteristics of primitive history.

Thus for our knowledge of this interesting period we depend for the most part on narratives " of which it is simply impossible for us at this time of day to establish the accuracy[1]." At the same time there is good reason for supposing that the book of Genesis, after every allowance has been made for the natural bias or defective information of the original writers, contains a life-like picture of an age which really existed, and we are so far justified in accepting the account of the patriarchal period as being in its broad outlines credible. A nomadic stage in the development of the Hebrew

---

[1] Prof. G. A. Smith, *The Preaching of the O.T. to the Age*, p. 37.

people, such as the book of Genesis describes, seems to be certainly presupposed in the later history. Moreover, recent archaeological discoveries, even if they do not actually confirm the Scriptural narrative in all its particulars, at least render perfectly credible the general course of events described in it. It is now practically certain that the age of Abraham, Isaac and Jacob, fell within the limits of a period of which important literary monuments are still extant[1] ; and it may be fairly maintained that our present knowledge, derived from different sources, corroborates the tenour of the Biblical tradition respecting the ancestry and original home of the Hebrew race. There is no cogent reason for doubting that the migration of Israel's ancestors from Mesopotamia was actually the starting-point of a higher faith, based on conceptions of the divine nature and character which afterwards formed the foundation of the pure and austere religion taught by Moses and the Prophets. He whom Moses was commissioned to proclaim to his oppressed fellow-tribesmen in Egypt as their saviour and deliverer was none other than *the God of their fathers, the God of Abraham, of Isaac, and of Jacob* (Exod. iii. 16).

On the whole there can be little question that the book of Genesis gives us in the main a vivid and truthful picture of the general conditions of patriarchal life. Traditions respecting the immigration into Canaan of a small Semitic tribe lingered around *General conditions of patriarchal life.* certain sacred spots supposed to be hallowed by a special presence of Deity. The ancestors of the Hebrews wandered southward through a land already occupied by numerous and powerful tribes, Canaanites, Amorites, and Hittites, a land which had long since felt the tread of Babylonian and Elamite armies, and had been used for ages as a thoroughfare between Western Asia and Egypt. Their habits and customs were such as may be witnessed to this day among the Bedawin Arabs.

---

[1] See Driver in *op. cit.* pp. 35 foll.

They dwelt in black goat-skin tents among their flocks and herds, for the most part avoiding the tumult of cities and preferring the freedom of the hills and open plains. Now and then some sudden raid would compel them to use their weapons, or some dispute among the women or children of the tribe would interrupt the placid course of pastoral life. Proud of their race, they shunned any alliance by marriage with the surrounding tribes. They clung to their ancestral traditions, their simple religious observances, their family priesthood, their peculiar social institutions. In many respects doubtless their religion was closely akin to that of neighbouring Semitic peoples. They had their sacred pillars, trees, and other emblems of the divine power and presence; they carried with them *teráphim*, which were apparently images venerated as household gods. In many of their beliefs and practices they did not rise above the general level of their age. But they bore upon them the mark of a special consecration, and in an age when every type of false and debased worship was rife in the East, they carried with them wherever they went the secret of future greatness, namely, a faith, rude perhaps and imperfect but sincere, in the true God, the Maker of heaven and earth[1].

These general observations may well serve as an introduction to a sketch of the events recorded in the book of Genesis, chh. xii.—l. But something must first be said respecting the origin and affinities of the Hebrew people.

The Hebrews were originally a nomad tribe, akin to the Aramaeans (or Syrians), Ammonites and Edomites, and belonging like them to the Semitic race. The name 'Hebrew,' according to the most probable account, means 'dweller on the other side,' and it came to be applied by other Semitic tribes to the Israelites, with reference either to their early migration from the eastern to the

Origin of the Hebrews.

[1] See an interesting passage in *The Hebrew Tragedy* by Col. C. R. Conder, R.E., ch. i. (Blackwood, 1900).

western side of the Euphrates, or possibly to their subsequent movement across the Jordan into Western Palestine[1]. If this view be correct we may suppose that while the Hebrews described themselves as *Benê Israel* in token of their descent from a reputed ancestor of that name, they were styled by foreigners *'Ibhri*, a term implying that   Their migrations. they were anciently regarded as immigrants or intruders into Palestine from a district 'beyond the river[2].' Whatever may have been the original home of the Hebrew race[3] the earliest notices of its history indicate that its primitive ancestors removed at a very early date from Chaldaea into upper Mesopotamia, and that after a long sojourn in this region they migrated into Palestine together with the ancestors of Moab, Ammon, and Edom.   They were led by their pastoral instincts to seek out the districts best suited for grazing purposes.   Thus one large group of these Semitic nomads moved eastwards and established itself in the fertile district east of Jordan (Moab and Ammon).   The remaining tribes migrated southward and ultimately descended into Egypt, where they retained their pastoral habits, their language and peculiar tribal institutions.   The hardships to which they were subjected in

[1] The precise meaning and origin of the name 'Hebrew' is still much disputed.   Prof. Hommel holds that the land 'beyond the river' (*'Ebir Nâri*) originally signified the region *West* of the Euphrates where Ur was situated, and that the name was eventually extended to the country West of Jordan (*Ancient Hebrew Tradition etc.*, Appendix).   In Gen. x. 21 foll. the Hebrews (*'Ibhri*) are represented as 'sons of Eber,' according to the common Semitic idiom which expresses the facts of geography or ethnography in the form of a genealogy.   Cp. Sayce, *Early History of the Hebrews*, p. 7. On the question whether the name *'Apuriu*, *'Apri*, or *'Epri*, which occurs in later Egyptian monuments, is identical with *'Ibhri*, see Hommel, *op. cit.* p. 259. Dillmann, *Comm. on Gen.* xi. 12, says, " It may now be considered certain that the *'Apuriu*...are not the Hebrews."

[2] Thus in Gen. xiv. 13 Abraham is called 'the Hebrew' (LXX. ὁ περάτης) as distinguished from Mamre, the Amorite.

[3] There are some indications that the Hebrews originally migrated northwards from the desert region south of Palestine.

Egypt impelled them to seek a new settlement; the events of the exodus consolidated the tribes into a nation, the history of which, in the strict sense, begins with the age of Moses and with the establishment of the Israelites in the land already occupied by the Canaanites, Amorites and Hittites—races widely distinct from each other in origin and characteristics, but apparently at one time intermingled in all parts of Syria.

Such seem to have been the origins of the Hebrew people. Their relationship to the Moabites, Ammonites, Edomites and Aramaeans is attested by the traditions which connected the founders of these races with the family of Abraham. It is probable that they were united by more remote ties to the Midianites and Amalekites; and though the Phoenicians and Canaanites are represented as belonging to another stock, there is no doubt that they, like the Hebrews, were Semites, and spoke a language akin to that of the tribes who invaded their territory from the East.

I. *The Hebrew tradition according to the Book of Genesis.*

There is a statement in the book of Joshua (xxiv. 2) which

Migration of
Terah from
Ur-Kasdim.

seems to embody the general belief of the Israelites respecting the original home of their race, *Your fathers dwelt of old time beyond the river* [Euphrates][1], *even Terah, the father of Abraham, and the father of Nahor: and they served other gods.* With this corresponds the ancient tradition preserved in Gen. xi. 26 foll. that Terah with his family lived at Ur of the Chaldees (Ur-Kasdim), an ancient and flourishing city of lower Mesopotamia lying on the right bank of the Euphrates, at no great distance from the mouth of the Persian Gulf[2]. Modern research has discovered

---

[1] ' Beyond the river' (*b'eber hannâhâr*) probably means the region *west* of the Euphrates, the writer's standpoint in Josh. xxiv. 2 probably being *east* of Euphrates. See Hommel, *The Ancient Heb. Tradition*, pp. 323 foll.

[2] Ur has been identified with the modern ruins of Mugheir, 150 miles

that Ur contained a famous temple dedicated to *Sin*, the Moon-god, and that besides being a chief centre of Babylonian culture, trade and civilization, its situation west of the Éuphrates rendered it easily accessible to the Semitic nomads of the Arabian peninsula.   There is some evidence that a Semitic dynasty at one time held power in the city of Ur, and possibly Terah belonged to the ruling class.   His migration from Ur to Haran, which lay east of the Euphrates some 600 miles further north in Padan-Aram, was the first stage in a movement of which Canaan was the goal (Gen. xi. 31).   At Haran Terah died, and his son Abram received a divine command to continue the journey westward.   Accompanied therefore by his wife Sarai, who was also his half-sister, and by Lot his nephew, Abram *went forth to go into the land of Canaan*[1].

Haran was a city inhabited by Semites, a centre of Babylonian commerce, and a chief seat of the worship

Haran.

of the Moon-god *Sin*, who was even known by the title *Ba'al-Kharran*, 'lord of Haran.'   Thus in its culture, law, customs and religion it closely resembled Ur, and the 'call' of Abram—the divine command which bade him seek a new country—was doubtless welcome to one whose purer conception of God made him dissatisfied with his heathen surroundings. Moreover there is reason to think that northern Babylonia itself was at this time greatly disturbed by a recent invasion of the Kassites, a mountain people related to the Elamites. While Nahor, Terah's second son, remained in Haran, Abram crossed the Euphrates, and, after probably making a short sojourn in the neighbourhood of Damascus, reached Canaan, and traversed the land in a southerly direction.   Certain sacred spots are specially mentioned in connection with his

from the mouth of the Euphrates, which seems to have formerly entered the Persian Gulf nearly a hundred miles to the north of the present coast (Sayce, *EHH* p. 9).

[1] Called in Heb. xi. 9 γῆ τῆς ἐπαγγελίας, with reference to the promise of Gen. xii. 1.

journey: such as the oak of Moreh, near Shechem, and a
Gen. xii.   place between Bethel and Ai, at each of which
1—9.   Abram halted and erected an altar to Jehovah.
At Shechem, we are told, the divine promise was renewed
Unto thy seed will I give this land.

In course of time the pressure of famine drove Abram
Abram in   and his tribe to take refuge in Egypt. It may
Egypt. Gen. be reasonably surmised that this incident took
xii. 10—20.
place during the period of the twelfth dynasty,
when intercourse between Egypt and Palestine was beginning
to be frequent, and groups of Semitic nomads occasionally
crossed the Egyptian frontier.   Abram was hospitably welcomed by the reigning monarch, chiefly as it seems for the
sake of Sarai, whom, in his fear for his own safety, he represented as his sister.   The discovery however by the Egyptian
king of Abram's deceit led to his expulsion from Egypt[1].

Returning northwards through Canaan, Abram and his
nephew Lot reached the central highlands in the neighbourhood of Bethel.   Here the multitude of their possessions
and the occurrence of disputes between their clansmen and
Separation   retainers compelled them to separate. Abram
of Abram and generously offered the first choice of a settle-
Lot: Gen. xiii.
ment to his nephew. *Is not the whole land
before thee? if thou wilt take the left hand, then I will go to
the right; or if thou take the right hand, then I will go to
the left.* Lot selected the fertile plains of the Jordan valley.
Abram, encouraged for the third time by Jehovah's promise,
removed to Kirjath-arba or Hebron in the *Negeb* (south-
country), which became his permanent place of abode, and
was marked as a sacred spot by the erection of an altar.

At Hebron, Abram *the Hebrew* (xiv. 13) fixed his encamp-

[1] It is most probable that the supposed repetition of this conduct on
Abram's part in connection with Abimelech (Gen. xx. 2 foll.), and the
similar story of Isaac (xxvi. 7 foll.), are both due to some variation of form
in the same original tradition.

ment beneath the oak of Mamre the Amorite, who, with his brothers Eshcol and Aner, became *confederate with Abram.* This alliance proved to be important in the next episode of the patriarch's career, his defeat of the Elamite army, whose incursion into the land is related in Gen. xiv. This narrative seems to be based on dim reminiscences or traditions of an era (about 2300 B.C.) when Mesopotamia and even Palestine had fallen under the conquering sway of the Elamites, a tribe whose original seat lay in the mountainous region south-eastward of the river Tigris. A powerful king of Elam, called Chedor-laomer (Kudur-lagarmar), aided by certain Chaldaean princes[1], is described as having invaded Canaan with the intention of punishing the rebellion of five vassal kings, who had thrown off the Elamitish yoke.

Marching swiftly southwards and dispersing the tribes who inhabited the highlands east of Jordan, the Rephaim in Bashan, the Zuzim and Emim of the district further south, and the Horites of Mount Seir, the invaders destroyed Kadesh and returned northwards along the western shore of

The campaign of Chedor-laomer: Gen. xiv.

the Dead Sea. In the vale of Siddim, at the northern extremity of the sea, they fell suddenly on the five Canaanitish princes. The kings of Sodom and Gomorrah were slain and Lot was carried away among the captives. On receiving tidings of the disaster, Abram instantly started in pursuit of the Elamites with 318 of his own retainers and his Amoritish

---

[1] The monuments mention four kings who seem to have been contemporary : *Kudur-lachgumal* of Elam, *Khammurabi* of Shin'ar (Babylonia), *Eriaku* of Larsa, and *Tudchula* of Gutim (in northern Babylonia). These are probably identical with Chedorlaomer, Amraphel, Arioch and Tidal of Gen. xiv. 1. Though the inscriptions make no mention of the particular expedition described in Gen. xiv. they testify that such an invasion of Palestine was a possible incident of the patriarchal age. There are however certain historical improbabilities in the narrative which make its accuracy questionable. See the careful summary of Driver, *op. cit.*, pp. 39—45.

allies.   He overtook the victorious host near Damascus, fell on
them by night and completely routed them.   Lot and the
other prisoners, together with the captured spoil, were recovered.   On his homeward way Abram was met in the valley
of Shaveh (afterwards known as 'the King's Dale') by the new

Melchi-
zedek: Gen.
xiv. 17 foll.

king of Sodom and by Melchizedek, king of
Salem, who combined in his own person the
offices of king and priest of his city.   The latter
brought forth bread and wine for the patriarch, and solemnly
blessed him in the name of *'El-'Elyon,* 'the Most High God.'
To Melchizedek in return Abram reverently *gave tithes of
all.*   With the king of Sodom, however, he declined to have
any dealings.   He refused to receive from him even his
rightful share of the spoil, and only demanded that his confederates Eshcol and Aner should be compensated for their
services.

Meanwhile Abraham remained childless, and knew not

The promise
of an heir:
Gen. xv.

how the promise of a glorious future for his
descendants was to be fulfilled.   He could
point to no heir of his house other than his
steward, Eliezer.   At this point, to encourage the patriarch's
drooping faith, Jehovah *brought him forth abroad, and said,
Look now toward heaven, and tell the stars, if thou be able
to tell them: and He said unto him, So shall thy seed be.*   And
Abram *believed in Jehovah, and He counted it to him for
righteousness.*   The covenant between Abram and Jehovah
which confirmed this promise was solemnly ratified by sacrifice, after which the future of Abram's posterity was revealed
to him in a vision, the land of Canaan being assigned to them
as their inheritance.

According to the narrative of Genesis, Abram became in

The rite of
circumcision.

due time the father of Ishmael by Hagar, Sarai's
handmaid; but Ishmael was not the promised
seed.   When the lad was thirteen years old the
covenant between Jehovah and Abram was sealed anew by

the institution of circumcision, a rite which, having been practised from very early times in Egypt and elsewhere, was now selected as the covenantal sign.   On this occasion, minutely described by the priestly compiler of Gen. xvii., the patriarch's name was changed from 'Abram' to 'Abraham,' which in xvii. 5 is explained to mean 'father of a multi-tude[1].'   'Sarai' also became 'Sarah,' i.e. 'princess.'   At the same time Abraham and his offspring pledged them-selves to a life of separation from the polluting rites and practices of heathendom.   Circumcision was to be the out-ward symbol of their vocation to a purer life and creed than that of the surrounding nations.   Gen. xvii. 1.
And thus the Bible connects with the name of Abraham the beginning of that life of friendship and communion between God and man in which true religion essentially consists[2]. Henceforth Abraham is admitted to a closer degree of inti-macy with Jehovah ; he converses with Him, pleads with Him concerning His judgments and receives repeated tokens of divine favour.   The narratives relating to his career in the book of Genesis are derived from different sources and are loosely strung together, but they form a series intended to depict the chequered experiences of the foremost among the *friends of God.*   Hence it is not surprising that the patriarch's character should be depicted in an ideal light, and that he should be portrayed as a prophet and a saint, as *the father of the faithful* and the ancestor of the Messiah.   The picture is evidently drawn in the light of a later age by devout narrators who discerned in Abraham's career an illustration of the great principles which lay at the root of Israel's re-ligion.   Not only in later Jewish theology, but in the traditions

---

[1] The real meaning of the name is uncertain.   The explanation given in Gen. *l. c.* represents a popular rather than an etymologically correct account of the word.   See Hastings' *DB*, s. voc. 'Abraham,' vol. I. p. 17, and Sayce, *EHH*, pp. 33, 34.

[2] See Isai. xli. 8, 2 Chr. xx. 7, James ii. 23.

of the whole Moslem world, 'the friend of God' is a great figure. *In glory*, says the son of Sirach, *was there none like unto him* (Ecclus. xliv. 19).

The reward of Abraham's faith was not destined to be much longer delayed. The narrative relates how in process of time three angelic visitors, one of whom was Jehovah Himself, appeared in human form to the patriarch as he sat at the door

The promise renewed, Gen. xviii. 1—15.

of his tent; how they accepted his proffered hospitality and at the same time announced that in the near future Sarah, though *well-stricken in age*, should become the mother of a son; how the patriarch's wife by her incredulous laughter drew upon herself a solemn rebuke.

This incident is followed by a description of the destruction

Destruction of the cities of the plain, Gen. xviii. 22 foll.

of *the cities of the plain*, or more strictly *of the circle*. The very site of these cities is uncertain, but it seems most probable that they stood at the northern end of the Dead Sea[1]. We are told of Abraham's humble and pathetic but unavailing intercession for the guilty inhabitants; of the tremendous overthrow itself; of the escape of Abraham's kinsman Lot and his two daughters from Sodom, and of the destruction of Lot's wife who *looked back from behind him, and became a pillar of salt.*

Gen. xix. 1—29.

And Abraham gat up early in the morning to the place where he had stood before the Lord: and he looked toward Sodom and Gomorrah, and toward all the land of the plain, and beheld, and lo, the smoke of the land went up as the smoke of a furnace. The natural cause of the catastrophe may well have been a violent storm of thunder and lightning, which, setting fire to the naphtha springs that oozed from the bituminous soil, produced a terrific conflagration[2]. The fate of the overwhelmed cities is frequently referred to in

[1] The question is carefully discussed by G. A. Smith, *Hist. Geography of the Holy Land*, pp. 505 foll.

[2] Other writers attribute the catastrophe to volcanic action.

the Old Testament; it was evidently regarded as a most awful and typical example of the divine judgment on human sin.

With the escape of Lot, and his settlement on the eastern heights overlooking the Jordan valley was con-   Origin of nected the origin of two tribes, Ammon and   Ammon and Moab, which were related to Israel by ties of   Moab. kinship; the tradition alluded to in Gen. xix. bears witness to the repugnance which later Israelites felt towards these frequently hostile neighbours. The district afterwards occupied by the Ammonites lay to the east of Mount Gilead, between the Jabbok and the Arnon; the Moabites were a larger tribe, whose borders extended from the Arnon to the district south of the Dead Sea. We are informed elsewhere that the possessions of Ammon had been previously occupied by a giant race called Zamzummim; those of Moab by the Emim (Deut. ii. 10, 20). These tribes were probably of the Amorite stock, and closely connected with the original population of western Palestine[1].

At this point the narrative mentions another movement of Abraham to the south. At Gerar in the *Negeb*, south of Gaza, where he next took up his abode, the Philistine Abimelech was king. Once more the patriarch, in fear of his life, represented Sarah as his sister; once more she was protected   Abraham at from injury and restored to her husband by   Gerar, Gen. Abimelech, though not without an indignant   xx. rebuke.

[1] The following table (taken from Hastings' *DB*, vol. II. p. 508), shows the relationships of Israel according to the account in Genesis.

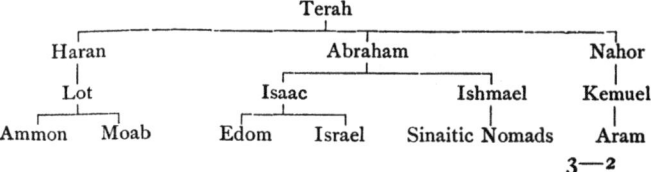

It was apparently at Gerar that Abraham's long-promised
son was born, circumcised on the eighth day
and named Isaac, 'laughter,' because Abraham
had 'laughed' with exultation at the prospect
of his birth[1]. At a feast which was held on the day when
the child was finally weaned, Sarah's jealousy was aroused
by the sight of the young Ishmael playing with Isaac. She
demanded the expulsion of Hagar and her son, lest *the son of
the bondwoman* should claim a share of the ancestral inheritance. Hagar and Ishmael were accordingly dismissed from
Abraham's tents. The youth, preserved by divine intervention
from perishing with thirst in the desert, became in due time
the reputed ancestor of the nomadic tribes of the Sinaitic
peninsula[2]. Meanwhile Isaac grew to manhood in the district
of Gerar. Abraham was on terms of friendly alliance with
Abimelech; a dispute which arose respecting the ownership of
a well digged by Abraham's servants was decided by a covenant at Beersheba ('well of the oath')[3], which thus became
one of the sacred spots specially connected with patriarchal
history, and was successively the home of Abraham, Isaac and
Jacob.

Birth of Isaac, Gen. xxi. 1—21.

[1] Gen. xvii. 17 ἐγέλασε, LXX. Cp. S. Jo. viii. 56 ἠγαλλιάσατο.

[2] The story of Abraham's marriage with Keturah (xxv. 1—7), by whom
he became the ancestor of Midian and other Arabian tribes, seems to
represent a different tradition. In both narratives we probably have an
instance of the way in which *tribal* incidents are described in the form of
personal history. "It is impossible to resist the conclusion," says Prof. Ryle
(in Hastings' *DB*, vol. I. p. 16 a), "that some of the references to Ishmael
and the allusion to Keturah contain an Israelitish picture of the relationship of the Arabian tribes and clans to the Hebrew stock rather than
the record of personal history." This mode of describing the affinity of
Israel to surrounding tribes is consistent with the general purpose of the
narrative to represent Abraham as not merely a great personality, but as
the leader of an important racial movement.

[3] Literally 'well of the seven,' because the two parties to the covenant
pledged themselves by setting apart seven things. See Dillmann on
Gen. xxi. 31.

And now came the culminating trial of Abraham's life. He felt himself impelled to sacrifice his son Isaac as a burnt-offering to Jehovah. Such an act was entirely in accordance with the ideas and $\qquad$ The offering of Isaac: Gen. xxii. 1—20.

practices of the Semitic tribes in that rude and primitive age. *God* we read, *did prove Abraham*: in other words He dealt with the prevalent custom in such a way as to test Abraham's faith and to raise and purify men's conception of the divine nature and requirement. He accepted the best that the patriarch could offer, and in doing so revealed to him a more excellent way of pleasing God. Journeying northward with his son for three days Abraham at length *lifted up his eyes and saw the appointed place afar off:* a mountain *in the land of Moriah*[1]. Here he built an altar and bound Isaac *upon the wood.* At the very moment when Abraham's hand was outstretched to slay his son, it was arrested by the voice of Jehovah calling to him and bidding him not to harm the lad, but to offer in his stead a ram which was caught by the horns in a thicket close at hand. Once more the covenant between Jehovah and the patriarch was solemnly renewed, and the far-reaching promise was repeated: *In thy seed shall all the nations of the earth be blessed; because thou hast obeyed my voice.* Then the father and son rose up and returned together to Beersheba, and from thence in course of time they removed to Kirjath Arba or Hebron, where Sarah died at the age of 127 years. The cave of Machpelah at Hebron was purchased by Abraham as *a possession* Death and burial of Sarah, Gen. xxiii.

of a burying place. The acquisition of this spot—the earnest of his promised inheritance—brought the patriarch into contact with the Hittites, who had apparently established themselves at Hebron, though that city lay within the borders of Amoritish

---

[1] *i.e.* probably either (1) equivalent to 'Moreh'=the highland country (ἡ γῆ ἡ ὑψηλή LXX.), or (2) used proleptically with the meaning 'shown by Jehovah' (cp. xxii. 14). The term is transferred to the Temple mount by the chronicler (2 Chr. iii. 1).

territory. A formal agreement was made with *Ephron the Hittite*, by which Abraham acquired the field for 400 shekels of silver. The cave which probably lay opposite to the site of Abraham's encampment naturally became one of the sacred spots of Palestine, venerated in later times alike by Jews, Christians and Moslems. Here Sarah was buried, and here not long afterwards Abraham himself was laid to rest by his sons Isaac and Ishmael.

Before the patriarch's death however one important duty remained to be discharged: namely, to find among Abraham's own kindred in Haran a suitable wife for Isaac, the heir of the promise. The vivid and poetical narrative of Gen. xxiv. relates the mission of Abraham's trusted servant, the steward of his house; it tells how he was providentially guided to the habitation of his *master's brethren*, Laban and his family; how

Isaac's marriage, Gen. xxiv.

Rebekah, Laban's sister, made her venture of faith and departed with the servant; how *Isaac went out to meditate in the field at the eventide,* and met the approaching cavalcade; how he brought Rebekah

Death of Abraham, Gen. xxv. 7—II.

into his mother Sarah's tent and she became his wife. And now at the age of 175 years Abraham *was gathered to his people,* and was buried in the cave of Machpelah by the side of Sarah his wife.

The life of Isaac as described in the book of Genesis is

Life of Isaac: Gen. xxiv. foll.

comparatively uneventful. He is not represented as a great nomadic chief or warrior like his father. His days were spent in the neighbourhood of Gerar, Beersheba and Hebron. At Gerar the oath which Jehovah *sware unto Abraham* was renewed to his son; Isaac and his children were thus made *heirs of the same promise* (Heb. xi. 9). The unworthy stratagem by which his father had deceived Abimelech is said to have been repeated by Isaac, who described Rebekah as his sister; and the old strife between the Hebrew herdsmen and those of the king of Gerar was renewed. Isaac's increasing prosperity in fact aroused the envy of the Philistines, and it seems that the stoppage of the wells formerly dug by Abraham's servants was intended as an act of hostility. Two wells belonging to Isaac were forcibly seized by the Philistines and were consequently named by him '*Esek* ('strife'), and *Sitnah* ('enmity'). Isaac consequently removed his encampment further to the south, and dug another well which he called *Rehoboth* ('open spaces'), because he was here left in undisputed possession of the territory. At Beersheba, Jehovah once more appeared to Isaac by night and blessed him. Here too he was visited by Abimelech, and a league was made between them which was confirmed by a solemn oath. According to an independent tradition the name 'Beersheba' was derived from this incident[1].

At this point Isaac is withdrawn from the foreground of the narrative. In Gen. xxvii. he is described as old, helpless, and preparing for his death, and henceforth the interest of the story is centred in Jacob, the younger of Isaac's twin sons. According to the Hebrew tradition the rivalry between the descendants of Jacob and Esau, which became so persistent a feature in later history, was foreshadowed even in the circum- stances of their birth. The younger of the twins was born holding the heel of the elder, as if already striving to hold him back from his rightful priority : hence he was named by his parents ' Jacob ' (supplanter)[2]. From the first the brothers differed in character and disposition. Esau is de- scribed as a *cunning hunter, a man of the field;* Jacob as a *plain* or *quiet man dwelling in tents*. It is clear from the sequel that the narrator intends to depict two different types

Birth of Esau and Jacob: Gen. xxv. 23, foll.

---

[1] It is evident that two different traditions existed among the Hebrews respecting the origin of Beersheba, 'the well of the oath.' One of these is preserved in Gen. xxi. 31 foll., the other in xxvi. 32, 33.

[2] Such was the idea suggested by the sound of the name 'Jacob' to a Hebrew ear : but the real meaning and origin of the name is obscure.

of human character, which find their counterpart in the Edom
and Israel of a later age. Esau is a type of
'the natural man'—the man of strong animal
instincts, free-handed and generous but un-
disciplined, unresponsive to spiritual ideas and impulses, and
therefore incapable of moral growth. He has none of the
faults which mar the character of Jacob, but also has none of
his capacity for greatness. Jacob on the other hand is a type
of 'the spiritual man,' whose higher nature is slowly and pain-
fully developed. In early life he is treacherous and cowardly,
conscious indeed that he is called to a high destiny, but
choosing his own wilful road to its attainment. Only when
he has paid a bitter penalty for his wrong-doing is he visited
by a vision of glory which transfigures him and lifts him to
greatness.

Their character.

In course of time an occasion arose when Jacob, taking
advantage of Esau's exhaustion after a day spent
in the chase, compelled his elder brother to
sell his birthright. To the Hebrew narrator the
heedless profanity of Esau appeared far more blameworthy
than the self-seeking greed of Jacob. When Esau *despised
his birthright,* he showed his incapacity for entering into the
spiritual hopes and aspirations cherished by the patriarchs.
Jacob on the other hand never lost sight of the blessing
promised to Abraham's seed, whatever may have been his idea
of its scope and the mode of its fulfilment. His act of deceit
brought its inevitable penalty, and the story of his life is a
kind of parable describing the painful but salutary discipline
by which the character of the 'supplanter' was transformed
into that of 'Israel', the hero who strives with God and pre-
vails[1].

Gen. xxv. 29—34.

In Gen. xxvii. a second incident of the same kind is related.
Isaac is here described as desirous of solemnly transmitting
the patriarchal blessing to his elder son. He accordingly

[1] See below, p. 44 note.

bids Esau go out to the field and take venison. *Bring it me,*
he says, *that I may eat, that my soul may bless thee before I die.*
At the instigation of his mother Rebekah Jacob deceives his
father by a cunning artifice, and secures the
blessing for himself. Esau returning from the   Jacob blessed by
field learns too late what he has lost, and utters   Isaac: Gen. xxvii.
an exceeding great and bitter cry of remorse. It
is noteworthy that "the contrasted blessings of Jacob and
Esau express clearly the different geographical and political
conditions of the countries owned afterwards by their respec-
tive descendants[1]." To Jacob are assigned the rich fields and
vineyards of Canaan, watered by *the dew of heaven* and bringing
forth *plenty of corn and wine.* He is also promised dominion
over the neighbouring nations and over his *mother's sons,* i.e.
the peoples nearest of kin to Israel, such as Edom, Moab, and
Ammon. The blessing reserved for Esau is such as might be
the portion of a race living *away from the fatness of the earth
and the dew of heaven*[2]. Only after prolonged subjection shall
Esau *shake* his brother's *yoke from off his neck.* In this incident according to a tradition that may have originated in
Edom, began the secular hatred that divided Esau or Edom[3]
from Israel. The story of Esau's profane levity in bartering
his birthright may represent that form of the story which
found favour in Israel.

The fear of Esau's vengeance compelled Jacob to fly—
Esau himself took up his abode in the region
of Mount Seir, the barren and rugged tract   Esau and his descend-
which extends southward from the Dead Sea to   ants, Gen. xxvi. 34, 35;
the gulf of Akabah. His alliances by marriage   xxviii. 6—9;
with the Canaanites, the Hittites, and certain   xxxvi.

---

[1] Driver in Hastings' *DB*, vol. II. p. 527 a.

[2] See Gen. xxvii. 39, R.V. marg.

[3] Gen. xxv. 30, where the traditional explanation of the name 'Edom'
is mentioned. The name, however, is probably due to the red colour of
the cliffs of Edom. Cp. Sayce, *EHH*, pp. 66, 67.

Arabian tribes are specially mentioned, together with the fact that he became an ancestor of the 'dukes' or sheiks of Edom. The general purport of these details is to show that the later Edomites belonged to a stock tainted at its source by inter-marriage with aliens. An incidental mention of the primaeval Horites who originally dwelt on Mount Seir shows that the tribe of Esau obtained possession of Edom by dispossessing or absorbing the former inhabitants.

Meanwhile the narrative is almost exclusively concerned

Cause of Jacob's flight, Gen. xxviii. with the fortunes of Jacob. Aware of Esau's resolve to be avenged after his father's death, Rebekah urges Jacob to take refuge with her brother Laban in Haran, and there to remain until Esau's resentment shall have subsided. In the account given by the 'Priestly' writer (xxvii. 46—xxviii. 6), which differs from the 'Prophetical' narrative (J), we find Jacob's departure as-cribed to his parents' anxiety that he should not follow Esau's example by taking to wife a woman of the Hittite race. He is solemnly charged by Isaac to form an alliance among his mother's kindred in Haran.

Accordingly, we read, Jacob departed from Beersheba and

The vision at Bethel, Gen. xxviii. *went toward Haran.* As he fared northwards *he lighted upon a certain place and tarried there all night because the sun was set.* The exact spot was the site of the city afterwards known as Bethel. On the rugged and desolate plateau Jacob lay down to sleep with a stone for his pillow. In his dream he beheld the rocks that lay about him shaping themselves into a mighty stairway reaching from earth to heaven, and the angels of God were ascending and descending on it. Jehovah Himself seemed to stand over the sleeper, and to address him with words of en-couragement, promising him a countless posterity and assuring him of unfailing mercy and protection throughout his wander-ings. Presently Jacob awoke to find the grey dawn stealing over the place of his repose, *and he said, Surely the LORD is in* *this place and I knew it not.* To mark the sanctity of the spot, he consecrated the stone which he had used for a pillow by pouring oil upon it. Such sacred stones (*Mazzeboth*), supposed to be the actual abode of Deity, were common in all parts of the Semitic world. The traditional pillar erected by Jacob was afterwards regarded as an object of special veneration, and was probably pointed out for centuries within or near the later sanctuary of Bethel[1].

The story of Jacob's arrival in Haran and of his first meeting with Rachel, the daughter of Laban, is one of those beautiful idylls in which the Old Testament is so rich. It is needless however to dwell upon details, or to describe particularly the lengthened probation by which Jacob finally won the object of his love. It was the experience of stern discipline and hardship that taught the 'supplanter' what it was to be himself deceived. After seven years' service for the hand of Rachel, Jacob was compelled by a ruse on Laban's part to wed her elder sister Leah ; he was only allowed to take Rachel also to wife on the understanding that he should serve his father-in-law for seven years more. At length after a sojourn of twenty years at Haran, Jacob determined to make his escape. With his two wives and his twelve children he took his departure across the Euphrates in the direction of Gilead, while Laban was engaged in sheep-shearing. On the highlands of Gilead he was overtaken by his father-in-law, who had hastily pursued him and now upbraided him with his flight. There, at a spot marked by a cairn of stones, a league was made between the Syrian and the Hebrew chiefs, which fixed the boundary line of the territories afterwards occupied by their descendants.

Jacob in Padan-Aram, Gen. xxix., xxx.

Jacob's flight: Gen. xxxi. 17 foll.

Proceeding on his way Jacob sent messengers to his brother Esau *unto the land of Seir, the field of Edom.* They soon

---

[1] On the details of Gen. xxviii. see a learned and suggestive essay, *Jacob at Bethel*, by the Rev. A. Smythe Palmer (Nutt, 1899).

returned with tidings that Esau was advancing to meet him with four hundred men.

In this hour of mortal fear, Jacob passed through a mysterious struggle by night with an angel at Peniel, overlooking the ravine of the Jabbok. When the day broke it seemed to Jacob as if God Himself had been his antagonist. *I have seen God face to face and my life is preserved.* In this crowning struggle of his life he received his new name. *Thy name shall be called no more Jacob, but Israel: for thou hast striven with God and with men, and hast prevailed*[1]. The appellation may be regarded as indicating not merely a moral change in the patriarch, but also the vocation destined for him and his descendants. The allusion of the prophet Hosea (xii. 3, 4) to this incident in Jacob's career shows that in the example of their ancestor the Israelites of a later age were intended to learn the true spirit of their religion and the goal towards which their existence as a nation pointed. The spiritual struggle which Jacob underwent during that memorable night was believed to have left its mark on his physical frame At sunrise, when he *passed over Penuel, he halted upon his thigh*, which had been *strained as he wrestled with* his antagonist[2].

Jacob's struggle at Peniel: Gen. xxxii. 22 foll.

Jacob's meeting and reconciliation with Esau is next described. By the generosity of his brother Jacob's fears are dispelled, but he declines Esau's offer of an escort, and is evidently uneasy at the presence of his armed retinue.

---

[1] The name 'Israel,' meaning literally 'God persists' or 'perseveres,' suggests the interpretation 'He who perseveres with God.' In this as in other cases, the explanation of the name is based on *sound* rather than on etymology. Gesenius and others explain 'Israel' as meaning 'soldier of God.'

[2] We may notice the fact that the narrator traces to this incident the Hebrew custom of not eating the sinew of the thigh of slain animals: the custom, though prescribed by the Mishna, is not mentioned elsewhere in the O. T.

After Esau's departure he removes his encampment first to Succoth on the east of Jordan and later to Shechem in the very heart of the promised land. At this point an incident occurs which leads to a treacherous assault on Shechem by Jacob's sons, and the cold-blooded murder of its inhabitants. It seems reasonable to suppose that this account of a personal transaction between 'the children of Israel' and Hamor the father of Shechem covers an obscure episode of tribal warfare; it is probable that many such conflicts took place between the Israelitish clans, who by this time must have formed a numerous and warlike community, and the inhabitants of the land which they were now invading.

Jacob in Canaan: Gen. xxxiii. 18—xxxiv. 31.

At Shechem Jacob caused his tribe to *put away the strange gods, teraphim,* and other emblems of idolatry which they had brought from Haran. He then journeyed to Luz or Bethel, where Jehovah had appeared to him at the beginning of his long exile. Here in fulfilment of his former vow he raised an altar to the *God of Bethel,* and once more, we read, *God appeared* unto him *and blessed him.* Continuing his journey towards the south he reached Ephrath (or Bethlehem), near to which spot Rachel, after giving birth to Jacob's youngest son Benjamin, died and was buried. At Hebron Jacob found Isaac at the point of death. Once more Jacob and Esau met for the purpose of burying their father in the cave of Machpelah [1].

Jacob reaches Bethel: Gen. xxxv. 1, foll.

Death of Isaac: Gen. xxxv. 27—29.

Jacob himself, we are told, settled at Hebron, but we hear of his sons being engaged in pastoral pursuits as far northward as Shechem. From this point onwards, however, Jacob's favourite son Joseph becomes the most prominent figure in the

---

[1] The chronological difficulties involved in the story of Isaac's old age and death are due to the combination of different strata of tradition, which the compilers of Genesis do not attempt to harmonize. See Ryle in Hastings' *DB*, vol. II., p. 484.

history; and the closing chapters of Genesis relate the successive events which led to the exaltation of Joseph and his house over the other Benê Israel.

A general outline of Joseph's personal history is all that

Joseph and his brethren: Gen. xxxvii.

need be attempted for our present purpose. Joseph, the son of Rachel, Jacob's best-loved wife, was the youngest but one of the patriarch's children, and in consequence of being his father's favourite, became an object of envy to his elder brothers. Two dreams which seemed to foreshadow his future greatness, and which were perhaps too eagerly related to his father by Joseph, only increased their ill-will. When a fitting opportunity arrived the brothers conspired against the object of their hatred. *Moved with jealousy against Joseph* they *sold him into Egypt* (Acts vii. 9), and persuaded their father that his favourite son had fallen a victim to wild beasts. Jacob was overwhelmed with grief, but the supposed calamity was destined to be overruled for good. Joseph was brought to Egypt by the Midianites or Ishmaelites to whom he had been sold as a captive, and became a slave in the household of Potiphar, the captain of Pharaoh's guard. The young Hebrew quickly gained his master's confidence and goodwill, but his prospects were soon blighted. Through the wicked intrigues of his master's wife he was disgraced and thrown into prison, where he remained for two full years, forgotten by his master but comforted by tokens that Jehovah was still *with him* (Gen. xxxix. 23).

At the end of this period, Joseph, who was now thirty years

Joseph in Egypt: Gen. xxxix. foll.

old, suddenly rose to great eminence. His reputation as an interpreter of dreams brought him to the notice of the reigning Pharaoh, who on a certain occasion was disturbed by two visions portending seven years of plenty, to be immediately followed by seven years of scarcity. Joseph's skill as an interpreter and his practical sagacity as an adviser were rewarded by signal marks of royal favour. He became *a father to Pharaoh and lord of all his house and ruler over all the land of Egypt* (Gen. xlv. 8). An Egyptian name, Zaphnath-pa'anea'ḥ ('revealer of secrets'), was bestowed on him, and the daughter of Potiphera, priest of the great temple of On (Heliopolis), became his wife. During the seven years of plenty which he had predicted Joseph prepared for the time of dearth by collecting grain and storing it in all the cities of the surrounding district.

When the famine began, it proved to be exceptionally severe and wide-spread, affecting Canaan and other adjacent countries. At this point the sons of Jacob, who knew nothing of Joseph's elevation, were driven by the pressure of scarcity to go down into Egypt for the purpose of buying corn. At first Joseph, though he recognized his brethren, dealt roughly with them as spies who had come *to see the nakedness of the land* (Gen. xlii. 9), and even detained Simeon, one of their number, as a hostage for the appearance of their brother Benjamin. On the occasion of their second visit Joseph invited the brothers to his palace and entertained them at his table, showing special favour to Benjamin, whom Jacob had reluctantly suffered to accompany the rest. On the next day they had already departed when they were summoned to halt by the steward of Joseph's house, who charged them with theft and insisted on their return to the presence of Joseph. The pathetic pleading of Judah on behalf of Benjamin, Jacob's best-loved child, moved Joseph to throw off his disguise. He could no longer refrain himself, and then and there *made himself known* to his brethren, who discovered to their terror that the great potentate before whom they had humbled themselves was none other than he whom they had once so cruelly wronged. Joseph however reassured and comforted them. *God*, he tells them, *did send me before you to preserve life. So now it was not you that sent me hither but God* (Gen. xlv. 5, 7). He then sent an urgent message to his father Jacob, inviting him to come down and make his abode in Egypt, together with his whole clan, his flocks, herds and other possessions.

The story of Israel's migration from Canaan is very simply

Israel goes down into Egypt: Gen. xlvi.
related, but it was a momentous crisis in the history of the tribes when *Israel came into Egypt and Jacob sojourned in the land of Ham* (Ps. cv. 23). The narrator relates how Jacob was encouraged by a vision to leave the promised land; how he arrived in Egypt with *all his seed, threescore and six souls*; how he was honourably welcomed by the reigning Pharaoh, who assigned to the Benê Israel a settlement in the land of Goshen, where they might carry on their pastoral pursuits in peace. It has been surmised that the monarch who thus favoured the Hebrew kinsmen of Joseph was one of the last kings of the Hyksôs dynasty, who being themselves of foreign (Asiatic) origin, were disposed to befriend a tribe of Semitic nomads. The district of Goshen was probably situated along the eastern bank of the Nile, near the north-eastern frontier of Egypt, and within easy distance of Tanis (Zoan), where the Hyksôs princes had fixed their residence.

The next incident recorded in Genesis is the sickness and

Last days of Jacob: Gen. xlviii., xlix.
death of the patriarch Jacob. Perceiving his end to be near at hand, he summoned Joseph to his side, and solemnly adopted Manasseh and Ephraim, the two sons born to Joseph in Egypt, as members of his own family. *Thy two sons*, he said, *are mine; even as Reuben and Simeon they shall be mine.* In blessing the lads however the patriarch gave to the younger, Ephraim, the preeminence—a prophetic act in which was foreshadowed the future destiny of Ephraim as the leading tribe of the Benê Israel. At the same time he assigned to Joseph a special portion of territory in the land of Canaan: a mountain slope which Jacob had taken from the Amorite with his sword and with his bow. The allusion is evidently to Shechem, which remained for so long the central sanctuary and meeting-place of the tribe of Ephraim[1].

[1] See Gen. xlviii. 22 (R.V.) marg.

The 'Blessing of Jacob,' addressed to all his sons, is a very ancient poem, foretelling in symbolic imagery the geographical situation, character and fortunes of each of the twelve tribes. The poet dwells on "the moral instability of Reuben, the disorganized social condition of Simeon and Levi, the ideal sovereignty and vine-clad territory of Judah, the maritime advantages enjoyed by Zebulun, the ignoble indifference which led Issachar to prefer ease to independence, the quick and effective attack of Dan, the warlike bravery of Gad, the richness of Asher's soil, the blessings of populousness, military efficiency, climate, and soil, which, in spite of envious assailants, are showered upon Joseph, the martial skill and success of Benjamin[1]." Jacob's final charge to his sons was a direction for his burial in the cave of Machpelah at Hebron. His body was therefore embalmed, and afterwards, accompanied by a great funeral procession in accordance with Egyptian custom, was carried into the land of Canaan and interred in the ancestral burying-place. The book of Genesis ends with a brief notice of Joseph's continued sojourn and prolonged life in Egypt, his kindness to his brethren, and his parting injunction to his fellow-tribesmen, that they should ultimately lay his bones in the plot of ground assigned to him at Shechem. *By faith, when his end was nigh, he made mention of the departure of the children of Israel, and gave commandment concerning his bones* (Heb. xi. 22). With the death of Joseph, the 'patriarchal age' of Israel's history, as described in the Old Testament, reaches its close.

II. *The historical substance of the patriarchal story.*

Having now briefly related the Hebrew tradition as recorded in the book of Genesis, we may enquire how far the story contains a strictly historical substance. Such a question is by no means easily answered.

General summary.

---

[1] Driver in Hastings' *DB*, vol. II. p. 532. The poem in its present form probably belongs to the age between the Judges and David.

It is probable that a large proportion of the names connected with Abraham and his descendants are those not of individuals, but of races and tribes, and that some at any rate of the prominent figures in the book of Genesis are only personifications of the races whose name they bear[1].   It has been pointed out that the Hebrew tradition itself dimly recognizes this fact in the case of Rebekah, who, before the birth of her twin sons, receives an oracle from God (Gen. xxv. 23) which runs as follows :

Two nations are in thy womb,
And two peoples shall be separated even from thy bowels :
And the one people shall be stronger than the other people ;
And the elder shall serve the younger.

Assuming therefore that the patriarchal period was one during which important though obscure tribal movements were in progress, there seem to be indications of at least three important migrations.

We first hear of an expedition of nomad tribes under the leadership of Abraham which started from Mesopotamia and ultimately entered Western Palestine.   Among these emigrants were probably not only the ancestors of Israel but those also of Moab, Ammon, and Edom.   The separation of Lot from Abraham may represent an eastward movement on the part of some of the immigrants, who, impelled by the prospect of luxuriant pasture for their flocks, crossed the Jordan, and within a comparatively brief space of time developed into distinct nations, afterwards known as Moab and Ammon.   The remaining members of the original expedition moved continually southwards, attracted by the rich pasturage to be found on the grassy steppes of Southern Judah.   When in course of time Western Palestine came within the sphere of Egyptian

---

[1] A parallel instance is the Greek tradition respecting Hellen, his two sons Dorus and Aeolus, and his grandsons Achaeus and Ion.   The same method of tracing tribal descent is found among the Arabs.

influence, another branch of the immigrants gradually expelled the Horites of Mount Seir, and consolidated themselves into a powerful nation (Edom) in a region that lay beyond the reach of Egyptian domination.

A second expedition from the original home of the Hebrew tribes is perhaps implied in the story of Jacob's return from Syria with his twelve sons.   A new branch of the Hebrew race migrated into Canaan and amalgamated with the remnant of the Abrahamitic tribes.   There is no convincing reason for doubting that Jacob himself, the leader of this expedition, was a historical person, who inherited the hopes and the faith of Abraham[1]; but as regards his twelve sons Dr Sayce is doubtless justified in saying that "the names of the ancestors of some of the Israelitish tribes may have been the reflex of the later names of the tribes themselves[2]."   In the absence of decisive evidence we can only suppose that the formation of the twelve tribes had already begun to take place before the Hebrews migrated into Egypt.   This would explain the third and last of the movements recorded in Genesis, the descent of Joseph and later of all the tribes into Egypt.

The tradition which describes the relations between Joseph and his brethren, their envy of the favour shown him by his father and its consequences, points to the occurrence of a contest for supremacy among the Hebrew tribes.   Whether Joseph himself is a historic personage has been questioned on perhaps insufficient grounds.   In any case it is probable that the tribe of which Joseph was the representative failed in an attempt to exercise the hegemony over the other tribes; and that it was forced to take refuge in Egypt, where it presently rose to a position of power and was ultimately joined by the rest of the

---

[1] On the other hand some authorities think that Jacob is merely a tribal name: that 'Jacob' and 'Israel' were in fact the designations of two distinct Hebrew tribes, the amalgamation of which gave rise to the tradition of Jacob's change of name.

[2] Sayce, *EHH*, p. 78.

Hebrews. This account of the facts explains the leading position assumed by the tribe of Joseph in the conflict for the possession of Canaan. It is in fact "difficult to deny that the narrative, like those of Ishmael and Jacob, has been coloured in some of its details by later events, and even that particular episodes may have originated in the desire to account for the circumstances and relations of a later age[1]."

It will thus appear that the historical nucleus contained in the patriarchal story cannot now be precisely determined. We have to content ourselves with broad outlines of early tribal history cast for the most part in genealogical and personal form. It must suffice that the biblical narrative gives us a dim picture of incidents and relationships which are unquestionably presupposed in the later stages of Israel's national development.

---

[1] Driver, in Hastings' *DB*, s. voc. 'Joseph.' See also the art. 'Genealogy' (vol. II. p. 121).

CHAPTER III.

ISRAEL IN EGYPT AND IN THE WILDERNESS.

A WORD of introduction is necessary before entering upon the period covered by the present chapter.

·Introductory.

Like the book of Genesis, Exodus is of composite structure, and bears traces of the handiwork of· three or even four different schools of writers. Instead of a contemporaneous account of the Exodus and the subsequent history of the Benê Israel, we find combined in a single book three different views or studies of that primitive age in the nation's history; studies deeply coloured by the circumstances of the much later period at which they were compiled, and pervaded by ideas that are fundamentally religious. It is impossible now to disentangle the real facts and incidents of the history from the interpretation put upon them by the different authors of the record. Each document has its peculiar standpoint and its own special merits. The two 'Prophetical' narratives lay great stress on the nature, character and requirement of Israel's merciful God and deliverer. They love to trace in the traditional story of the wanderings, the divine providence guiding, sustaining and chastening the tribes as they traversed those 'paths of ancient pilgrimage' that led them through the desert to Canaan. They insist upon the moral conditions of Jehovah's covenant with Israel: the need of righteousness, obedience, and faith in those who would render Him acceptable service.

The document of the 'Priestly' writer, probably compiled in the Exilic or post-Exilic period, cannot claim to possess independent value as a narrative of incidents that occurred in so remote an age. It is rather the work of a devout idealist who ascribes to primitive times the peculiar laws and institutions befitting a purely religious community such as Israel became after its return from Babylon. The writer loses sight of the rough and simple conditions of the nation's childhood; he depicts the facts, actual or traditional, of the wilderness life in such a way as to exhibit their typical significance. He traces to the Mosaic age ceremonies, laws and forms of worship which foreshadowed the spiritual realities of the kingdom of God. Valuable as his representation is from a purely religious point of view, it would be a mistake to employ it as a historical document. It bears witness to the faith, the devotion, the aspirations of Judaism; it is not in any strict sense a record of the facts of primitive Hebrew history.

The present chapter will for the most part describe the events of the Exodus and the wanderings in accordance with the Hebrew tradition, without attempting to distinguish minutely between the actual incidents of the history, and the form in which they have been clothed by the devout idealism of the writers[1].

It is characteristic of the biblical history that large tracts of time are occasionally passed over in silence.

Israel in Egypt. We do not know what interval elapsed between the settlement of the Benê Israel in Egypt and the accession of the *new king over Egypt which knew not Joseph.* It may be fairly assumed that Joseph's elevation took place under one of the later Hyksôs or Shepherd kings, a foreign dynasty whose capital had been fixed at Zoan, a city in the Delta. The Hyksôs were of Asiatic origin, and their invasion of Egypt (about the year 2100 B.C.) had opened the

[1] A symbolic narrative of the kind here alluded to is the sublime account of the Vision of Jehovah in Exod. xxiv. 8—11.

country to Semitic and specially to Canaanitish immigrants. Accordingly the Hebrews were for a long time peacefully engaged in pastoral pursuits, observing in all probability their own peculiar religious and social customs; but they were left unmolested by the Egyptian government, which treated them with benevolent neutrality.   Meanwhile their numbers and wealth continually increased.   In time however circumstances arose which rendered them formidable to the Egyptians.   At the period when the Hebrew tribes first entered Palestine, the Pharaohs were busily engaged in extending their conquests in Western Asia.   The reign of Thothmes III. (*c.* 1503—1449) may be specially mentioned as one of exceptional splendour. He claimed the suzerainty of the whole of Palestine; he even received tribute from Assyria and extended his conquests as far south as the Soudan.   It is noteworthy that among the titles of Palestinian cities which brought tribute to Thothmes, and of which a list is inscribed on the great temple of Karnak, occur those of two places called *Jacob-el* and *Joseph-el*: names which seem to imply some reminiscence of Hebrew patriarchs or tribes.   After the death of Thothmes, however, the influence of Egypt in Western Asia declined.   Some of the vassal princes of Palestine revolted, and we hear of the rise of a powerful Hittite kingdom in Northern Syria.   After an ineffective campaign, Sethos (Seti I.), one of the earliest kings of the nineteenth dynasty, was compelled to recognize the independence of the Hittites, and to content himself with securing the allegiance of the petty states of Palestine.   His son Ramses II. renewed the struggle with the Hittites, but though he claims to have broken their power, he was in reality obliged to conclude a treaty of peace with Khata-sar 'the great king of the Hittites' on equal terms, and peace was presently cemented by the marriage of Ramses with the daughter of his adversary.

As the Hebrews had now grown from being a mere family of settlers into a powerful community of organized tribes, we can understand the distrust with which Ramses II.—*the new king* of Exod. i. 8—regarded them. He naturally feared

The oppres-
sion of the
Hebrews.

that in the event of war with an Asiatic power these Semitic settlers on the north-eastern frontier of his kingdom might prove dangerous allies of the enemies of Egypt. He accordingly altered the indulgent treatment which the Hebrews had hitherto experienced. He needed labourers for the immense military and architectural enterprizes by which he had resolved to strengthen and adorn his kingdom[1]. The Hebrews were taken from the care of their flocks and herds, were subjected to a system of forced labour, and employed in the laborious construction of public works. Severe measures were taken to restrict their numbers and to crush their proud spirit of independence. Taskmasters were set over them, who compelled them to toil under the lash, and made their lives *bitter with hard service, in mortar and in brick, and in all manner of service in the field.*

Thus the Hebrews exchanged the condition of nomadic freedom for the miserable lot of Egyptian serfs, and it was inevitable that they should eagerly look for some opportunity of escape from their intolerable servitude.

The Pharaoh who took these coercive measures was almost certainly Ramses II. It is not clear however how long the oppression lasted, nor is it now possible to determine the precise date of the exodus. The most probable view is that the departure of the Hebrews from Egypt took place during the reign of Ramses II.'s son and successor, Merenptah or Meneptah, early in the thirteenth century before Christ[2]. A large slab of granite, engraved by order of Merenptah, and discovered at Thebes in 1896, has been supposed to indicate that the Israelites had already quitted Egypt and had

---

[1] The 'treasure cities' of Pithom and Raamses seem to have been towns in the Delta which Ramses was anxious to fortify strongly.

[2] The date of the exodus has been approximately fixed by Prof. Sayce at the year 1277 B.C.

disappeared in the wilderness. "The Israelites"—so run the concluding lines of this famous *stelè*—"are spoiled so that they have no seed; the land of Khor (southern Palestine) is become as a widow for Egypt, all lands together are in peace[1]."

This statement however is too vague to be regarded as an indisputable reference to the exodus. It is only certain that whenever the event took place it was the outcome of a revolt on the part of the Benê Israel against their oppressors, and that the leader and champion of his fellow-tribesmen in this movement was Moses.

The life of Moses falls into three periods, each lasting forty years. His father Amram belonged to the tribe of Levi. We first hear of him as saved from death by the care of his mother Jochebed, when an attempt was made by Pharaoh's orders to destroy all the male children of the Hebrews. The child was hidden in *an ark of bulrushes*, which lay concealed among the flags by the brink of the Nile. Here he was discovered by the daughter of Pharaoh. Moved with pity at his helpless plight, she adopted the child, gave him an Egyptian name[2], and brought him up as her own son. In the palace of the princess Moses grew to manhood. He *was instructed in all the wisdom of the Egyptians*[3], and tradition represents him as a youth of conspicuous stature, beauty and valour. But he could not be indifferent either to the sufferings or to the

  Birth and education of Moses, Ex. ii.

---

[1] On this famous 'Israel-stelè' see some remarks in *The Hexateuch according to the Revised Version* (Longmans, 1900), vol. I. p. 170. Cp. Driver in *Authority and Archaeology*, etc., p. 63.

[2] Moses, or Mosheh, is probably the Egyptian *Messu*, 'son': to Hebrew ears it suggested the meaning 'drawn out' from a verb *mâshah* (Exod. ii. 10). See Sayce, *EHH*, p. 161. According to Josephus the name of Pharaoh's daughter was Thermuthis (*Antiq.* II. 9).

[3] Acts vii. 22. The wisdom of the Egyptians, especially of the priestly caste, was proverbial (1 Kings iv. 30. Cp. Isai. xix. 11, 12). Moses would probably be educated in natural science and magic, astronomy, medicine, and geometry.

hopes of his own kindred, and we are told that when he reached man's estate he resolved to see for himself how his brethren, the children of Israel, fared.   An impetuous deed of bloodshed done in defence of a fellow-Israelite who was being ill-treated by an Egyptian, compelled Moses to flee from Egypt.   He found refuge in the land of Midian, where he was hospitably received by Reuel or Jethro, *the priest of Midian*, who gave to Moses his daughter Zipporah in marriage, and employed him in tending his flocks.   For many years Moses remained hidden in the solitudes of the desert, till an **Moses** incident occurred which necessitated his return **at Horeb,** to Egypt.   *When forty years were fulfilled an* **Ex. iii.** *angel appeared to him in the wilderness of Mount Sinai, in a flame of fire in a bush* (Acts vii. 30).   Here he received the divine commission to be the *ruler and deliverer* of his oppressed fellow-tribesmen ; here too a new revelation of God was vouchsafed to him.   He whom the patriarchs had worshipped as '*El Shaddai*, 'God Almighty', now disclosed Himself as *JAHVEH*, the self-existent God of grace, the God who pledges Himself to be with His people throughout the course of their history, as their leader and saviour[1].   This divine Name cannot have been wholly strange to the Hebrew clans.   Probably it was already familiar to the tribe of Levi, to which Moses himself belonged, nor was it altogether unknown beyond the limits of the Hebrew people.   But its infinite and far-reaching significance was henceforth to be progressively unfolded, and the solemn proclamation of it to Moses unquestionably marks the beginning of a new epoch in the history of religion.

----

[1] The best account of the name *Jahveh* is that it means 'He who will be' (cp. Exod. iii. 12, 14, 15).   This is evidently the view of the writer of the passage in the book Exodus.   *What* God would prove Himself to be is left unexpressed.   Time only would gradually unfold it.   In the onward course of history God would be continuously manifested as 'creator, saviour, strengthening guide.'

The task enjoined upon Moses was one before which his spirit naturally quailed. He was commanded by   The Mission
God to appear in the dreaded presence of the   of Moses, Ex.
Pharaoh, and to claim for the Israelites the right   iv.
to journey three days' journey into the wilderness for the purpose of offering sacrifice to Jehovah. Three signs were accordingly vouchsafed to confirm the truth of his mission[1]. But Moses still hesitated : he had no gift of eloquence. *Slow of speech and of a slow tongue*, how should he persuade Pharaoh, or even convince his brethren ? In reply to his questioning he was bidden to take his brother Aaron with him as spokesman or *prophet*[2]. Aaron should be to him *a mouth*; Moses should be to Aaron *as God*. Thus encouraged, Moses with his wife and sons set out on his return to Egypt. In the wilderness near *the mountain of God*, Aaron met him, *and Moses told Aaron all the words of the LORD wherewith He had sent him.* Together the brothers reached Egypt, and after summoning the elders of the Israelitish tribes, told them of the divine purpose of deliverance. Jehovah *had visited the children of Israel and had seen their affliction.* On hearing the welcome message *the people believed:* and *they bowed their heads and worshipped.*

Moses and Aaron now ventured to approach the Pharaoh, and asked permission to lead the Hebrews into   Moses before
the wilderness. Their first attempt utterly failed,   Pharaoh :
and indeed only resulted in a cruel aggravation   Exod. v.
of the sufferings already endured by the people. Moses and Aaron were bitterly reproached by the Hebrews for this ill-success. *Ye have made our savour to be abhorred in the eyes of Pharaoh and in the eyes of his servants, to put a sword in their hand to slay us.* Pharaoh had hardened his heart, though the signs of divine authority which he demanded of Moses

[1] Exod. iv. 1—9.
[2] Exod. vii. 1 Heb. *Nâbhi*, i.e. one commissioned to speak on another's behalf or in another's name.

were not withheld (Exod. vii. 8 foll.). It remained to be seen

The plagues of Egypt, Exod. vii. 20 —x. 29. whether the king's obstinacy would be finally overcome by the plagues which in rapid succession fell upon his land and nation. These visitations are described in great detail: in their nature they are such as would fall with peculiar severity on a people like the Egyptians, with their rigid ideas of cleanliness and ceremonial purity, their veneration of certain animals, their dependence on the waters of the sacred Nile and on the produce of the soil. "There was nothing in the plagues themselves," says a modern writer, "that was either supernatural or contra-natural. They were *signs and wonders*, not because they introduced new and unknown forces into the life of the Egyptians, but because the diseases and plagues already known to the country were intensified in action and crowded into a short space of time[1]." It was only the last of these plagues—probably a sudden and violent outbreak of pestilence —that effectually weakened the resolution of the king. The

The last plague, Exod. xi., xii. 1—36. death of his first-born son was a blow which finally humbled his pride. He consented to the departure of the Israelites and even urged them to leave Egypt with all speed. What preparations for their flight had been previously made we do not know. Moses had probably gathered information about possible routes through the wilderness from the tribes of the Arabian desert. The Hebrew women had been enjoined to request of their Egyptian neighbours jewels of silver and gold, and the statement that Jehovah *gave the people favour in the sight of the Egyptians* (Exod. xi. 3) may imply that Israel's departure was more deliberate than the narrative at first sight suggests. In any case the exodus began one night during the month Ahib or Nisan (March—April), while the land of Egypt was stricken with the terrors of the last and most fearful of the plagues. Tradition connected with this occasion the institution

[1] Sayce, *EHH*, p. 169.

of the Passover-meal,—an institution ever afterwards regarded as the solemn commemoration of that momentous *night of the LORD* which was *to be much observed of all the children of Israel throughout their generations* (Exod. xii. 42).

The precise route followed by the Israelites cannot now be traced with certainty. Apparently they started from Rameses (Zoan or Tanis) and made their first encampment at Succoth, in a district probably adjacent to the city of Pithom. They then

The exodus: Exod. xii. 37 foll., xiii. 17— xiv. 31.

abandoned the main route leading from Egypt to Palestine[1], and reached the Gulf of Suez at a point near the present town of Suez, where it was possible by crossing the sea to pass the southernmost extremity of the line of Egyptian fortifications which at that time apparently extended along the isthmus from north to south. Here, at a spot called Migdol, on the shore of the gulf, they were overtaken by the army of Merenptah, who seems to have already repented of his hastily given consent to the departure of the Israelites.

From the desperate situation in which they found themselves placed between their pursuers and the sea, the Hebrews were marvellously extricated. A strong east wind arose and blew during the night with such force that it left the shallow waters of the

The passage of the Red Sea: Exod. xiv. 21— 31.

sea low enough to be forded on foot. Under cover of darkness the fugitives advanced, and before the dawning of another day the whole host had reached the eastern shore. The Egyptian forces, finding that the Hebrews had escaped, pressed after them in hot pursuit, but their heavy chariot-wheels sank deep in the soft sand; the wind shifted to another quarter; the waters rolled back, and the horsemen of Pharaoh were overwhelmed in the depths of the sea. Thus Jehovah *saved Israel*

---

[1] Exod. xiii. 17, 18. South Palestine and the sea-coast were at this time in the uncontested possession of Egypt. On the light thrown by Egyptian inscriptions on the topography of Exod. i.—xiv., see Driver's essay in *Authority* etc., pp. 54—65.

*that day out of the hand of the Egyptians ; and Israel saw the
Egyptians dead upon the sea shore*[1]. With a song of triumph
the tribes of Israel, now welded by their escape from servitude
into a powerful nation, hailed the overthrow of their oppressors[2].

Just as the precise point at which the passage of the Red
Sea took place is uncertain, so the route afterwards followed by the Israelites is a matter of
dispute. It is a question whether they journeyed
southward along the eastern shore of the Gulf of Suez, or
whether they crossed the Sinaitic peninsula at once in an
easterly direction[3]. It has been held that the latter route
would be the natural one for fugitives from Egypt, and that the
Benê Israel would in the ordinary course of things avoid the
western part of the Sinaitic peninsula, since it was garrisoned
by Egyptian troops to whom was assigned the duty of guarding
the copper-mines of that district. The Hebrews would naturally be eager to find a refuge as speedily as possible among
their kinsfolk in Edom, whose territory lay beyond the range
of Egyptian domination. There seems however to be no
convincing reason at present for abandoning the ordinary view,
according to which the Hebrews journeyed southward until
they halted at the foot of the traditional Mount Sinai.

Whatever may have been their precise route, the life of the

*The route of
the Israelites.*

---

[1] In some passages of the O.T. there is apparently a confusion between
the *Yâm Sûph* 'Reedy Sea' (Exod. xv. 4), which corresponds to the modern
Gulf of Akabah, and the 'Egyptian Sea' (Isai. xi. 15) or modern Gulf of
Suez. In course of time the distinction between the two arms of the Red
Sea seems to have been forgotten. Cp. Sayce, *EHH*, pp. 182, 183.

[2] The magnificent 'Song of Moses' (Exod. xv.) probably formed part
of an ancient collection of national songs. Both its triumphant tone and
its somewhat antique style point to its composition in the Mosaic period,
but it bears distinct traces of later modification and expansion. See Driver,
LOT, p. 30.

[3] This seems to be implied in Num. xxxiii. 10, if it be rightly assumed
that *Yâm Sûph* means the Gulf of Akabah.

Hebrews in the wilderness was that of ordinary nomads.   They
encamped at various places, a few of which have been identified
with more or less confidence by modern travellers: Marah with
its bitter waters, Elim with its wells and grove of palm-trees, the
wilderness of Sin where the murmurings of the tribes and their
yearnings for *the flesh-pots of Egypt* were silenced   Israel in the
by the gift of *manna* and the appearance of im-   wilderness:
mense flights of quails; Rephidim where the   Exod. xv. 22—
people thirsted for water and *strove with Moses*,   xvii. 16.
reproaching him as the author of their sufferings.   Here at
Jehovah's command Moses with his wonder-working rod smote
the rock, which yielded water in abundance.   In memory of
the distrust by which they *tempted Jehovah*, the spot was called
Massah, 'tempting,' and *Meribah*, 'strife.'   At Rephidim also
the advance of the Hebrews was resisted by the Amalekites, a
powerful and widely-dispersed tribe of nomads whose original
home was in the desert of Paran, and with whom the Israelites
more than once came into collision[1].   Owing to
the prolonged intercession of Moses, whose hands   The struggle
were supported in the attitude of prayer by Aaron   with Amalek.
and Hur, and to the valour of Joshua, now mentioned for the
first time as the acknowledged captain of the Hebrew warriors,
the Amalekites were discomfited.   The issue of the battle was
recorded *for a memorial in a book*, and to mark the scene of
the victory an altar was erected called *Jehovah-nissi*, 'Jehovah
is my banner.'   The treacherous hostility of Amalek was never
to be forgotten.   *The LORD hath sworn: the LORD will have
war with Amalek from generation to generation* (Exod. xvii. 16;
cp. 1 Sam. xv. 2, 3).

With the Midianites, on the other hand, whose king-priest
Jethro was Moses' kinsman by marriage, the Benê   Jethro's visit
Israel formed an alliance.   Jethro, accompanied   to Moses:
by Zipporah, the wife of Moses, and her two sons,   Exod. xviii.
who had perhaps been temporarily entrusted to his protection,

[1] Cp. Num. xiv. 45.

visited the camp of the Hebrews, and rejoiced to hear the story of their deliverance, in which he recognized the unique power of Jehovah, as *greater than all gods.* It was at his father-in-law's suggestion that Moses, who had hitherto borne the burden of leadership alone, took the first steps towards a systematic organization of the tribes with a view to a more thorough administration of justice. By these arrangements the people were to some extent prepared for the more complete and detailed legislation of Sinai. Jethro was now anxious to return *into his own land* (Exod. xviii. 27), but apparently he and his clansmen were induced to remain in the Hebrew camp and to act as guides to the Israelites during their wanderings[1].

The open expanse at the foot of Mount Sinai was reached

Arrival at Sinai: Exod. xix.

at the end of the third month after the exodus. We have already noticed that the situation of the biblical Sinai is a matter of some uncertainty. Some scholars incline to the view that the mountain mentioned in the book of Exodus lay on the frontiers of Edom, eastward of the desert of Paran[2]. If the Israelites crossed the Sinaitic peninsula they would naturally make their first prolonged halt in this region. On the other hand an early and constant tradition favours Jebel Mûsa, in the south of the peninsula, as the mountain on which the Law was delivered, and upon the whole this locality best satisfies the required conditions. In any case it is likely that the mountain was already venerated as a sacred spot, and derived its name from *Sin*, the Moon-god of Babylonia. The interest of the question as to its actual

[1] Cp. Num. x. 29 foll. There seem to have been two traditions respecting the name of Moses' father-in-law. One account calls him *Jethro* or *Reuel* (which possibly was a priestly title meaning 'Shepherd of God'); another speaks of him as *Hobab ben Reuel* (Num. *l.c.*). Some however suppose that *Hobab* is the name of Jethro's son. Cp. Judg. iv. 11, R.V. marg.

[2] This view finds some support in the language of the most ancient Hebrew poetry. Cp. Judg. v. 4, 5; Deut. xxxiii. 2.

situation is but slight when compared with the importance of the event which made it for ever famous. Sinai was in fact the birthplace of Israel's nationality, law, and religion.

Upon their arrival *before the mount* the Israelites were bidden to prepare for the approaching manifesta- tion of Jehovah's presence. Moses was called up into the mountain and charged to deliver the divine message to the people : *Ye have seen what I did unto the Egyptians, and how I bare you on eagles' wings, and brought you unto myself. Now therefore, if ye will obey my voice indeed, and keep my covenant, then ye shall be a peculiar treasure unto me from among all peoples: for all the earth is mine: and ye shall be unto me a kingdom of priests, and an holy nation* (Exod. xix. 4—6). On the third day, after a due interval of ceremonial purification, the awe-struck Israelites beheld the descent of Jehovah *in fire* upon Mount Sinai, amid the darkness and terrors of a thunderstorm and *the voice of a trumpet exceeding loud.* Then from the very mouth of God proceeded the 'Ten Words' which were to form the basis of the covenant[1] between Himself and Israel. The solemn and awful circumstances under which they were delivered imparted a unique and inviolable authority to the Ten Commandments. Not only were they uttered by the voice of Jehovah Himself, but they were believed to have been afterwards graven by His finger on two tables of stone[2]. Whatever may have been their original form, it is of vital importance to notice that the earliest legislation consisted of a series of plain *moral* precepts. As the charter of a higher religion than the world had yet known, the 'ten words' stood alone and supreme[3]. From the first, Israel's religion was based on a nobler conception of God, and therefore demanded a higher morality, than that of other nations.

The Theo-phany at Sinai.

The ten words: Exod. xx. 1—17.

[1] Cp. Deut. v. 2.
[2] Exod. xxxi. 18; Deut. iv. 13.
[3] Deut. v. 22; Jer. vii. 22.

O. H.   5

The Decalogue in fact laid down in large general outline the primary duties of a *holy nation*: fidelity and loyalty in the service of Jehovah, as the one and only God acknowledged by Israel; a pure and spiritual worship, consistent with His nature and essential holiness; reverence, humanity, purity, justice and good faith in the different relationships of human life. Thus the Law of Sinai declared, in an age when the notion was as yet wholly new and unfamiliar, that religion and morality, truth and righteousness, are vitally and indissolubly connected.

It is impossible to determine what parts of the legislation contained in the Pentateuch are to be ascribed to Moses himself. It is however practically certain that the highly elaborate ordinances connected with sacrificial worship existed, if at all in that primitive age, only in germ. But the so-called 'Book of the Covenant' (Exod. xx. 22—xxiii. 33) represents in all probability the earliest code of Hebrew law, and considering their rudimentary character the precepts contained in this passage may fairly be regarded as Mosaic. Among them are some which give a sanction to existing customs, such as the law of retaliation (Exod. xxi. 23—25); others are designed to protect human life in a rude and barbarous age. The greater part of the enactments however are applicable to an agricultural rather than to a nomadic condition of life. The state of society contemplated in the legislation is still simple and primitive but not altogether uncivilized. The conception that God Himself is the immediate source of judgment (Exod. xxi. 6, xxii. 8, 9) marks the archaic character of the code, while the injunction to observe three feasts in the year (Exod. xxiii. 14—19) may represent a custom which the Hebrews had practised during their sojourn in Goshen. Speaking generally however the most important features of the 'Book of the Covenant' are its comparative silence in regard to points of worship and ritual, and its insistence on fundamental duties of morality. "The principles of civil and criminal justice are

'The Book of the Covenant,' Exod. xx. 22—xxiii. 33.

those still current among the Arabs of the desert." The code "contains precepts adapted, as our Lord puts it, to the hardness of the people's heart. The ordinances are not abstractly perfect and fit to be a rule of life in every state of society, but they are fit to make Israel a righteous, humane and God-fearing people, and to facilitate a healthy growth towards better things [1]."

The conditions of the covenant which Jehovah purposed to make between Himself and the ransomed people were communicated to them by Moses. They were taught at Sinai the real meaning and object of their deliverance from Egypt; at the same time there dawned upon them a new and worthier conception of the God of their fathers. The experience of the exodus had taught them that Jehovah was a Being incomparable or unique among gods (Exod. xv. 11). The redemption of an enslaved race from the bondage of Egypt had manifested both His grace, and His 'holiness [2]'; His pity for the oppressed, and His unapproachable majesty. But at Sinai Israel learned the further lesson that this God of grace and power was also a Being who delighted in justice and humanity, a defender of the cause of the poor and helpless, the chastiser of falsity, cruelty and oppression. There were doubtless many elements of imperfection in Israel's idea of Jehovah. He was popularly conceived as Israel's tribal deity, marching with His people to battle against their enemies, more powerful indeed than the deities of the heathen, but having stern attributes akin in some respects to theirs. But the arm of Jehovah had as it were been laid bare in the marvels of the exodus, and the legislation of Sinai formed the foundation of higher and purer moral ideas, which the great prophets of later ages expanded and developed. Thus the revelation of God's essential character and requirement was

The revelation of God at Sinai.

[1] Robertson Smith, *OTJC*, pp. 341—343.

[2] The original meaning of 'holiness' as applied to God seems to be *transcendence*, or *separateness from created things.*

progressive, and it is the teaching of the Gospel that finally crowns and completes the gradual disclosure of the Old Testament.

The ratification of the covenant now took place. *Under the mount* Moses erected an altar on which burnt-offerings and peace-offerings were sacrificed. The blood was sprinkled partly on the altar, partly on the people in token of the bond which now united them to Jehovah. They on their part pledged themselves to obedience. Finally, chosen representatives of the nation, Moses, Aaron and his two sons, together with seventy of the elders of Israel, were admitted to a mysterious communion-feast with "the very God, the Highest," and even to a vision of celestial glory—a symbolical foretaste of the future blessings of the divine kingdom. *They beheld God, and did eat and drink.*

Ratification of the covenant: Exod. xxiv. 1—11.

Moses alone with his minister Joshua remained for forty days and nights in the mount. It was believed that during this time the divine pattern of the future tabernacle and its furniture was delivered to him. Meanwhile however the first signal act of apostasy on the part of the newly-enfranchised nation took place. Restless and alarmed at the prolonged absence of their leader, the people demanded of Aaron that he should make them a god to go before them. Aaron yielded to their pressure, and taking the golden ear-rings offered by the Hebrew women he fashioned a molten calf, built an altar before it, and proclaimed a feast to Jehovah. On the morrow sacrifices were offered, and *the people sat down to eat and rose up to play.*

The golden calf: Exod. xxxii.

This worship of the national God under the symbol of a metal calf or bull was a breach of the second rather than of the first commandment[1]. In any case it was necessary that the

[1] The origin of the bull-worship is not to be traced to Egyptian influence. It is more likely that it was rooted in the religious tendencies of the Hebrews themselves. "Among an agricultural people there would be

people should be severely punished for their speedy violation of Jehovah's covenant. Moses unexpectedly reappeared in the camp. He had already been warned by God of what had occurred and had already pleaded for the pardon of the guilty people. When he approached the scene of shameless riot he cast down in hot anger *the tables of the testimony*, and broke them to pieces *beneath the mount*. At his summons his kinsmen of the tribe of Levi rallied to his side, and he employed them as the ministers of vengeance on the guilty. Three thousand of the offenders were slain. The molten calf was ground to powder by Moses, and the fragments strewed upon the water which the people drank. Then he *returned unto Jehovah* to renew his intercession for the people, and was finally rewarded by the acceptance of his prayer and by the assurance of Jehovah's continued presence with His erring people. The broken tables of the covenant were replaced, and to Moses himself was vouchsafed the privilege of a closer communion with Jehovah, and a fuller unveiling of the divine glory. It is significant that the wonderful declaration of Jehovah's 'Name' in Exod. xxxiv. 6, 7 is placed   The 'Name' of Jahveh. by the compilers of the book in very close connection with the account of Israel's act of apostasy. The sin of man as it were brought into higher relief two essential truths of the divine nature. On the one hand God is invisible: *man shall not see me and live*. On the other hand, in God are inseparably conjoined the two attributes so seldom perfectly blended in man: mercy and truth, perfect love and perfect righteousness.

A large portion of the book of Exodus (chh. xxv.—xxx. and xxxv.—xl.) is devoted to a description of the   The Tabernacle and its worship. Tabernacle and its furniture, the institution of the priesthood and the ordinances of worship. Of all these it was believed that the pattern had been revealed

no more natural symbol of strength and vital energy than the young bull." Hastings' *DB*, s.v. 'Golden Calf.'

to Moses in Mount Sinai (Exod. xxv. 40). The worship of a national God implied the erection of a national sanctuary, to be a visible emblem or pledge of Jehovah's presence in the midst of His people, and connected with it, such primitive rites and ceremonies as might be suited to the conditions of life in the wilderness. The earliest tabernacle or tent was probably very simple in its structure and arrangement. In form it was like an ordinary nomad's tent. It was surrounded by an open court—an enclosure formed by curtains suspended from pillars of wood. This portable tent consisted of two chambers, the outer one being lighted by a lamp, while the inner sanctuary remained in total darkness. As its name implies, the Tabernacle was regarded as the actual dwelling-place of Jehovah, the spot where He was pleased to manifest Himself to His people. *There I will meet with the children of Israel; and the tent shall be sanctified by my glory* (Exod. xxix. 43)[1]. 'The tent of meeting' as it was called (Exod. xxvii. 21) served also to shelter the most sacred of Israel's possessions, 'the ark of the covenant[2].' The ark was venerated as a visible token of Jehovah's unfailing presence with His people. It accompanied the Hebrews throughout the period of their wanderings; it was even carried into battle, as being a sure pledge of victory over their foes; by Hebrew poets it is spoken of as the seat on which Jehovah sits enthroned. To the tribe of Levi were assigned the care of the sanctuary and the duties of ministration, while Aaron and his sons exercised the priestly office. It was only by degrees

[1] The description of the Tabernacle in the book of Exodus which represents it as a highly elaborate and gorgeous structure is probably idealized. It occurs in the work of the 'priestly writer' and seems to be coloured by reminiscences of Solomon's Temple. But the existence of a simple 'tent of meeting' in the wilderness cannot be disputed.

[2] Josh. iii. 6, 8 etc. The older name for the ark was 'ark of Jehovah,' or 'ark of God.' The later title 'Ark of the Testimony' had reference to the Tables of the Law deposited in the ark. It has been thought that the primitive ark contained some sacred image, or stone, representing Jahveh Himself.

that the ordinances of worship were developed into an elaborate and complex system. During the period of Israel's sojourn in the wilderness the services of the Tabernacle were necessarily simple. The main duties of the priesthood con- The priest-sisted in the offering of sacrifice, the consultation hood. of the divine oracle and the communication to the people of instruction (*Torah*) concerning the divine will or decisions (*Toroth*) in particular cases of difficulty. To the priests was assigned the duty of summoning religious assemblies and of giving the signal for journeying and for battle by a blast of the sacred trumpets. To them also belonged the right of blessing the people in Jehovah's name. The fundamental idea that inspired the legislation of Moses in all its details was that Israel belonged to God by right of redemption, that its peculiar ordinances and institutions were prescribed by Him, and that He was present in the midst of His people to direct, guide and govern them according to their need. Thus the priests, like Moses himself, were the organs of the divine sovereignty; they were ministers through whom God made Himself known to Israel as its lawgiver, judge, and king (Exod. xxix. 46)[1].

The materials needed for the construction of the Tabernacle were provided by the people themselves, who freely offered of the wealth they had brought from Egypt. Tradition also preserved the names of the artificers who superintended the work, Bezalel of the tribe of Judah, and Oholiab of the tribe of Dan.

At length the appointed sign for departure from Sinai was given: after a year's sojourn before the Mount The march *the cloud was taken up from over the tabernacle* resumed, *of the testimony;* in regular order of march, each Num. x. 11—36. tribe being marshalled under its proper ensign, the Israelites *set forward out of the wilderness of Sinai.* Guided by Hobab the Midianite and preceded by the sacred

---

[1] This immediate and direct government of the nation by God Himself was in a much later age called a 'Theocracy.' Josephus, *c. Apion.* ii. 16.

ark, they journeyed from Sinai into the wilderness of Paran. A few typical incidents of the desert journey are recorded, as

St Paul says, *for our admonition* (1 Cor. x. 11).

Taberah,
Num. xi. 1.

Taberah ('burning'), which was apparently the first resting place of the host, derived its name from the *fire of Jehovah* (lightning) which slew those who

Kibroth-
hattaavah:
Num. xi. 4—
35.

murmured against God. At Kibroth-hattaavah ('graves of lust') *they buried the people that lusted* for the plenty of Egypt and were surfeited by the flesh of quails. At this spot took place the

appointment of seventy elders of Israel to share with Moses the heavy burden of government. Hazeroth was the scene of

Hazeroth,
Num. xii.

a jealous contention against Moses on the part of Aaron and Miriam. *Hath Jehovah indeed spoken only with Moses?* they asked. *Hath he not spoken also with us?* This led to a direct vindication by Jehovah of His servant's authority. Miriam was smitten with leprosy and only healed through the supplication of Moses. We do not read elsewhere of the Ethiopian (Cushite) wife of Moses, who was made the pretext of complaint against him. But Josephus preserves a tradition which implies that as an Egyptian prince Moses was at one time brought into contact with the Ethiopians[1].

The 'desert-wearied tribes' came almost within sight of

Kadesh,
Num. xiii.,
xiv.

Canaan when they reached the ancient sanctuary of Kadesh-barnea (the En-Mishpat of Gen. xiv. 7), which was situated in a rich oasis near the

northern boundary of the wilderness of Paran. After Sinai, Kadesh was the most important halting place of the Israelites, and here apparently they abode *many days* (Deut. i. 46). There is even reason for supposing that throughout the 38 years of the wandering the Tabernacle remained at Kadesh, and formed a centre to which the widely-dispersed tribes

---

[1] *Antiq. of the Jews*, bk. ii. 10.

resorted for purposes of worship and direction.   From Kadesh
in due time were sent forth twelve spies to explore the
promised land.   They penetrated at least as far as Hebron,
and returned after the lapse of forty days bring-
ing with them a huge cluster of grapes and   *The report of the spies.*
other products of the land.   Their account of
the land however was *evil.   It is a land*, they declared, *that
eateth up the inhabitants thereof;* all the people that they had
seen were of unusual stature, some of them apparently being
descendants of the ancient *Nephîlîm* or giant race of aboriginal
Palestine.   This report so discouraged the people that they
refused to advance further and even clamoured for a return to
Egypt.   Caleb and Joshua, two of the spies, vainly endeavoured
to stem the torrent of disaffection, and narrowly escaped being
stoned to death.   The faithless and timorous distrust of the
tribes brought upon them a heavy chastisement.   The intercession of Moses availed indeed to avert from the rebellious
host the doom of utter destruction, but a divine sentence of
exclusion for forty years from the land of promise was passed
upon the whole 'congregation' with the exception of Caleb
and Joshua, while a plague consumed the remaining spies
whose evil tidings had led to the outbreak.

The panic-stricken mood of the people quickly passed away,
but repentance came too late.   They made a desperate attempt
to force a passage northwards into the land, but the complete
discomfiture of their warriors taught them that they were as yet
no match for the fierce and hardy inhabitants of the hill-
country.   A swarm of Amalekites and Canaanites burst upon
them *and smote them and beat them down even unto Hormah*
(Num. xiv. 45, Deut. i. 44).

It was at Kadesh in all probability that the serious rebellion
of Korah and his associates took place.   The
account in the book of Numbers implies that   *The rebellion of Korah, Num. xvi.*
with a civil rebellion against the authority of the
Lawgiver was combined a religious revolt against

the influence of the Aaronic priesthood[1]. The revolt against Moses was led by Dathan and Abiram, of the tribe of Reuben[2]. As members of the oldest tribe they resented his supremacy, and rudely reproached him with his unfitness for the leadership. Their rebellion was fearfully punished. The earth *clave asunder* under them and *swallowed them up* with their wives and children. Korah on the other hand demanded on behalf of the whole tribe of Levi, to which Moses and Aaron belonged, the right to exercise priestly functions. His adherents, however, who had presumed to offer incense upon the sacred altar, brought upon themselves speedy retribution.

The renewed murmurs of the people were chastised by the outbreak of a pestilence, in which more than fourteen thousand perished, and which was finally stayed through the mediation of Aaron, who stood with his kindled censer between the living and the dead making atonement for Israel's guilt[3].

How long the sojourn in Kadesh continued we do not
Death of Miriam, Num. xx. 1. know. Two other incidents seem to have occurred before the wanderings were resumed: the death and burial of Miriam, whom tradition represented as sharing with her two brothers the burden of leadership (Mic. vi. 4); and the sin of Moses and Aaron at *the waters of strife.* Again the people complained of a scarcity
The waters of strife, Num. xx. 2-- 13. of water, and their murmurs provoked Moses to speak *unadvisedly with his lips* (Ps. cvi. 33). Instead of obeying the divine command to *speak to the rock that it give forth water* he cried to the people *Hear now, ye rebels: shall we bring you forth water out*

---

[1] Cp. Deut. xi. 6 foll.

[2] Gen. xlix. 3 foll. shows that Reuben as the oldest tribe claimed a position of hegemony among the Israelites, which however had been justly forfeited.

[3] The account in Num. xvii. of the miracle which vindicated the claim of Aaron and his family to hold the priestly office, belongs to the priestly document, not apparently to the earliest tradition.

of this rock? and twice smote the rock with his staff. For this failure of patience and faith both Moses and Aaron forfeited the privilege of leading the Israelites into the promised land.

The long sojourn in the wilderness of Paran at length reached its close. The years during which Israel abode in this region were of great importance for its future destiny. At Kadesh the vigorous but undisciplined tribes were slowly consolidated into a warlike host; the legislation of Moses was probably completed and put to the test of practical experience; the religion of Jehovah took deep and permanent root in the heart of the ransomed nation. A poet of a much later age in Hebrew history looks back with devout interest on that creative epoch in Israel's career [1]:

> *For Jehovah's portion is his people;*
> *Jacob is the lot of his inheritance.*
> *He found him in a desert land,*
> *And in the waste howling wilderness;*
> *He compassed him about, he cared for him,*
> *He kept him as the apple of his eye:*
> *As an eagle that stirreth up her nest,*
> *That fluttereth over her young,*
> *He spread abroad his wings, he took them,*
> *He bare them on his pinions:*
> *Jehovah alone did lead him,*
> *And there was no strange god with him.*

(Deut. xxxii. 9 foll.)

In the arid solitudes of the wilderness the generation which escaped from the bondage of Egypt was gradually replaced by a hardier race. The desert life was indeed a necessary stage in the nation's moral and religious development,

---

[1] It is doubtful whether the 'Song of Moses' is of earlier date than the age of Jeremiah. See Driver, *LOT*, p. 96 foll.

and prepared it for the conflict by which the promised land was afterwards won. In the wilderness Israel's character was gradually disciplined by a simple and pure moral code, while its faith was moulded and invigorated by those austere conceptions of God which are natural to the desert nomad[1]. Thus the Hebrews slowly gathered the force and vitality necessary for the task of subduing the nations of Palestine, and appropriating the gifts of Canaanitish culture and civilization.

From Kadesh Moses sent messengers to the king of Edom, asking permission to pass through his territory. The request was peremptorily refused, and Israel was consequently forced *to compass the land of Edom*[2].

On the summit of Mount Hor Aaron breathed his last, and Eleazar his son was invested with the priestly office. In this wild, dreary and barren region *the soul of the people was much discouraged because of the way.* Obliged by the unbrotherly conduct of Edom to turn southward from Canaan, when their goal was almost within sight, they slowly journeyed towards the shores of the Gulf of Akabah. The narrative touches briefly but vividly on their sufferings; the scarcity of food and water led to renewed murmurings, which were punished by the visitation of the *fiery serpents*. The memory of this scourge and of the remedy divinely-provided was preserved to a late period; for the brazen serpent which Moses was enjoined to set upon a pole or standard before the eyes of the people seems to have been actually preserved for centuries, and to have become an object of superstitious reverence[3].

Death of Aaron: Num. xx. 22 foll.

The brazen serpent: Num. xxi. 4—9.

---

[1] Cp. G. A. Smith, *HGHL*, p. 88.

[2] The encounter (Num. xxi. 1—3) with the Canaanitish king of Arad, a city in the *Negeb* (south country), probably took place before the departure of the Israelites from Kadesh.

[3] The brazen serpent is said to have been destroyed by Hezekiah 2 Kings xviii. 4. We may here have an example of a later tradition respecting a monument the origin of which was wholly forgotten.

No clear tradition respecting the wanderings from this point onwards is preserved. A list of stations at which the tribes encamped is recorded in Num. xxxiii. (cp. Deut. x. 6, 7), but the actual route followed by the Israelites is quite uncertain. On the whole the most probable view is, that having journeyed southwards towards the Gulf of Akabah, on the western side of Mount Seir, they returned northwards on the eastern side, thus completing the circuit of Edom (Deut. ii. 1). At length we hear of them as crossing the brook Zered, which formed the northern boundary of the desert and the southern limit of Moab. They next halted on the brink of the deep defile through which the Arnon rushes eastward into the Dead Sea. A reminiscence of this memorable stage in their journey is preserved in a fragment of a national ballad quoted in Num. xxi. 14, 15, which recalls the dim memories of

> *Vaheb in Suphah,*
> *And the valleys of Arnon,*
> *And the slope of the valleys that inclineth toward the*
>   *dwelling of Ar.*

They were now at length in a territory comparatively well-watered and fertile[1]; but their advance was threatened by the hostility of the Amorite chief Sihon, who had apparently made an incursion into the territories of Moab and Ammon, and established a powerful kingdom with Heshbon as its centre. At this point therefore the Israelites were once more engaged in fierce warfare. Sihon not only refused them a passage through his territory, but resisted their further advance by force of arms. A decisive campaign ensued. Sihon was slain in battle and his land *from Arnon unto Jabbok* fell into the hands of the Israelites. The

Conquest of Sihon and Og: Num. xxi.

---

[1] The 'song of the well' (Num. xxi. 17, 18) may recall some incident of the desert wanderings which had now reached their close, or may express the naive delight with which the Israelites entered a land where wells could be effectually sunk.

capture of Heshbon, Sihon's stronghold, was celebrated in another ancient war-song, of which we perhaps possess a fragment in Num. xxi. 27 foll.[1] This success was followed by the overthrow of Og the king of Bashan, an Amoritish chief who had seized on a tract of territory north of the Jabbok, and had fixed his capital at Edrei. By this conquest the Israelites gained possession of the greater part of Gilead[2]. The tribes

Num. xxxii.   of Reuben and Gad, and the half-tribe of Manasseh, were allowed to occupy the conquered district (which was luxuriantly fertile and well-suited for the grazing of cattle), on condition of their duly assisting the other tribes to subdue the territory west of Jordan.

A firm footing had now been secured by the invaders on the eastern side of the Jordan valley. In the *plains of Moab* opposite to the city of Jericho the main body of the Israelites was securely encamped. Their rapid and decisive conquests had naturally struck terror into the Moabites, who apparently

The story of Balaam: Num. xxii.— xxiv.; xxxi. 8, 16.   abstained from any hostile action[3], and allowed the invaders a free right of passage through their territory. In his alarm and perplexity Balak, the king of Moab, sent an embassy to Balaam, a famous eastern soothsayer who dwelt at Pethor on the Euphrates, imploring him to come and pronounce a curse (i.e. cast some malignant spell) upon the Israelites. The account of this episode is very remarkable though somewhat obscure and contradictory in minor details. The mention of

---

[1] It is a matter of dispute whether this song (Num. xxi. 27—30) refers (1) to the victory of Israel over Sihon, or (2) to a later conquest of Moab, or (3) whether it is part of an *Amorite* war-song recounting the invasion of the region of Moab by Amorites from the west side of Jordan.

[2] The *Havvoth Jair* ('tent-villages of Jair') situated in *the region of Argob* ('stony') afterwards called Trachonitis, apparently formed part of the kingdom of Bashan: but the conquest of this district probably took place at a later period, when the Israelites were already settled west of Jordan. See Num. xxxii. 39—41.

[3] Cp. Deut. ii. 9.

the *elders of Midian* seems to imply that Moab was at this time partially occupied, as in later times, by hordes of Midianites [1]. We are told that the Israelites were seduced from their allegiance to Jehovah not only by the attractions of the licentious worship offered to the Moabitish deity Baal-Peor, but by the *wiles* of the Midianites (Num. xxv. 18). The wrath of Jehovah fell heavily on the camp of the Israelites, and it was only the righteous zeal of Phinehas the priest that saved them from utter destruction. A speedy and overwhelming vengeance overtook the Midianites. Twelve thousand men of Israel led by Phinehas, and accompanied by *the vessels of the sanctuary* (i.e. the ark), fell upon the host of Midian; the five chieftains were slain, and Balaam himself, who had counselled the Midianites to ensnare Israel into idolatry, perished in battle [2]. The encampments and villages of the tribe were destroyed, and the remnant which escaped the sword was driven back into the desert.

The famous prophecy of Balaam calls for a passing word of comment. In its present form it probably belongs to the age of the early monarchy, though doubtless it is based on some more ancient Balaam's prophecy. tradition. It reflects the thoughts and hopes which were popularly connected with the establishment of the monarchy. The prophecy thus takes its place in the series of 'Messianic' predictions. The main thought of the poem is that Israel is a people protected by the favour of the Almighty against the evil designs of all its enemies, and that future dominion is its rightful and certain portion. In the allusion to *the star* destined to *come forth out of Jacob, and the sceptre* that should one day *rise out of Israel*, we may trace a reference to some individual king, possibly David himself, through whom Israel's magnificent destiny is to be realized. The prophecy belongs

[1] Cp. Judg. vi. 1—6.
[2] Gen. xxxvi. 32 mentions 'Bela, son of Beor' as an early king of Edom. Possibly he is to be identified with Balaam. See Sayce, *EHH*, 229.

to a time when the Messianic vision in its strict sense—the vision of a Davidic king exercising world-wide sovereignty, and triumphant over foes—had already dawned upon Israel.

In the plains of Moab the final work of Israel's great leader and lawgiver was accomplished. Nothing is more probable than that Moses supplemented the legislation of Sinai and Kadesh by enactments adapted to the altered conditions of the tribes which had now finally emerged from the wilderness. The appointment of six cities of refuge for persons who might have unwittingly or unintentionally shed blood may be confidently ascribed to this period, as also may the assignment of certain cities to the Levites, not for their exclusive possession, but for the purpose of distributing them duly among the districts occupied by the tribes. The book of Deuteronomy doubtless belongs to an age several centuries later than that of Moses himself, but its hortatory 'recapitulation' of the Law may well be based on a traditional account of the last words of the great lawgiver [1].

End of the wanderings.

The noble 'Song of Moses' (Deut. xxxii. 1—43) has been described as a kind of "prophetic meditation" on the lessons which lay on the surface of Israel's earlier history. Its imagery seems to have been suggested by reminiscences of desert life. If we discern in this striking poem an ideal picture of Israel's transition from a nomadic life in the wilderness to that of agricultural settlers in a new country we may regard it as most suitably placed at the close of the book of Deuteronomy [2].

'Song' and 'Blessing' of Moses: Deut. xxxii., xxxiii.

The *blessing wherewith Moses the man of God blessed the children of Israel before his death* (Deut. xxxiii.), marked as it is

[1] The title (first employed by Philo) is derived from the Greek version of Deut. xvii. 18, where the words rendered in R.V. *a copy of this law*, are translated τὸ δευτερονόμιον τοῦτο.

[2] Cp. G. A. Smith, *HGHL*, pp. 8₅, 86. As to the date of the 'Blessing' see Driver, *LOT*, p. 98.

by a highly idealised conception of the tribes and a thrilling
tone of martial enthusiasm, is probably more ancient than
the 'Song.' It bears traces of having been composed at
a period when Ephraim and Manasseh (the descendants of
Joseph) stood foremost among the tribes in power and
prestige. It may be regarded as a war-song, intended to keep
alive in the hearts of the tribes the memory of the glorious
days when *Jeshurun* (the 'righteous nation' i.e. Israel), as
a strong and united people, loyal to its God and devoted to its
leader Joshua, marched from one scene of victory to another,
and at length rested from its martial toil, secure in the sense of
Jehovah's favour and protection. The tone and spirit indeed
of the 'Blessing' differ widely from those of the 'Song.' In
the latter Israel is described as having fallen into apostasy and
brought upon itself the consuming anger of Jehovah. The
'Blessing' on the other hand reflects the aspirations and
temper of a prosperous and powerful people.

> *Happy art thou, O Israel:*
> *Who is like unto thee, a people saved by Jehovah,*
> *The shield of thy help,*
> *And that is the sword of thy excellency !*
> *Thine enemies shall submit themselves unto thee ;*
> *And thou shalt tread upon their high places.*
>
> (Deut. xxxiii. 29.)

And now the closing scene of Moses' life was at hand. He
received the divine command to get him up into Mount Nebo,
one of the heights of the *'Abârim* (the ranges running east of
the Jordan valley), and there to behold with his eyes the land
of promise in its entire breadth and length. Here on the
barren height or summit (*Pisgah*) of a mountain, he yielded
up his spirit, and was buried *in the valley in*   Death of
the land of Moab over against Beth-peor: but no   Moses; Deut.
man knoweth of his sepulchre unto this day. His   xxxiv.
prayer for a successor qualified to be a true shepherd of the

congregation, *to lead them out* and *to bring them in,* had already
been answered; before his departure he had
been commanded to lay his hands upon
Joshua, the son of Nun, and to *give him a
charge.* For the difficult task that now lay before them, the
tribes of Israel were provided with a leader whose very name,
'Jehovah's salvation,' was a pledge of divine aid and of ultimate
triumph.

Num. xxvii.
17, 23.

CHAPTER IV.

THE CONQUEST OF PALESTINE.

THE account of the invasion of Western Palestine by the Israelites is contained in the first half of the book of Joshua, chh. ii. 1—xi. 23. There are also scattered notices in later parts of the book and in Judges, ch. i. The narratives are not in every particular clear or consistent, but the main facts can be ascertained without much difficulty. The invasion appears to have been a simultaneous movement of all the tribes under the leadership of the Ephraimite Joshua; the Jordan was crossed at a point near the city of Jericho, which was the first place that succumbed to Israel's impetuous onset. The inhabitants of the important stronghold of Gibeon, situated on the central plateau some six miles north-west of Jerusalem, were panic-stricken at the speedy fall of Jericho, and hastened to come to terms with the conquerors. Gilgal, in the plain between Jericho and the Jordan, was selected by the Israelitish leader as the site of his central camp, and from this base a further campaign was directed against the Canaanites. A coalition of petty kings was hastily formed in the hope of checking the advance of the Hebrews, but the Canaanitish forces were completely overthrown and scattered near Beth-horon in Central Judaea. After this the operations of the

The conquest of Western Palestine— its general course.

invaders were divided : the tribes of Judah and Simeon, aided by the Calebites, overran and occupied the highlands of central and southern Judaea ; while Joshua at the head of the powerful tribe of Joseph, penetrated by way of Ai, Bethel and Mount Ephraim, into the plain of Esdraelon, and finally defeated a confederacy of northern kings at the waters of Merom.   The subjugation of Palestine however was apparently by no means completed at Joshua's death.   By that time indeed the Israelites had gained a permanent footing on Mount Ephraim and on the highlands of southern Canaan, but most of the larger cities, together with the cultivated valleys and the maritime plain, were still in the possession of the Canaanites.   The effects of this partial occupation were in many respects disastrous, but they only became fully apparent in the subsequent age of the Judges.

There is little reason to doubt that the Jordan was actually crossed opposite to Jericho.   After due prepara-

The crossing of Jordan : Josh iii.—v. 9. tion for this important crisis in the history of the nation, the Hebrew host, headed by the priests bearing the ark, marched across the bed of the stream, the waters of which, as in the case of the Red Sea, were *wholly cut off*, thus enabling the people to pass over dryshod [1]. The passage of the Jordan was commemorated by the erection at Gilgal on the western bank of a cairn or circle of twelve stones taken from the bed of the river.   At Gilgal Joshua fixed a permanent camp, and here the rite of circumcision, which had been neglected during the later period of the wanderings, was again enforced [2], and the ordinance of the Passover was observed.   Thus the Israelites were prepared,

---

[1] Sayce mentions that a parallel phenomenon is recorded by an Arabic historian as having happened in 1267 A.D., when the river was suddenly dammed up by a landslip (*EHH*, p. 249).

[2] Gilgal means 'cairn' or 'circle' of stones.   A popular etymology explained the name by the rite of circumcision which 'rolled away' the reproach of Egypt.

and as it were consecrated, for their approaching conflict with the Canaanites.

The first city which confronted the invaders was Jericho— a strongly fortified place lying near the foot of the steep central range, and commanding the fords of Jordan. After an interval which Joshua employed in sending two spies to ascertain the strength of the city and the temper of its inhabitants, he led the Israelites to the attack. The biblical account of the fall of Jericho seems to be an instance of the way in which a graphic or poetic figure of speech may become in process of time hardened into a circumstantial narrative. The statement that the wall of the city *fell down flat* at the sound of the great shout which the Hebrews raised at a given signal, evidently implies that Jericho yielded almost at the first onset. Throughout its history indeed, the city has never been able to resist the pressure of a siege: the enervating effect of its tropical climate and luxuriantly fertile soil, together with its low-lying and exposed situation near the entrance of a steep mountain-pass— these always rendered Jericho an easy prey to its assailants. "That her walls fell down at the sound of Joshua's trumpets is no exaggeration, but the soberest summary of all her history[1]." The city was razed to the ground, and a curse was pronounced upon its very site. None of the inhabitants were spared, except the household of Rahab, who had hospitably received the spies and aided them to escape. Rahab was admitted into the Hebrew community, and by her subsequent marriage with Salmon of the tribe of Judah became the ancestress of David[2].

The pass into the hill-country was now open, and the Israelites advanced westward towards the level plateau on which the strongholds of Bethel and Ai were situated. An attack on the latter city failed in the first instance owing to the trespass of Achan, the

(margin note:) The fall of Jericho; Josh. ii., vi.

(margin note:) Capture of Ai, Josh. vii., viii.

[1] G. A. Smith, *HGHL*, p. 267.
[2] St Matt. i. 5.

son of Carmi, of the tribe of Judah, who had secreted a part
of the spoil captured at Jericho, and had thus trespassed by
taking of the devoted thing (*ḥêrem*, i.e. property laid under the
ban). When the crime had been expiated by the destruction
of Achan together with his household and all his possessions,
Ai was successfully surprised by a stratagem and burnt, its
inhabitants were put to the sword and its king was hanged on
a tree.

The moral effect of this decisive blow, following the
overthrow of Jericho, was demonstrated in the

The league
with Gibeon;
Josh. ix.

alacrity with which the Gibeonites hastened to
make terms with the invaders. They trembled
for the safety of their city, which, as it lay somewhat to the
south of Ai, appeared likely to be the next object of assault.
By a crafty device the Hebrew leaders were entrapped into
concluding an agreement with Gibeon, which, with three other
adjacent cities, submitted to tribute on condition that the lives
of the inhabitants should be spared. But the action of Gibeon,
which was reckoned *a great city, as one of the royal cities,*
roused the fears of Adonizedek, king of Jerusalem. In order
to resist the advance of the Israelites he hastily formed a
league with four other petty chiefs of southern Canaan, with
the intention of punishing the Gibeonites for their abandon-

Battle of
Beth-horon;
Josh. x.

ment of the common cause. Upon receiving an
urgent summons from the Gibeonites to come to
their aid, Joshua, after a forced march, arrived
suddenly before the city, and fell suddenly on the besieging
army. The Canaanites gave way before the fierce onset of the
Israelites, and were driven from the plateau over the height on
which upper Beth-horon stood, and down the valley of Ajalon
as far as Makkedah in the *Shephelah*[1]. The discomfiture of
the Canaanites was completed by a fearful hailstorm in which
many perished; and the signal victory of Joshua was crowned

[1] i.e. the low hill-country which lies between the central range and the
maritime plain.

by the capture and slaughter of the five confederate kings who had taken refuge in a cavern at Makkedah. A fragment of an ancient ballad, taken from the 'Book of Jashar,' commemorates the standing still of the sun at Joshua's prayer:

Sun, stand thou still upon Gibeon;
And thou, Moon, in the valley of Aijalon.
And the sun stood still, and the moon stayed,
Until the nation had avenged themselves of their enemies.

(Josh. x. 12, 13.)[1]

This victory was followed up by the subjugation of other districts of southern Palestine, a work which, according to the narrative in Judges, seems to have been accomplished mainly by the tribes of Judah and Simeon assisted by the Kenites and the Calebites[2], while the conquest of the north was achieved by the tribe of Joseph under the leadership of Joshua himself. The important city of Hebron was captured by Caleb, who drove out the three giants Sheshai, Ahiman, and Talmai (Josh. xv. 14); Debir or Kirjath-Sepher, which was probably a chief centre of Canaanitish culture, fell into the hands of Othniel, his kins-

Conquest of Southern Palestine. Judg. i. 1—21.

man; the tribes of Judah and Simeon advanced from the camp near Jericho and gradually acquired the district which was afterwards formally allotted to them. A great victory at Bezek, and the capture and punishment of its barbarous king Adoni-bezek, virtually gave them the command of the hill-country and of the *Negeb* (Judg. i. 1—7)[3]. Possibly the whole

[1] The cry *Sun, stand thou still* (lit. 'be silent') was probably a request not that the daylight might be prolonged, but that the darkness of the storm might continue. The 'Book of Jashar' (i.e. 'the upright one,' 'the hero,' or in a collective sense 'heroes') was a collection of ballads relating the achievements of ancient Israelitish worthies. Cp. 2 Sam. i. 17—27.

[2] The Calebites were apparently a family distinct from the tribe of Judah, but ultimately coalesced with it. Caleb, one of the twelve spies, seems to have belonged to the Edomite tribe of Kenaz. See *Encyclopaedia Biblica*, s.v. 'Caleb.'

[3] i.e. the 'dry' or comparatively waterless district south of Judah.

or part of the stronghold of Jebus fell into the hands of *the children of Judah* (Judg. i. 8 ; cp. Josh. xv. 63). The Simeon-ites pressed further south and established themselves in the *Negeb.* Among them the Kenites (the tribe of Moses' father-in-law) apparently found a settlement[1].

Meanwhile a powerful coalition of Canaanitish kings had been formed in northern Palestine, and had only been prevented from joining the league of the southern princes by the rapidity of Joshua's movements.   Under the leadership of Jabin, King

The battle of Hazor: Josh. xi. 1—15.

of Hazor in Galilee, the Canaanitish host mus-tered near the waters of Merom.   Again Joshua with his army took the enemy by surprise.   The Canaanites were completely routed and fled in all directions, some across the Jordan into Gilead, others westward as far as Sidon on the coast.   The Canaanitish chariots were destroyed ; Hazor itself was taken by assault and burnt, and all its in-habitants were put to the sword : *neither left they any that breathed.*   This victory was the crowning achievement of Joshua's life[2].   Before his death, however, the Tabernacle was

The gathering at Shechem. Josh. viii. 30-35.

erected at Shiloh in Mount Ephraim, which formed the natural centre of the newly-conquered territory[3]; and at Shechem, a few miles further north, a great gathering of the tribes took place for the purpose of carrying out one of the last injunctions of Moses[4].   *An altar of unhewn stones* was erected on Mount Ebal, overlooking the city of Shechem ; when sacrifices had been duly offered, the stones were covered with plaster, and a copy of *the Law of Moses* (probably the Decalogue) was inscribed upon them. Certain blessings and curses were then recited by the Levites

---

[1] The Kenites were always regarded as closely allied to the Israelites. See Hastings' *DB.* s.v.

[2] According to some modern authorities Joshua took no personal part in the expedition against Hazor.   His work consisted solely in the conquest of the Ephraimitic territory.

[3] Josh. xviii. 1.   [4] Cp. Deut. xxvii.

in the hearing of the tribes, six of them being stationed on Mount Gerizim and six on Mount Ebal. Each blessing or curse was answered by a solemn *Amen*. At Shiloh, Joshua apparently confirmed the provisional arrangements he had already made for the partition of the land between the tribes. But the actual settlement of the people in the different districts allotted to them was only gradually and partially carried out. Several of the tribes seem to have failed to dispossess the Canaanites, and were ultimately compelled to dwell side by side with them. This was specially the case with the tribes of Zebulun, Asher, and Naphtali, whose territory lay to the north of the great plain of Esdraelon. Many centuries later, the prophet Isaiah gives to the district occupied by Zebulun and Naphtali the title 'Galilee of the nations' (Is. ix. 1), evidently because the Canaanitish population still maintained to some extent its position alongside of the Israelites. Again, it is evident that the Danites failed to dislodge the Amorites who held the maritime plain, and hindered their access to the sea. Nevertheless, when the period of the Judges opens, we find most of the tribes occupying, at least provisionally, the territory assigned to them. The Levites, as we have seen, were distributed in forty-eight different cities, and their maintenance was provided for by the tithe-offerings of the whole community.

The book of Joshua closes with two prophetic exhortations ascribed to the great leader himself, who was aware that his end was near. In the first of these Israel is warned, in the spirit of the book of Deuteronomy, of the dangers likely to result from fraternization with the Canaanites; the

Exhortations ascribed to Joshua. Josh. xxiii., xxiv.

second, addressed to a gathering of the tribes at Shechem, recapitulates for their encouragement the story of the divine dealings with the nation from the very dawn of its history. In response to Joshua's appeal, the people, through its representatives, made a vow of fidelity to Jehovah, and a great stone was set up *by the sanctuary of Jehovah* as a memorial of the covenant thus renewed.

At the age of 110 years Joshua passed away. The sacred historian observes that his influence continued to be a powerful force during the first generation after Israel's invasion of Canaan. At his death, the Ephraimites held a paramount position among the tribes. The Tabernacle erected at Shiloh was under their protection ; Shechem, situated at the very heart of the land, and the natural meeting-place of the tribes, lay within their borders. Here, probably in the local sanctuary of the tribe, the bones of Joseph, which had been brought up from Egypt by the children of Israel, were deposited. Joshua himself was buried at Timnath-heres in Mount Ephraim. The memory of his achievements was gratefully cherished[1], but the conquest of Canaan was far from being complete at the time of his death. He had brought Israel into the land of promise, but his victories won for them only a partial and troubled rest after the toils of their desert-pilgrimage[2]. Even when his own share in the work of conquest was accomplished *Jehovah said unto him, There remaineth yet very much land to be possessed* (Josh. xiii. 1).

Death of Joshua.

One significant incident recorded in the book of Joshua remains to be mentioned. Before he died Joshua dismissed with his blessing the tribes to which settlements had been already assigned in the trans-Jordanic territory: Reuben, Gad, and the half-tribe of Manasseh. Before they crossed the Jordan, which formed the natural border separating them from the Israelites in Western Palestine, these tribes resolved to erect an altar as token of their devotion to Jehovah, and of the religious ties that bound them to their brethren in Canaan. They feared lest at a future time it should be said to their descendants by the other tribes, *What have ye to do with*

The altar of the trans-Jordanic tribes: Josh. xxii.

---

[1] Cp. Ecclus. xlvi. 1—8.
[2] Cp. Heb. iv. 8.

Jehovah, the God of Israel? for Jehovah hath made Jordan a border between us and you, ye children of Reuben and children of Gad; ye have no portion in Jehovah (Josh. xxii. 25). The erection of the altar was however mistaken by the other tribes for a schismatic act of rebellion against both Israel and its national God[1]; preparations were accordingly made for immediate war. As a precautionary measure, however, Phinehas the priest, with ten *princes of the congregation*, was sent to enquire into the meaning of the act which had roused such resentment : they returned satisfied with the explanation of the three tribes. It was clear that the altar was intended only to be a monument of the common faith of all the tribes: it was *a witness that Jehovah* was *God*. Thus Israel escaped the disasters and dangers of a fratricidal strife.

It will be convenient at this point to give a brief description of the land which had now passed by right of conquest into the possession of the Israelites. To this subject the remainder of the present chapter will be devoted.

The southern portion of Syria was known to the Hebrews as 'the land of Canaan,' and its inhabitants as 'the Canaanites.' The name 'Canaanites' was very ancient: it had been used by the Egyptians to denote the dwellers on the Phoenician coast, and was gradually extended so as to include first the inhabitants of the entire coast-line[2], and at a later time the population of the whole country west of Jordan. Another ancient name of Palestine was 'land of the Amorites' (*Amurru*). The Amorites seem originally to have occupied the highlands east of Phoenicia, but the name was (like Canaan) gradually extended to the dwellers in the entire hill-country south of the Lebanon.

Original inhabitants of Palestine.

When however the Israelitish invasion took place (some time during the twelfth century B.C.), the population of Canaan, owing to intermarriage and obscure tribal movements, already

---

[1] Josh. xxii. 19, 22.

[2] The original meaning of Canaan is probably 'sunken' or 'low-lying.'

consisted of a heterogeneous mixture of races.   It was the land
of *the Amorite, the Hittite, the Perizzite, the Canaanite, the
Hivite and the Jebusite* (Exod. xxiii. 23).   The Hittites, who
had crossed the Orontes westward, had even before the patriarchal age displaced the 'Amorites' of northern Palestine[1],
but though this part of the country long continued to be their
principal seat, the Israelites found groups of them established
in the south ; indeed the narrative of Abraham's intercourse with
'the children of Heth' (Gen. xxiii.) implies that they were
believed to have inhabited the district about Hebron even in
patriarchal times.   Moreover the maritime plain east of Judaea
had, shortly before the arrival of the Israelites, been invaded
by the Philistines, a sea-faring nation of alien (non-Semitic)
race[2], which had made settlements on the coast, and had
gradually gained possession of the whole plain.   Strangely
enough this comparatively unimportant people ultimately gave
its name to the entire country.   The Greeks first, and afterwards the Romans, entering the country by way of the coast
and becoming first acquainted with the race that inhabited the
maritime plain, naturally called the whole region of southern
Syria by the name of Palestine.

The district which the Israelites in course of time acquired
and which is so closely identified with their history, was bounded,
roughly speaking, by the range of Lebanon on the north, and
the desert of Paran on the south.   The western limit of the
land was the Mediterranean ; its eastern, the Arabian desert.
The portion, however, mainly occupied by the Israelites was

---

[1] Cp. Josh. i. 4 ; Judg. i. 26.

[2] The Philistines probably migrated into Palestine from the coast of the
Egyptian Delta, or (according to some authorities) from the island of Crete.
By some scholars they are identified with the *Purasati*, "a piratical people
who, with other sea-faring tribes from the coast of Asia Minor or the Aegean
isles, made a descent upon Egypt in the time of Ramses III. (*after* the
Exodus)," and afterwards established themselves in Canaan.   See Driver
in *Authority and Archaeology*, p. 46 ; G. A. Smith, *HGHL*, ch. ix.

that which lay westward of the Jordan. Its length (from Dan to Beersheba) was about 180 miles; its breadth (from the coast to the Jordan) from 30 to 50 miles. As compared with the vast desert of which Canaan forms the north-western boundary, the general character of the whole region is mountainous. From the plains of Moab, where the Israelites encamped before crossing the Jordan, the district lying westward of the river presented itself as a long, elevated range of barren hills extending northwards towards the Lebanon. From this point of view the whole land is described as *that goodly mountain and Lebanon* (Deut. iii. 25).

General features of Palestine.

The great central plateau of the land wears the aspect of a mountain rampart overlooking the valley of the Jordan. In point of fact, however, the differences of elevation in different parts of Canaan are very marked, and the historical consequences of this diversity have been important. The land is split up into portions differing so widely in soil, scenery and climate, that any permanent social or political union between the various tribes or races inhabiting Palestine has always been found impracticable. Even to the modern traveller Palestine appears to be a land of strange and startling contrasts[1]. We cannot wonder that Israel's conquests were only slowly and partially extended; and that the tribes, once settled in their allotted districts, remained for all practical purposes distinct. We understand the causes which inevitably paved the way for the speedy disruption of Solomon's kingdom[2].

The writer of the introductory chapters of Deuteronomy enumerates (besides *the hill country of the Amorites*) four distinct districts, namely, (1) the *'Arâbah* or Jordan valley,

---

[1] "Palestine deserves the name of the land of contrasts; here is found gathered together everything between a sub-tropical climate and the region of eternal snow." Cornill, *History of the People of Israel*, p. 12. Cp. G. A. Smith, *HGHL*, ch. iii.

[2] Cp. G. A. Smith, *HGHL*, ch. ii.

(2) the *Shephelah* or lowlands, (3) the *Negeb* or south country, and (4) the *sea shore*.   Each of these districts has its peculiar features, and the names correspond to clearly-marked divisions of the land.

    1.   The name *'Arâbah* (from a root probably meaning 'dry') was applied to the deep depression through which the Jordan runs from its sources to the Dead Sea, and which extends southwards as far as the Gulf of Akabah.   This singular valley or cleft is enclosed by two mountain ranges, spurs respectively of the Lebanon and anti-Libanus.   These ranges run parallel, roughly speaking, to the coast, and form a double barrier separating Palestine from the desert.   From the foot of Mt Hermon the valley of the Jordan[1] rapidly sinks below the level of the Mediterranean ; in the sixty miles between the lake of Galilee (680 ft. below sea-level) and the Dead Sea (1290 ft. below sea-level) the river falls some 600 feet.   From this point the *'Arâbah* is prolonged southward over a comparatively low watershed and again sinks to the Gulf of Akabah.

    (1) The Jordan valley.

    Of the two ranges by which this great cleft is bounded on the east and west, the eastern divides itself into three main districts, the plateau of Bashan to the north of the river Yarmuk, the hill-country of Gilead watered by the Jabbok, and the level table-land of Moab extending southwards to the Arnon.   The western or central range runs southward from the Lebanon ; it is interrupted by the great plain of Esdraelon, which has always afforded a convenient outlet or passage from the Jordan valley to the shore of the Mediterranean.   South of the plain the range sends out a lateral spur to Carmel on the coast, but the main portion continues to run southward. "Scattering at first through Samaria into separate groups, it consolidates towards Bethel upon the narrow table-land of

---

[1] The name *'Arâbah* seems to have been applied to the whole of that portion of the valley which lies between the Sea of Galilee and the Gulf of Akabah (*Encycl. Biblica*, s.v.).

Judaea with an average height of 2400 feet, continues so to the south of Hebron, where by broken and sloping strata it lets itself down, widening the while, on to the plateau of the desert of the wandering[1]."

It was this portion of the mountain district which was first conquered by the Israelites, and which perhaps owing to its rugged natural features made the deepest impression on the character of the conquering race. The most powerful tribes occupied parts of the range, and gave their names to different districts. Thus *the hill-country of Ephraim*[2] was the name of the plateau between the plain of Esdraelon and Bethel; *the hill-country of Judah*[3] was that portion of the range which lay between Jerusalem and the district called the *Negeb*.

2. A range of low hills called the *Shephelah* ('lowlands') lay between the maritime plain and the highlands of the central range. The *Shephelah*, strictly speaking, formed part of the territory of Judah; it was a fertile and open district, but the least secure of Judah's possessions, as it was naturally much exposed to the incursions of the Philistines. The *Shephelah* is separated from the 'hill-country' of Ephraim and Judah by a series of valleys running north and south, while access to the central range is afforded by several defiles, the most important being *the vale of Aijalon* down which the Canaanites fled precipitately after the battle at Beth-horon (Josh. x. 10—12); the *vale of Sorek*, by which the Philistines usually made their inroads during the days of the Judges; and the *vale of Elah*, leading to a small open plain[4], whence a narrow pass runs in a north-easterly direction towards Bethlehem.

(2) The Shephelah.

---

[1] G. A. Smith, *HGHL*, p. 47.

[2] Josh. xvii. 15. Ephraim included the district of Samaria.

[3] Josh. xxi. 11. Similarly *The hill-country of Naphtali* was that part of the central range which lay north of the plain of Esdraelon. Josh. xx. 7.

[4] This was probably the scene of David's encounter with Goliath. 1 Sam. xvii.

3. The south-country (*Negeb*, lit. 'dry' or 'parched land')[1]
is the name of a well-defined region, about
seventy miles long by forty or fifty broad, extending southwards from Hebron.   The *Negeb* falls
from the central range in a series of terraces or steppes to the
wilderness of Paran, of which Kadesh may be regarded as the
northern limit.   As compared with the fertile plains of Philistia
this region is rough, barren and desolate, and affords only scanty
and occasional pasturage for flocks.   It naturally depends to
an unusual extent on its few springs and on the annual rains.
The *Negeb* had however a few important towns, of which
Beersheba was the most ancient, being a sacred spot closely
connected with the history of the Hebrews from patriarchal
times.

(3) The
Negeb.

4. The maritime plain (the northern part of which was
called the plain of Sharon, the southern part
Philistia) extends from Carmel southwards, gradually widening from a breadth of six to a breadth
of twenty-five miles.   The southern limit of this great plain is the
so-called 'brook of Egypt' (Wady el 'Arîsh)[2].   At its northern
extremity it is united by several easy passes to the great level
expanse of Esdraelon.   One of these passes, formed by the
plain of Dothan, opened a direct road to the Mediterranean
from the region beyond Jordan.   By this route the Ishmaelites,
to whom Joseph is said to have been sold by his brethren,
carried their wares down into Egypt (Gen. xxxvii. 25); by this
too, the Philistines were repeatedly enabled to penetrate to the
very heart of the land.   The two great plains of Esdraelon and
Sharon were in fact continuous, and formed a "historical
highway between Asia and Africa," between the Nile and the
Euphrates.   "It has ever been," we are told, "one of the most
famous war-paths of the world[3]."

(4) The mari-
time plain.

[1] Num. xiii. 17, 22.
[2] Isai. xxvii. 12.
[3] G. A. Smith, *HGHL*, ch. viii. pp. 149 foll.

The plain of Esdraelon itself may be appropriately noticed at this point. It has been well compared to a great gulf of the sea breaking with its broad fertile expanse into the hill-country and thus completely interrupting the long, central range. It is drained by one important stream, the river Kishon, running in a north-westerly direction nearly parallel to the range of Carmel. This plain formed a natural battle-field. At the river Kishon the host of Sisera was discomfited by Barak ; and some centuries later at Megiddo, on its western side, Josiah was slain in attempting to resist the advance of Pharaoh Necho towards the Euphrates. At the south-eastern extremity of the plain lay Mt Gilboa, from which Gideon made his sudden descent upon the Midianites, and drove them down towards the Jordan in panic-stricken flight. Here also Saul and his sons met their untimely end in a last desperate conflict with the Philistines. The most conspicuous city of the plain was *Jezreel*, over-looking the long sloping defile which led eastwards into the Jordan valley. The two principal gateways (so to speak) of the great plain were at Megiddo and Jezreel. " Megiddo guarded the natural approach of Philistines, Egyptians and other enemies from the south ; Jezreel that of Arabs, Midianites, Syrians of Damascus, and other enemies from the east[1]."

The plain of Esdraelon.

The Israelites, as we have seen, found the maritime plain already occupied by the powerful race of the Philistines, which was too strong to be dislodged from its possessions, and effectually excluded the invaders from the chance of gaining a hold upon the sea coast. The plain, though often traversed by armies, was well cultivated ; its southernmost portion had however an evil reputation for unhealthiness. The district north-east of the Delta was notorious in ancient times as the home of the plague.

To the north of the headland of Mount Carmel along the

[1] G. A. Smith, *HGHL*, p. 391.

Mediterranean coast lay Phoenicia with its cities—a narrow

Phoenicia.   strip of the coast about 120 miles in length and 20 miles at most in breadth.

The Phoenicians were a Semitic people of remarkable industry, intelligence and enterprise. They were for a long period the exclusive navigators of the Mediterranean and became the great commercial people of antiquity. Greece owed to these busy traders and colonists some important elements of her early culture and civilization. The Phoenicians were the merchants of Palestine[1]; the Israelites found a market for their products at Tyre and Sidon; Abibal and Hiram I. were the friends and allies of David and Solomon; Ahab married the daughter of Ethbaal. But though Solomon for a while maintained a navy which perhaps inspired the Israelites with dreams of commercial greatness, they had no lasting opportunity of becoming a seafaring people. They never established themselves on the coast, and the successors of the Philistines and Phoenicians in the possession of the maritime cities were ultimately the Greeks.

The most important features of the land, so far as Old Testament history is concerned, have now been described. Neither the noble mountain Hermon, which forms the most conspicuous object in the landscape looking north-east, nor the sea of Chinnereth (Galilee), so closely associated with the Gospel record, call for special notice in connection with the Old Testament history. A few words however may be added, in order briefly to describe the situation of the two cities which became respectively the capitals of the northern and southern kingdoms.

Jerusalem was virtually a mountain-city, lying on the

Situation of Jerusalem.   barren and scantily-watered plateau due west of the northern end of the Dead Sea. It stood at a height of 2600 feet above the sea, on a spur of the central range sharply defined by the valleys of Hinnom and

---

[1] In Hos. xii. 7 a 'Canaanite' means a 'merchant.'

the Kidron. The city sloped gently to the south, and was surrounded on three sides by ravines which forbade any extension of its boundaries. On the fourth side (the north and north-west) it was strongly fortified. On the east it was overlooked by the Mount of Olives. But its most striking feature was its seclusion. It lay apart from the great highways of commerce, and from the route trodden by alien armies in their passage to and from the further east. It was connected only by rough mountain-paths with Egypt on the one side, and Syria on the other. It was almost entirely cut off from the opportunities of that close intercourse with foreign lands which was so fatally easy for its rival Samaria. In fact the austere surroundings and isolated situation of Jerusalem qualified it for its future destiny as a unique centre of religious influence. It was not so much a home of culture and civilization as a stronghold and sanctuary of faith.

The situation of Samaria was strikingly different. The city lay on a flat-topped hill in a wide and verdant basin, encircled on three sides by lower heights **Samaria.** of the central range, and opening into the plain of Sharon. This hill, commanding a wide prospect to the west, was selected by the sagacious and powerful king Omri in preference to Shechem, the natural centre of the land, because of its comparative proximity to the sea. The district to which Samaria gave its name was uniformly rich and fertile, and it was in later times guarded by a chain of important fortified towns. The danger of Samaria lay in the openness of its situation; it was easily overrun by invaders from east or west, and its population yielded too readily to the corrupting influence of foreign heathenism. "The surrounding Paganism poured into her ample life; and although to her was granted the honour of the first great victories against it—Gideon's and Elijah's—she suffered the luxury that came after to take away her crown[1]."

[1] G. A. Smith, *HGHL*, p. 331.

It is obvious that Palestine was specially qualified to be the
home and source of a world-wide religion. It
occupied a central position among the nations of
the earth, yet was separated from other lands, on the west by
the sea, on the east and south by the desert, on the north by
a mountain range; it was at once "near to and aloof from the
great streams of human life[1]." The maritime plain on which
the heights of Judah looked down was a highway of the world's
commerce and often a battlefield of contending nations. Thus
Israel watched, without the power of controlling, the restless
movements of the gigantic empires which lay to the east and
to the south-west of Palestine. Though in a sense *the fewest of
all peoples*, Israel was conscious of a vocation which placed it
above all peoples that are upon the face of the earth (Deut. vii.
6, 7), and which made its small and rugged territory *the glory
of all lands* (Ezek. xx. 15). To the home which God had
assigned to them, the Jewish people owed much of their
physical and mental vigour, their habits of industry, their
stubborn individuality, their reckless courage. In exile their
hearts turned towards the land which they had lost with
passionate regret, and with unutterable yearnings for the fulfilment of the cherished ideal of prophecy,

Summary.

> *The Lord will have compassion on Jacob,*
> *And will yet choose Israel, and set them in their own land.*
>
> (Isai. xiv. 1.)

---

[1] G. A. Smith, *HGHL*, p. 112.

CHAPTER V.

THE AGE OF THE JUDGES.

WE have already seen that the Canaanites were far from being exterminated by the conquests of Joshua. The coast-land remained in the possession of the Philistines and Phoenicians; the strong fortress

towns of central Canaan were still held by their former inhabitants; there were many districts in which the Israelitish invaders were allowed to have a footing, but not supremacy. In fact it was only the lack of cohesion among the demoralized Canaanites that enabled the Hebrews to hold their ground. A united and determined effort on the part of their foes might have swept them back into the deserts from which they had emerged. For the most part they lived in 'villages' or open encampments, like those to which they had been used during their wilderness life, with the result that they came into more frequent contact with the Canaanitish peasantry than with the dwellers in towns. Moreover the relations subsisting between the different tribes were as yet undefined and insecure. They were weakened by their want of organization, by their tenacious love of independence, and by their unfamiliarity with the habits of a settled people. Conquerors and conquered soon became inextricably intermingled; Israel still to a great extent imbued with the ideas and beliefs it had inherited from Moses; the Canaanites possessed of a superior culture, but deeply debased

by the corrupting taint of Semitic heathenism[1]. For a time it
was doubtful which type of civilization would prevail. For as
the Hebrews naturally learned from the Canaanites the necessary arts of husbandry, so they were inevitably introduced by
them to the local sanctuaries (*bamoth* or 'high places'), at
which were practised the foul rites of the heathen deity who
was regarded as the author of fertility, and the giver of corn,
wine and oil to his worshippers[2]. The Hebrews did not
indeed openly abandon their allegiance to Jehovah, but they
co-ordinated, and sometimes even identified, their national
Deity with one or other of the gods of Canaan, and thus the
simple and pure worship of Jehovah was gradually corrupted
by the admixture of usages and symbols borrowed from the
nature-worship of the Canaanites. The compilers of the Book
of Judges, however, writing some five or six centuries after the
events of this period, regarded Israel's religious retrogressions
as even amounting to a formal apostasy from Jehovah[3].

Two features of this stage in Israel's career, during which it
was transformed from a powerful horde of nomads into an
agricultural people, call for attention at the outset. First, the
bonds of union between the different tribes were
quickly dissolved when they found themselves
dispersed in different districts, and when the
conditions of warfare were finally exchanged for a state of
security and peace. The peculiar formation of the land itself
with its sharp contrasts of mountain and plain, table-land and

*Disunion of
the tribes.*

---

[1] The Tel el-Amarna letters shew that the Canaanites were both in race
and language closely akin to the Hebrews. Isaiah even describes Hebrew
as 'the language of Canaan' (xix. 18).

[2] "When we speak of *Baal* as the principal god of the Canaanites, it is
not to be understood that there was one god, Baal, whom all the Canaanites worshipped, but that the many local divinities were all called by this
significant name." (Moore in *Polychrome Bible* on Judg. ii. 13.) The
Ba'al of a place is the god to whom it belongs, just as the citizens of a
town are its *ba'alim*, 'proprietors.'

[3] See *e.g.* Judg. ii. 12, x. 6.

valley, intensified the tendency to isolation. Yet there remained elements of cohesion which could occasionally be appealed to with effect : faith in Jehovah as the God and champion of the Hebrews, reverence for the traditional Law of Sinai, and the existence of a central sanctuary at Shiloh. The 'Song of Deborah' (Judges, ch. v.) bears witness to the fact that the influence of the national religion was powerful enough to unite six of the tribes in common action against their northern oppressor.

Again, the rule of the so-called 'Judges' was not merely a social necessity : it was a safeguard of religion. The Judges (*Shophetim*)[1] were not so much ad-ministrators of law and government as tribal chiefs, who from time to time undertook to vindicate the inde-pendence of Jehovah's people and to proclaim anew the truths of His religion. They contended not merely against the foes that threatened Israel from without, but against the spirit of heathenism within it. Most of the Judges were strong, rough men, stirred by heroic zeal for Jehovah's cause, and eager to defend the peculiar principles which sharply distinguished the religion of Israel from that of Canaan. That the higher con-science of the nation was still active in the days of the Judges is sufficiently proved by the stern vengeance which the Ben-jamites suffered at the hands of the other tribes for the outrage perpetrated at Gibeah[2]. Thus it may be said with truth that the task laid upon Israel at this period was chiefly that of "*spiritual* self-assertion against the genius of the Canaanitish nation[3]." The age of the Judges was in short an age of trans-ition, in which, humanly speaking, Israel's higher life depended upon the force of character and singlemindedness of individual

Religious function of the Judges.

---

[1] 'Judges' were an institution peculiar, so far as we know, to the Semitic world. The chief magistrates of Carthage were called *Sufetes*. Cp. Sayce, *EHH*, p. 288.

[2] See Judg. xx.

[3] E. König in Hastings' *DB*, art. 'Judges, Book of.'

leaders.   Such men when they appeared were rightly regarded as heroes raised up by Jehovah not merely to deliver the nation from the yoke of its oppressors, but also to keep alive the standard of worship and morality which Israel had inherited from Moses.   In the belief that the Judges had on the whole faithfully fulfilled their appointed task, the men of a later age blessed their memory[1].

Some incidents mentioned in the Book of Judges throw a vivid light on the disorganized condition of the Hebrew tribes, and explain the impulse which tended towards the establishment of a monarchy.   The narratives which form a kind of appendix to the book (chh. xvii.—xxi.) are apparently intended to illustrate the truth and the consequences of the fact that *in those days there was no king in Israel: every man did that which was right in his own eyes*[2].

The strange story of Micah the Ephraimite presents us with a picture of a domestic sanctuary or 'house of God,' furnished with its *'Ephod*[3] and *Teráphim*, and served by a consecrated priest.   It forms a preface to the account of an interesting tribal movement.   The Danites, hard pressed apparently by their Philistine neighbours, resolved to abandon the territory assigned to them on the coast, and ultimately found a new settlement in the north, near the foot of Mount Hermon.   The narrative relates how the Danite explorers, in crossing Mount Ephraim, paused to consult the oracle in Micah's house for guidance in their quest; and how, when the main body of the tribe had migrated to their new home, they persuaded the Levite, who acted as Micah's household priest, to accompany them, and to bring with him the sacred images.   Micah made a fruitless attempt to recover his 'gods,' which were triumphantly carried

Micah and
the Danites.
Judg. xvii.,
xviii.

---

[1] See Ecclus. xlvi. 11, 12.

[2] Judg. xvii. 6, xxi. 25 ; cp. xviii. 1, xix. 1.

[3] An *'Ephod* seems to mean some kind of oracular image, but the word has never been quite satisfactorily explained.

off. They were eventually placed in a permanent sanctuary belonging to the new city of Dan (formerly Laish), and committed to the charge of the Levite and his descendants. The sanctuary soon became notorious, and a dangerous rival to the 'house of God' established at Shiloh. The priest who was first appointed was a grandson of Moses[1]; we are told that he and his sons held this tribal priesthood *until the day of the captivity of the land*[2].

The moral degeneracy which resulted from Israel's contact with the Canaanites was signally exemplified in the crime committed at Gibeah, which brought upon the tribe of Benjamin a fearful vengeance.

The fate of the Benjamites. Judg. xix., xx.

In their abhorrence of the deed, the other tribes demanded that the perpetrators should be delivered up and put to death. This demand the Benjamites peremptorily rejected, and threatened to meet force with force. In the hostilities that ensued the tribes were at first defeated; in a second battle however the Benjamites were deceived by a stratagem, and worsted; Gibeah was captured and burnt, and the guilty tribe was almost exterminated. The victors however were moved to pity by the reflection that *there should be one tribe lacking in Israel.* Accordingly the males who had survived the general massacre were provided with wives by expedients which illustrate the reckless cruelty and lawless violence of that rude age. The capture of the maidens who attended the vintage festival at Shiloh finds a parallel in the Roman legend of 'the rape of the Sabines'[3].

If this state of anarchy and disorganization had been allowed to continue, Israel must have finally lost all elements of cohesion, and have fallen into the helpless degeneracy which had

---

[1] Judg. xviii. 30. The reading *Manasseh* (R.V. marg.) for *Moses* is probably due to an alteration of the text in later times.

[2] *i.e.* till the deportation of the northern tribes by Tiglath Pileser (734) or the overthrow of Samaria (721).

[3] Judg. xxi. 19 foll. Cp. Liv. *Hist. Rom.* i. 9 foll.

already overtaken the former inhabitants of the land. But when, in course of time, the Canaanites recovered to some extent from the paralyzing effects of Joshua's conquests, and put forth new efforts to regain their old supremacy, the successful invaders found themselves again compelled to fight for their existence. Moreover the nomad peoples inhabiting the desert eastward of Gilead, the Midianites, Amalekites and others, were constantly pressing upon Israel's eastern border. The Moabites waited for an opportunity of dislodging the tribes of Reuben and Gad from their newly-acquired possessions, while the Philistines naturally watched with alarm the settlement of a warlike race of invaders on the highlands which overlooked their own low-lying territory.

Earlier ' Judges,' such as Othniel, Ehud and Shamgar dealt

The early Judges : Judg. iii.

isolated blows at various heathen oppressors but we are not told how far their authority extended, nor do we know the precise range of

Othniel.

the tyranny which they resisted. *Othniel,* the brother of Caleb, was a Kenizzite, and was therefore of Edomitish origin, though reckoned as belonging to the tribe of Judah. He is mentioned as the first of those 'saviours' who was successively raised up to deliver Israel from a foreign yoke, the pressure of which must have hindered them from any extension of their conquests. Othniel succeeded in checking the armies of Cushan-rishathaim, king of northern Mesopotamia[1], which apparently invaded Syria soon after Joshua's death and overran

Ehud.

the whole country. *Ehud,* of the tribe of Benjamin, was a left-handed man, who by a perilous act of daring delivered Israel from the tyranny of Eglon, king of Moab. Eglon had made himself master of Jericho and the neighbouring districts. Ehud, who had been commissioned to deliver the tribute which Eglon exacted from the Hebrews, found a means of secretly gaining access to the Moabite king,

---

[1] Lit. '*Aram Naharaim,* (R.V. marg.) 'Aram between the two rivers' (probably the Euphrates and the Chaboras).

and assassinated him in his own house. He then placed himself at the head of his fellow-tribesmen, and succeeded after a
short struggle in throwing off the Moabite yoke.   Shamgar.
Shamgar, the son of Anath, is mentioned as the
hero of an exploit achieved during some raid of the Philistines.

It is evident however that the first decisive success gained
by the Israelites was the overthrow of the great   Deborah
confederacy of northern Canaanites[1] of which   and Barak:
for the second time Hazor, near the waters of   Judg. iv., v.
Merom, was the rallying point. For twenty years Jabin, king
of Hazor, the possessor of nine hundred chariots of iron, had
mightily oppressed the northern Israelites. When rumours of
revolt reached the ears of Sisera, the leader of the Canaanitish
host, he lost no time in occupying the most important strongholds of the plain of Esdraelon, thus effectually hindering any
conjunction of the northern tribes with those of the south.
The miseries of Israel's condition at this crisis are alluded to in
Deborah's song. Life in the 'villages' or unwalled encampments became impossible; the peasantry were forced to find
refuge in dens and caves; the highways were deserted, and *the
travellers walked through byways*. The Hebrews, moreover,
were almost destitute of weapons, and they had lost the inspiration which strict fidelity to Jehovah had formerly given
them. It was a religious impulse that was needed to con-
solidate the tribes and to nerve them for resistance.

The impulse came from a woman, Deborah the prophetess,
who *judged Israel at that time*, and who dwelt between Ramah
and Bethel in Mount Ephraim. In Jehovah's name she summoned Barak, a man of Kedesh-Naphtali in Galilee, to rally the
tribesmen to his standard, and to concentrate his force on Mount
Tabor, overlooking the plain of Esdraelon. Six of the tribes
sent detachments, but the greater part of Barak's army was
drawn from Zebulun, Naphtali and Issachar, the three tribes
which suffered most acutely from the tyranny of the Canaanites.

[1] Judg. v. 19, 'the kings of Canaan.'

In his camp on Mount Tabor, concealed by a forest of oaks, Barak secretly equipped and trained a band of ten thousand men. Meanwhile Sisera marshalled his host along the banks of the Kishon, which flows north-westward across the great plain. Barak seized his opportunity. The impetuous onset of the Israelites threw the cavalry of Sisera into wild confusion. A sudden storm caused the river to rise and to overflow its banks. The horses and chariots, impeded by the marshy ground, were swept away by the swollen stream, and the discomfiture of the Canaanites was complete. Sisera himself fled from the field and sought refuge in the camp of the friendly Kenites, but was treacherously slain by Jael, the wife of Heber, the Kenite chief, as he lay *fast asleep and weary* on the floor of her tent.

Battle of the Kishon.

It is clear that, for the time at least, the power of the Canaanites was effectually broken by this disaster. The splendid ode (Judg. v.) which commemorates the triumph of Barak's army, is one of the most ancient fragments of Hebrew literature and bears every mark of being the work of a contemporary poet[1]. It is evidently a product of the newly-kindled spirit of patriotism and religious fervour which impelled six of the tribes to unite in striking a blow on behalf of Israel's freedom. The poet bitterly denounces the faint-heartedness and love of ease which restrained the tribes of Reuben, Gad, Asher and Dan from sharing the peril and the glory of the contest. Altogether, the ode is a worthy monument of a crisis in Israel's history which was never forgotten. "Its verses go tumbling on, foaming like the waves of the Kishon upon whose banks the victory was won[2]." The benediction upon Jael's act is in keeping with

The Song of Deborah: Judg. v.

---

[1] The account which this ode gives of Barak's victory differs in some details from the later prose narrative of ch. iv., especially in regard to the manner of Sisera's death.

[2] E. König in Hastings' *DB, ubi sup.*

the tone of fierce triumph which rings through the poem. The poet does not rise above the moral level of the rude and barbarous age in which he lived :

> *Blessed above women shall Jael be,*
> *Blessed shall she be above women in the tent.*

Such an estimate of Jael's foul deed was possible only in the age of tents.

The name of Gideon, the most prominent, and in some respects the most typical figure among the Judges, is connected with another important crisis in the history, when the Israelites were suffering from the periodical incursions of the Midianites, who *Incursions of the Midianites : Judg. vi. 1—6.* habitually came up in vast swarms from the Arabian desert and overran the richest and most fertile districts of Palestine. Year after year the Israelites, by this time inured to the regular cultivation of the soil, saw snatched from them the fruits of their labour. The villages were again deserted as in the days of Canaanitish oppression : the peasants were forced *because of Midian* to hide in the dens and caves of the hill-country[1]. The wild 'children of the East' came up with their multitude of camels and *destroyed the increase of the earth till thou come unto Gaza, and left no sustenance for Israel, neither sheep, nor ox, nor ass.* There was danger lest through sheer discouragement the Israelites should be induced to return to the nomadic habits which they had now outgrown.

The deliverer raised up in this sore strait was Gideon, an Abiezrite of the tribe of Manasseh. In his case, even more clearly than in that of other Judges, *Gideon.* the purpose of the biblical narrator is to bring two points into

---

[1] Prof. G. A. Smith (*HGHL*, p. 8) points out that Syria was exposed by its geographical position to such incursions of desert tribes. "She lay, so to speak, broadside on to the desert ; part of her was spread east of the Jordan, rolling off undefended into the desert steppes....The loose humanity of the Semitic world has therefore been constantly beating upon Syria, and almost as constantly breaking into her."

prominence: first, the fact that Israel's 'saviours' were men directly chosen and inspired by Jehovah; secondly, that the divine will could be executed even by lowly and despised instruments[1]. Gideon's family however had already suffered grievous injury at the hands of the Midianites, who in one of their raids had captured and slain two of his brothers (Judg. viii. 18 foll.).

The angel of Jehovah, we are told, suddenly appeared to Gideon as he was secretly threshing wheat in the winepress at Ophrah, *to hide it from the Midianites.* As a test of his moral courage and of his fitness for the heroic work of a deliverer, he was commanded to destroy the altar which his father Joash had erected to Baal, together with the *ashêrah*, or sacred pole, that stood beside it; he was then to build an altar to Jehovah, and to offer upon it a bullock taken from his father's herd. Gideon's obedience to this command involved an attack upon the established worship of Baal, and was a bold defiance of tribal prejudice. The men of Ophrah clamoured for his blood, but Joash refused to yield up his son to their resentment. If Baal was a god, he said, he was well able to defend his own cause. *Let him plead for himself because one hath broken down his altar.* The issue of this adventure won for Gideon the name of *Jerubba'al* ('Let Baal plead')[2].

> *The call of Gideon, Judg. vi. 11 foll.*

Gideon was now free to fulfil his appointed mission. His first step was to collect an army. The men of his own clan, Abiezer, quickly responded to his summons and, four tribes in all, sent detachments. Encouraged by a sign that promised him success, he encamped with his forces beside the spring of Harod, near the foot of Mount Gilboa. Here he was directed to reduce his army from

> *Attack on the Midianites, Judg. vii., viii.*

---

[1] This is perhaps the point of Judg. vi. 15, vii. 2.

[2] The name should probably be explained 'Baal contends'; but the true reading may be *Jeruba'al* 'Baal founds' or 'establishes' (Moore on Judg. vi. 32).

32,000 to 300 men, and with this little band he prepared for a nocturnal attack on the Midianites who *lay along in the valley like locusts for multitude*. First, however, with his armour-bearer he crept stealthily down to the Midianite camp, and overheard a man telling his comrade a dream : how *a cake of barley bread tumbled into the camp of Midian, and came unto the tent and smote it that it fell*. The meaning of the omen was clear : Gideon returned to his camp and roused his men. Dividing the three hundred into three bands, he provided each man with a pitcher and a lighted torch. Thus equipped, the Hebrews surrounded the Midianite camp. At a given signal three hundred torches flashed, three hundred pitchers fell crashing to the ground, and a great shout rang through the darkness of the night, *The sword of the Lord and of Gideon !* The un-disciplined hordes of Midian fled in wild panic and confusion. Some of the fugitives were intercepted by the Ephraimites at the fords of Jordan, where two chieftains, Oreb and Zeeb, were slain. The pursuit however was continued beyond the river. At Karkor the Midianites attempted to make a stand, but were again put to flight. Zebah and Zalmunna, the two *kings of Midian*, who had been the actual murderers of Gideon's brothers, were put to death by his own hand. After the victory, the men of Succoth and Penuel who, perhaps in fear of Midianite vengeance, had refused to assist their brethren of Manasseh or even to supply them with food, were cruelly punished. Meanwhile the jealousy of the Ephraimites had already been aroused by the growing strength and prosperity of the younger tribe Manasseh. They now complained bitterly of the small part assigned to them in the recent conflict. By his soft answer to their reproaches Gideon soothed the wounded pride of the haughty tribe. *Is not*, he said, *the gleaning of the grapes of Ephraim better than the vintage of Abiezer ? God hath delivered into your hand the princes of Midian, Oreb and Zeeb : and what was I able to do in comparison of you ?* (Judg. viii. **3.**)

The heroism of Gideon had important consequences. The tribes of central Palestine were anxious to estab-

Gideon's rule.

lish a permanent monarchy as a guarantee of future protection against the incursions of Midian, and offered Gideon the crown. He is said indeed to have declined the title of king, and reminded the Israelites that their sole king was Jehovah; but he could not fail to hold a very influential position as tribal Judge, and possibly even exercised priestly powers. At Ophrah, his native place, he built a sanctuary, and set up an *'ephod* overlaid with gold taken from the Midianitish spoils. In taking this step Gideon himself seems to have had no idolatrous intention, but by the judgment of a later age his action was naturally condemned, as having been the occasion of a widespread religious apostasy[1]. At length he died, in a good old age, and was buried in the sepulchre of his fathers at Ophrah.

The tendency towards the establishment of a monarchy became more decided as time went on. An

The career of Abimelech, Judg. ix.

actual attempt to found a kingship over Israel was made by Abimelech, a son of Gideon by a Shechemite concubine. He relied for success partly on his father's prestige, partly on the support of his mother's Shechemite kinsfolk. Appealing at once to their family pride and to their self-interest, he secured their goodwill. Was it better for them, he asked, that they should be ruled by all the sons of Jerubbaal or by one? Let them remember also that he was their bone and their flesh. The Shechemites readily supplied him with money, which enabled him to raise a band of hired mercenaries, *vain and light fellows, which followed him*[2]. By the wholesale murder of his brethren, Abimelech raised himself to a position of precarious power, which lasted

---

[1] Judg. viii. 27.

[2] The Shechemites were apparently on terms of friendly alliance with the Hebrews, and worshipped Baal-berith ('Lord of the covenant') in token of the fact. Judg. ix. 4, 46.

for three years. The parable uttered by Gideon's surviving son
Jotham (Judg. ix. 7 foll.), telling how *the trees*   Jotham's
went forth to anoint a king over them, was intended   parable, Judg.
to upbraid the Shechemites with their ingratitude   ix. 7 foll.
towards Gideon; but it also proved to be a true prophecy.
The Shechemites became discontented with Abimelech's rule,
and began to form plots against him. During his temporary
absence from the city an open revolt broke out, instigated by
one Gaal, the son of Ebed. The king however inflicted a
severe defeat on the troops hastily raised by Gaal, and gained
an entrance by a stratagem into Shechem. After a fierce
conflict it was captured; a number of the inhabitants, who had
taken refuge in the sanctuary of El-Berith, perished in the
flames which consumed the building. The city
was razed to the ground. Its destruction was   Destruction
an important incident, marking the successful   of Shechem.
repression of a movement which seems to have been an
endeavour on the part of the Canaanitish population to regain
their former ascendancy. Abimelech, originally
the self-constituted champion of this movement,   Death of
soon afterwards perished ignominiously at the   Abimelech.
siege of the neighbouring town of Thebez. When he approached close to the wall, a woman hurled down a stone
upon his head, inflicting a mortal wound. He hastily bade his
armour-bearer slay him, lest it should afterwards be said that
a woman slew him. Thus ended the first attempt to found
a monarchy. As yet the tribes were so sharply divided by
mutual jealousies and conflicting interest, that union under the
sceptre of a single ruler was quite impracticable.

Of the remaining Judges the figures of only two stand out
with any distinctness amid the obscurity that envelopes the
period following Abimelech's fall. The tribes seem to have
again relapsed into a state of social disorganization and religious
degeneracy. The names of lesser Judges, Tola, Jair, Ibzan,
Elon and Abdon are recorded, but without any clear indication

of their date, their achievements, or the extent of their influence. The pressure of the Ammonites on the east however, and afterwards of the Philistines on the west, brought into prominence two distinguished leaders, *Jephthah* and *Samson*.

During the pre-Israelitish period, the Ammonites had been

Jephthah and the Ammonites, Judg. xi.

compelled by Sihon and the Amorites to evacuate a large portion of the trans-Jordanic district which they originally claimed as their own. They now made a determined effort to recover their hold upon this territory which, with Sihon's other possessions, had passed into the possession of the Israelites. Accordingly they attacked the land of Gilead, which had been occupied since the conquest by the warlike half-tribe of Manasseh[1]. In their extremity the chiefs of Gilead summoned to their aid Jephthah, a Gileadite warrior, who had been unjustly outlawed and had become the captain of a band of freebooters in the land of Tob (probably a district of Eastern Syria)[2]. Jephthah consented to lead an expedition against the Ammonites on condition that he should be afterwards appointed *head and chief* of the Gileadites. After fruitless negotiations with the enemy[3], Jephthah led his forces to the attack, and smote the Ammonites *from Aroer to Minnith with a very great slaughter*. The victory however was marred by the tragic incident which followed,—an incident characteristic of Jephthah's age—the sacrifice of his daughter in fulfilment of a rash vow. Jephthah's misfortune in the hour of his triumph gave rise to a custom *that the daughters of Israel*

---

[1] Josh. xvii. 1.

[2] The most probable explanation of the statement *Gilead begat Jephthah* (Judg. xi. 1) is that it conceals an incident of tribal history under the guise of a domestic event, "Jephthah's relations with the other inhabitants of Gilead being represented as his relations with the legitimate sons of his father Gilead." (Driver in Hastings' *DB*, s.v. 'Gilead.')

[3] A curious passage gives an account of Jephthah's parley with Ammon (Judg. xi. 12—28). There is good reason to suppose that the account was inserted by a compiler, using the narrative in Num. xx. and xxi. as an authority.

went yearly to lament the daughter of Jephthah the Gileadite four days in a year.

After Jephthah's successful campaign, the tribe of Ephraim, which had apparently declined to aid the Gileadites in their struggle with the Ammonites, complained in an insolent and menacing tone as they had done on a former occasion (Judg. viii. 1) of not having been invited to take part in the war. A tribal conflict between the Gileadites and Ephraimites ensued, in which the latter were completely worsted (Judg. xii. 1—7); many of the fugitives were ruthlessly slain in cold blood at the fords of Jordan.

Around the name of *Samson* a whole cycle of traditions must have gathered. He was probably a hero belonging to the tribe of Dan, and his exploits were closely connected with the earliest occasion when Israel came into collision with the Philistines. The Philistines, as we have seen, had migrated from their original home, probably some part of the coast-line of the Egyptian Delta, and had settled in the great plain which separated the *Shephelah*, or low hill-country of Judah, from the sea. By the expulsion of the Avim, who already occupied the plain, they had gradually extended their borders as far north as Gaza. Their five principal cities, Gaza, Ashkelon, Ashdod, Gath and Ekron, lay on or near the great thoroughfare which connected Egypt with the far East. It was inevitable that the expansion of the Philistine territory should bring them into collision with some of the Israelitish tribes. The Philistine wars did in fact extend over a considerable space of time, and the ultimate effect of them was to precipitate the foundation of the Hebrew monarchy. We first hear of the Philistines as making hostile incursions into the adjacent territory of Dan and Judah. With this stage of the struggle the name of Samson the Danite was connected; but his valour at the best merely served to keep in check the formidable pressure of the Philistine power.

History of Samson: Judg. xiii.—xvi.

The Philistines.

8—2

For the purposes of more permanent defence against hostile inroads from the plain, a stationary camp seems to have been formed between Zorah and Eshtaol[1], two towns situated on the heights commanding the *Shephelah*, which was usually the scene of this border warfare. Samson's personal career is not of much significance in the history of the period. Tradition described him as a Nazirite[2], the secret of whose superhuman strength lay in strict fidelity to his vow of self-dedication to Jehovah. His fitful and impetuous deeds of valour were exactly of the kind which would appeal to popular fancy. In the accounts of his career—of his amours, his adventures, and his feats of strength—there is an element scarcely consistent with sober history. The manner of his death, however, involving as it did a wholesale destruction of his inveterate foes, won him an honourable place among the ancient worthies of Israel. The cycle of narratives relating to Samson was probably of gradual growth and it is chiefly valuable as illustrating a side of Israelitish life and character of which we otherwise know but little.

The Book of Ruth, a beautiful idyll of pastoral life connected with Beth-lehem, describes an incident supposed to have occurred in the days of the Judges, and forms a pleasing counterpart to the rough and stormy history of that period. The latter part of the Book of Judges, as we have noticed, is probably intended to give a picture of the state of anarchy which prepared the way, and gave birth to the desire, for a stable monarchy. The Book of Ruth, describing the ancestry of the first true and typical king of Israel, serves to connect the books of Judges

The Book of Ruth.

---

[1] Judg. xiii. 25.

[2] See Num. vi. Naziritism seems to have been the outcome of reaction against the disastrous influence which Canaanitish heathenism had exercised upon Hebrew religion. The Nazirites endeavoured by an example of asceticism to restore the austere simplicity of faith and manners which Israel had learned in the wilderness.

and Samuel[1]. Boaz, an upright and generous citizen of Beth-lehem, takes to wife Ruth the Moabitess, and from the union springs the line of David. One object of the book is apparently that of witnessing to the moral glory of David's house. The law of Deut. xxiii. 3 forbade the admission of a Moabite into *the congregation of the Lord, even to the tenth generation.* The story of Ruth shows how faithful love to Israel, and devotion to Israel's God, won for a lowly maiden, belonging to a despised and hostile race, a place of pre-eminent honour in the annals of the chosen people.

The name of David, with which the Book of Ruth closes, opens a new chapter in the history. The troubled period of the Judges—the age of Israelitish romance—was verging towards its close. The tribes of Israel had, by fusion with the Canaanites, become a large and vigorous though not as yet a united people. Their habits of life, their modes of thought and even of worship had undergone a gradual transformation, and the primitive tribal organization under which a single chief administered justice and settled disputes between the tribesmen, had in course of time given way to a system of government by the elders or ruling families of a district or tribe. In many respects, of course, the period of the Judges was an age of iron, in which rude violence, treacherous dealing, murder and robbery were scarcely regarded as crimes, and even human sacrifice was within the range of possibility. But on the other hand Israel's contact with the civilization of Canaan developed in it the trading instinct, widened the horizon of knowledge, and even gave some impetus to art. To this period may probably be

Survey of the age of the Judges.

---

[1] The Book of Ruth forms part of the *Hagiographa* in the Hebrew canon. It was probably composed at a period long subsequent to the compilation of Judges: but it is reasonable to suppose that it preserves a genuine tradition respecting the descent of David. It has been thought by some scholars that the book was written with a polemical object about the time of Ezra's reforms. See note on p. 236.

ascribed the beginnings of Hebrew literature and the common use of writing.

As regards Israel's religious condition at this time, there can be no doubt that the simple and austere faith which it had learned in the wilderness, had undergone serious corruption since the conquest of Canaan. The Hebrews still held fast to their national deity; but their perception of the distinction between Jehovah and the multitudinous *Ba'alim* of the Canaanites had gradually faded away. There was a popular tendency to identify Israel's God with the various local deities. Jehovah was actually worshipped under the title of *Ba'al*, 'lord'; the ancient sanctuaries of Canaan were frequented by the Hebrews as recognized holy places. Thus, as the psalmist says, *they were mingled among the heathen and learned their works* (Ps. cvi. 35). The usages and symbols of Canaanitish idolatry were freely borrowed in the worship of Jehovah: the *mazzeboth* or sacred pillars which were venerated as the abode of deity; the *ashêrim* or sacred poles which served as emblems of the goddess of fertility. In appropriating the 'high places' and altars of the Canaanites, Israel permanently adopted these and other adjuncts of heathen worship; indeed it was not till the reign of Josiah that they were finally abolished.

In earlier times the worship carried on at the high places was regarded by the Hebrews themselves as offered to Jehovah, though they probably associated with it the cult of Baal as the god of the new country in which they were now settled, and as the author of its fertility. It was only by degrees, when the Canaanites had been completely subdued or exterminated, that they recognized Jehovah as the true Lord and owner of the land. As regards the practice of image-worship, the conduct of Gideon in fashioning and erecting an *'Ephod* may not have been altogether an innovation, but it gave an impetus to a practice which soon became common. At the same time we must remember that the Tabernacle with its sacred ark still existed at Shiloh; and attached to the sanctuary was a community of priests which traced its origin to an ordinance of Moses himself. Since we hear nothing of any image of Jehovah in connection with Shiloh, it may be presumed that during this age of political disorder and religious disintegration, there was an inner circle of faithful Hebrews who still cherished the religious traditions of the Mosaic age.

CHAPTER VI.

THE ESTABLISHMENT OF THE MONARCHY.

THE desultory warfare with the Philistines had hitherto consisted chiefly of a series of sudden blows inflicted by the Hebrews as occasion offered. This state of things however was only the prelude to a serious and determined conflict for supremacy. The Philistines at length resolved to make a decisive movement, their object being to secure a footing on the hills that overlooked the central plain of Esdraelon. With this end in view they advanced northward from the plain of Sharon and encamped at Aphek on its northern border. The

The battle of Aphek: 1 Sam. iv.

Israelitish army occupied a strong position on the hills. Two encounters took place, the first of which resulted unfavourably for the Hebrews, who lost about 4000 men. It was this defeat which induced them to fetch the ark from Shiloh. *Let us*, was the cry, *fetch the ark of the covenant of Jehovah out of Shiloh unto us, that it may come among us, and save us out of the hand of our enemies.* The only effect however of this act of superstition was a far more disastrous repulse. Of the Israelites, 30,000 were slain, including Hophni and Phinehas, the official guardians of the ark, which fell into the hands of the Philistines. The calamity was complete and overwhelming; it involved for Israel nothing less than the loss of honour, country and freedom. The Philistines now had access northward to the plain of Esdraelon, and westward to the highlands of Mount Ephraim. Shiloh was apparently destroyed, and the entire land occupied by Philistine garrisons. Israel thus found itself practically placed under a foreign yoke, helpless, dispirited, and even disarmed[1].

This condition of things seems to have lasted for nearly twenty years. It was plainly attributable to the disunion which tribal jealousies had produced. The utter demoralization of the Hebrew army however was mainly due to its lack of a leader, and the drift of events pointed more and more clearly to the urgent need of a single ruler, who might be able to unite and organize the scattered forces of the different tribes.

At this juncture all eyes were directed towards *Samuel*, as the only man capable of guiding the nation through this critical epoch in its history. Samuel ('God heareth') was a son granted beyond hope to the prayers of his mother Hannah. The circumstances of his birth marked him out for a high destiny. His childhood was spent at the sanctuary of Shiloh. Here, under the direction of Eli the priest, to whose care he had been consigned by his mother, he *ministered unto the Lord*, and was an eyewitness of the iniquities by which Hophni and Phinehas, the unworthy sons of Eli, desecrated their priestly office[2]. When Samuel was twelve years old, God revealed to him in a vision the impending doom of Eli's house. From thenceforth *all Israel knew that Samuel was established to be a prophet of the Lord.*

Birth and childhood of Samuel: 1 Sam. i.—iii.

The overwhelming disaster at Aphek and the capture of the ark, Eli's death and the ruin of Shiloh, happened in due course; but history relates nothing either of Samuel's movements or of the general condition of the land during the next twenty years. It only gives an account

1 Sam. v., vi.

---

[1] 1 Sam. xiii. 19.

[2] It is a matter of doubt whether Samuel was, like Samson, a Nazirite, dedicated by a special vow of consecration to Jehovah's service. He is nowhere expressly called a 'Nazirite' in the O.T., but it is quite probable that he actually was one. See 1 Sam. i. 11.

of the adventures that befell the ark : how it was a source of danger and trouble to the Philistines, and how it was eventually sent back into the Israelitish territory and deposited at Kirjath-jearim, on the northern frontier of Judah.

At last Samuel perceived that his opportunity had arrived,

Samuel's appearance as leader: 1 Sam. vii.

and he again came forward in the capacity of a preacher of repentance to his fellow-countrymen. At Mizpeh he inaugurated his judgeship by summoning an assembly of the tribes, at which he exhorted them to *put away* their *strange gods* and to solemnly renew their covenant with Jehovah. He insisted on these as the only conditions under which they would be able to shake off the Philistine yoke. This gathering of the Hebrews evidently roused the suspicion of their oppressors, who at once prepared to maintain their supremacy by force of arms. A conflict seems to have actually begun while Samuel was engaged in offering sacrifice ; but the Philistines were repulsed with heavy loss, and the victory kindled anew the hopes of the Israelites. A brighter day seemed to have dawned. Samuel was enabled to re-establish the reign of law and order, and the regular administration of justice was carried on by him and his two sons.

The want of a military leader, however, was still unsupplied,

The demand for a king.

and according to a later account of the foundation of the monarchy (contained in 1 Sam. viii., x. 17 foll., and xii.), the maladministration of Samuel's sons was made the pretext for a formal request on the part of the tribes that a king might be appointed. To the prophetic historians of a later age, such a demand would appear to be nothing less than an act of defection from Jehovah. It would imply the abandonment of the ideal which Moses had originally set before the nation, namely that of a 'theocracy,'—the immediate sovereignty of Jehovah, exercised through human instruments, such as Moses or the Judges. The demand for a king would be regarded as a virtual acknowledgment on Israel's part, of failure to rise to the height of its true vocation. It is questionable however whether Samuel himself took the view afterwards ascribed to him[1]. The older narrative (1 Sam. ix. 1—x. 16) implies that in this transaction he shared the general *desire of all Israel*. He doubtless perceived the urgent need of the moment—the union and consolidation of the divided and undisciplined tribes under the strong hand of a single ruler. By no other means could the oppressive yoke of the Philistines be broken. Thus Samuel's conduct at this juncture seems to have been guided by the spirit of a true optimism. He believed that the institution of a monarchy might after all prove to be perfectly compatible with the fulfilment of Israel's special destiny.

But Samuel rendered an even greater service to Israel than the inauguration of the monarchy. He was the restorer of its religion. Tradition points to him as in a real sense the first of 'the goodly fellowship of the prophets[2]'—an order of men which was destined to discharge an important function in Israel's subsequent history.

The 'schools of the prophets.

It is certain that the pressure of Philistine domination excited among the Hebrews an ardent spirit of religious and patriotic enthusiasm, which, as Samuel clearly perceived, might be enlisted on the side of the religion of Jehovah. An order of prophets (*Nebîim*) was an institution which the Hebrews originally shared with the heathen nations of Canaan and of other Semitic lands. The gods of Phoenicia had their 'prophets'—fanatical devotees of whose frenzied zeal we catch a glimpse in such passages as 1 Kings xviii. 28. In many respects akin to the Canaanitish prophets were the companies of *Nebîim* of whom we read in the first book of Samuel[3].

---

[1] On the probable date of this later narrative see Driver, *LOT*, pp. 175—177; H. P. Smith in *The International Critical Commentary* on 1 Sam. *ll. c.*

[2] See Acts iii. 24.

[3] See 1 Sam. x. 5 foll., xix. 20 foll.

They seem to have been in the habit of traversing the land in a state of wild and ecstatic excitement, probably preaching a patriotic crusade against Philistine oppression, and enlisting recruits for the defence of Jehovah's land and people[1].

This outburst of enthusiasm might have been merely a passing incident in Israel's history, but it is clear that Samuel resolved to utilize the newly-kindled zeal. He was not himself regarded as one of the *Nebîim*. He is described as a seer (*Ro'eh*), a name which had most probably been familiar to the Hebrews before the invasion of Canaan. But Samuel devoted himself to the task of regulating the turbulent and ecstatic element in the behaviour and character of the *Nebîim* in order to turn their peculiar gift to good account. By forming the so-called 'schools of the prophets' at various religious centres, such as Bethel, Jericho and Gilgal, he made provision for the training and perfecting of the prophetic gift, and also for the systematic religious instruction of the common people. The *Nebîim* doubtless did good service in diffusing among their countrymen a knowledge of the essential truths which Moses had taught. Meanwhile the gift of inspiration was kindled and nurtured among them, though it was not exclusively confined to them. In their schools they seem to have cultivated the art of sacred music, and they may have taken part in writing or compiling the annals of the national history. But their main duty was that of keeping alive in Israel, by their public teaching and by the example of their dedicated lives, *the light of Jehovah*[2]. We hear again of *the schools of the prophets* in connection with Elijah and Elisha, a fact which shows that the *Nebîim* were obedient disciples of men greater than themselves[3]. When

[1] The behaviour of the *Nebîim* was very similar to that of eastern dervishes preaching a crusade against the 'infidels.'

[2] Isai. ii. 5.

[3] To these leaders the *Nebîim* gave titles of special honour: *e.g.* 'Master' or 'Father' (2 Kings ii. 3, 12 etc.). They seem, like the mendicant friars of the middle ages, to have depended for their maintenance on charity.

in course of time they became a professional class, it was only occasionally that individuals arose among them who played a striking or heroic part in history.

We now return to the work of Samuel in connection with the new monarchy. The circumstances of Saul's election as king are by no means clear. There are two accounts of the transaction, one of which (1 Sam ix. 1—x. 16) describes the anointing of Saul by Samuel in obedience to a divine command. According to this narrative, the primary object of Saul's election was to deliver Israel from the tyranny of the Philistines. Another account (1 Sam. x. 17—27) represents the choice of Saul as having taken place by lot at a formal assembly of the people held at Mizpeh. We must suppose either that tradition varied respecting the mode of Saul's appointment; or that the private act of Samuel was afterwards ratified by popular election. There is no question however as to the impression produced by the new king: his gigantic stature, his ardent temperament, and the modest dignity of his bearing won him instant acceptance. *All the people shouted and said, God save the king*[1].

Saul elected king: circ. 1020.

No long time elapsed before Saul found an opportunity of proving his quality. The Ammonites were emboldened by the divided and distressed state of the Hebrew tribes to attempt the conquest of Gilead, and accordingly they marched upon the city of Jabesh-Gilead and closely invested it. The inhabitants however were allowed, before submitting to the barbarous terms of the Ammonite king Nahash, to appeal for aid to the tribes west of Jordan. Messengers from the distressed city arrived at Gibeah of Benjamin, the home of Saul and his family[2]. The king himself was ploughing in the fields when the urgent

Deliverance of Jabesh-Gilead: 1 Sam. xi.

---

[1] 1 Sam. x. 24.

[2] At Gibeah a Philistine prefect was posted with a garrison—a visible token of the humiliating bondage into which the Hebrews had fallen.

message from Jabesh reached his ears. Instantly hewing his oxen in pieces, he sent the portions in all directions, thus summoning the tribes to rally to the relief of Jabesh with the threat, *Whosoever cometh not forth after Saul and after Samuel, so shall it be done unto his oxen.* The people hastened to obey the summons, and Saul was enabled to strike a swift blow. With his army he fell suddenly on the Ammonites, and scattered the forces of the besiegers. This victory confirmed Saul's title to the throne. At Gilgal the monarchy was inaugurated afresh, and hailed with general rejoicing.

The real task however which Saul had been chosen to undertake was the conduct of the war against the Philistines. The flame of revolt against them was kindled by a bold and decisive venture on the part of Saul's son, Jonathan. In order to command the important pass which leads from the Jordan into the heart of Mount Ephraim, Saul had divided his forces into two detachments. Two thousand men were under his own command at Michmash on the northern side of the gorge, and a thousand were with Jonathan at Geba on the southern side. Jonathan gave the signal for a general rising of the Israelites by destroying the pillar which the Philistines had erected as a trophy of their supremacy at Gibeah. The Philistines were alarmed, and hastily concentrated an overwhelming force at Gibeah. For the moment the movement of revolt was crushed. Saul found himself forced to retreat from the heights to Gilgal in the Jordan valley, while the deserted stronghold of Michmash fell into the hands of the Philistines, who at once proceeded to overrun the country in different directions. But the position of affairs was quickly altered. With a small force of six hundred men Saul managed to effect a junction with Jonathan, who had apparently remained at Geba. An heroic adventure on Jonathan's part, who, accompanied only by his armour-bearer, scaled the steep cliffs of the defile and made a sudden assault on the Philistine

Campaign against the Philistines:
1 Sam. xiii., xiv.

garrison at Michmash, led to a renewal of the struggle for independence. Panic-stricken by Jonathan's impetuous attack, the Philistines gave way. Saul hastened to bring up his scanty forces and completed their discomfiture. The Philistines were driven from Michmash, and the Israelites who had been forced to take refuge in the hill-country turned against their oppressors. This memorable occasion, however, was in danger of being marred by the headstrong impetuosity of Saul, who, in his eagerness to follow up the pursuit of the Philistines, invoked a curse on any of his people who should touch food till evening. Jonathan, ignorant of his father's vow, and exhausted by the pursuit, refreshed himself by tasting some honey which he found dropping from a forest tree. When Saul consulted the oracle and discovered what Jonathan had done, he was on the point of putting him to death, and was only prevented from doing so by the energetic opposition of the people. The rash conduct of Saul was an ominous incident, which boded ill for the future of the new monarchy. This decided success how-ever had only a temporary effect[1], for we are told that *there was sore war against the Philistines all the days of Saul* (1 Sam. xiv. 52). The consequence of these continual hostilities was that Saul made it his chief object to attach to himself all who could claim distinction for their strength or valour. "War," it has been truly observed, "was at once the business and the resource of the new kingdom."

It was apparently during a temporary cessation of hostilities that Saul was commanded to conduct a campaign against the Amalekites, whose marauding excursions were a constant menace to the southern borders of Judah. The enmity between Israel and Amalek dated from the period of the exodus, and

Saul and the Amalekites. His rejection: 1 Sam. xv.

---

[1] The exact sequence of events narrated in 1 Sam. xiii., xiv. is difficult to determine. There is evidently some confusion in the Hebrew text between Geba and Gibeah. I have adopted what seems to be the most probable explanation of *Netsibh* in 1 Sam. xiii. 3, 'pillar' or 'trophy.'

it is likely that some barbarous deeds of violence or treachery on the part of these warlike nomads were the immediate occasion of Saul's expedition. The Amalekites were defeated, their king Agag was captured, and those who escaped wholesale slaughter were scattered as far as the frontiers of Egypt. Unfortunately, however, Saul's victory was again marked by an act of wilfulness which led to a final breach between Samuel and the king.   Already Saul's imperious self-will had displayed itself in the camp at Gilgal, where, owing to Samuel's delay in joining him, he had usurped priestly functions and offered sacrifice (1 Sam. xiii. 8—14).   In the present case he considered it expedient to spare the Amalekite king and the best part of the captured spoil—an act of leniency which to the men of Saul's age seemed nothing less than a heinous robbery of God.   Saul had been warned already by Samuel that his kingdom should *not continue* (1 Sam. xiii. 14).   His conduct in regard to the Amalekites now brought upon him a sentence of final rejection. *Because thou hast rejected the word of the Lord, he hath also rejected thee from being king. Samuel,* we read, *came no more to see Saul until the day of his death* (1 Sam. xv. 23, 35).

This incident led to an unhappy change in Saul's demeanour and character.   Harassed as he doubtless was by the unrelieved pressure of the war with the Philistines, he now found himself bereft of Samuel's guidance.   A spirit of strange and fitful melancholy came over him, and occasionally impelled him to acts of frenzied violence.   His servants suggested music as an alleviation or possible cure of his malady ; and according to one account it was David's skill as a player on the harp that first commended him to the notice of Saul.   David was apparently a mere stripling when the king sent for him, and attached him closely to his person. *He loved him greatly; and he became his armour-bearer* (1 Sam. xvi. 21).   Moreover when the evil spirit troubled him, the music of David's harp brought

Saul and David: 1 Sam. xvi. 14 foll.

him refreshment and health.   At the same time the narrative itself suggests a different explanation of David's appearance at the court of Saul.   He belonged to a Judahite family, being the youngest son of Jesse the Bethlehemite, and the great-grandson of Boaz the husband of Ruth.   It is therefore probable that David was one of the gallant and soldierly youths whom Saul took pains to discover in different parts of his kingdom, and gathered about his person (1 Sam. xiv. 52). He was renowned as *a mighty man of valour, and a man of war, prudent in speech and a comely person* (1 Sam. xvi. 18). He was evidently a man of more than ordinary mental and physical gifts, and was therefore likely, apart from his skill in music, to find his way to the court.

Another tradition however depicts David as an unknown and inexperienced youth, who had hitherto been engaged in tending his father's sheep, and who at a critical moment of the war with the Philistines came forward as the Israelitish champion against the giant Goliath of Gath[1].   David's prowess not only attracted the favourable notice of Saul, but raised him at once to a position of unbounded popularity with his country-men.   For the death of Goliath[2] was followed by a decisive

---

[1] It is very difficult to harmonize the narrative of David's first appear-ance in the valley of Elah and of Eliab's contemptuous notice of him (1 Sam. xvii. 28) with the tradition preserved in xvi. 1—13, which relates David's solemn unction by Samuel.   Perhaps the best account is that this latter incident occurred at a later time, and has been transferred to the period when David was still a shepherd-lad at Bethlehem.   The historian, for reasons of his own, places the story of David's anointing in close connection with the rejection of Saul.

[2] It may suffice here to mention the well-known difficulty that in 2 Sam. xxi. 19 the death of Goliath is attributed to a Bethlehemite called Elhanan.   Possibly Goliath was slain on some later occasion by one of David's warriors, and the victory was ascribed by popular tradition to David himself.   The passage, 1 Sam. xxi. 9, however, shows that Goliath was slain while Saul was still king.   In 1 Chron. xx. 5 where *the brother* of Goliath is slain by Elhanan we perhaps find a later attempt to harmonize two conflicting traditions.

defeat of the Philistines, and from that time forward David, the chosen son-in-law of the king, and the captain of his body-guard, became the most conspicuous figure in the kingdom, while ties of the closest friendship bound him to Jonathan, the heir to Saul's throne.

David now occupied a position which exposed him to the jealous fears of Saul—fears doubtless aggravated by the malady that disordered his brain. It seems improbable that the estrangement began immediately after David's encounter with Goliath. But it is clear that his growing influence and popularity, together with his uniform success in war, rapidly changed Saul's good-will into bitter hatred. The intercession of Jonathan only aggravated the king's suspicions: he began to look upon David as a rival, who aspired to the throne[1]. Finally David was driven from the court by a determined attempt upon his life; but though he thus became an exile and an outlaw, he did not cease to be regarded as a popular hero. Many stories of his adventures became current, fragments of which have reached us in the concluding chapters of the First Book of Samuel[2]. He seems once indeed to have sought refuge at a place called Naioth, where Samuel had planted one of the schools of the prophets'; and it is related that the messengers sent to apprehend David, and even the king him-self, presently coming in person, were overcome by the prophetic *afflatus*, while their intended victim escaped (1 Sam. xix. 18 foll.). But it is probable that after his final breach with the king, David fled southwards from Gibeah towards the territory of his own tribesmen. The priests of Nob supplied him with weapons, and even allowed David and his men to use the sacred shew-bread for food. This act of friendliness however brought upon *the city of the priests*

David at Saul's court.

His exile.

Saul's ven-geance on the priests of Nob: 1 Sam. xxi. 1—9, xxii. 6 foll.

[1] 1 Sam. xx. 30 foll., xxii. 13.
[2] See 1 Sam. xxi—xxxi.

a cruel vengeance.   Informed by Doeg the Edomite, his chief
herdsman, of the welcome which David had received at Nob,
Saul summoned Ahimelech the priest to his presence, taxed
him with an act of conspiracy, and gave orders for the immediate massacre of the entire priestly clan.   When the
king's officers hesitated to execute the sacrilegious order,
Doeg himself undertook the task.́ The priests and all the
other inhabitants of the city of Nob were put to the sword.
Abiathar the son of Ahimelech alone escaped, and fled to
David in the wilderness of Judah, bearing with him the oracular
'ephod.

The cave of Adullam in the *Shephelah*, somewhat to the
westward of Hebron[1], provided David with a stronghold
within the borders of his own tribe.   Here he was joined
by his family and kinsfolk, and also by a band of distressed
debtors and malcontents of every class, the total number
of his adherents gradually amounting to four hundred men.
His parents meanwhile sought protection with the king of
Moab[2].

The Hebrew tradition gives only a vague account of David's
movements from this point onwards ; but before
he left the neighbourhood of the *Shephelah* he
was enabled to strike a blow at the Philistines.

David at
Keilah:
1 Sam. xxiii.

Hearing that they had made an assault upon the frontier-town
of Keilah, David, having consulted the sacred oracle, marched
to the place and drove the enemy away with great slaughter.
But the fear of being betrayed to Saul by the ungrateful inhabitants of Keilah forced him again to flee eastwards to the
desolate region overlooking the Dead Sea.   Owing however to
the treachery of the Ziphites, who informed Saul of David's

---

[1] See G. A. Smith, *HGHL*, p. 229.

[2] Jesse must have had connections of kinship with Moab if we accept
the genealogy of Ruth iv. 18 foll.   The story of David's visit to Achish,
king of Gath (1 Sam. xxi. 10—15) seems to be certainly misplaced.   It
may well have occurred at a later period in David's career.

hiding-place in the hill of Hachilah, he retreated further south into the wilderness of Maon after narrowly escaping capture by Saul.   To this period probably belongs the incident related in

David and Nabal: 1 Sam. xxv. 1 Sam. xxv.   Nabal the Calebite was a wealthy sheep-owner whose flocks pastured on the plateau of Carmel, south-east of Hebron in the Negeb. David had repeatedly done good service to Nabal by protecting his possessions from the nomad tribes of the wilderness, and asked for a recompense on behalf of himself and his men. Nabal's churlish refusal of this request provoked David to avenge the insult; and Nabal would have paid dear for his 'folly' (1 Sam. xxv. 25), but for the intervention of his prudent wife Abigail, who by soft words and a generous gift appeased David's anger.   After her husband's death Abigail joined David and became his wife.   This alliance not only enriched him, but also formed a useful link of connection between the family of the future king and the powerful tribe of Calebites.

David seems now to have fixed his stronghold at Engedi on the western shore of the Dead Sea.   In the neighbourhood of this place he had more than one romantic adventure.   On one,

David spares Saul's life: 1 Sam. xxiv., xxvi. or possibly on two different occasions, Saul fell into his opponent's power, but David steadily refused to harm *Jehovah's anointed* (1 Sam. xxiv. 6)[1].   Apparently the king was for the moment touched by David's generosity and by his passionate protestation of innocence.   *Then said Saul, I have sinned; return, my son David: for I will no more do thee harm, because my life was precious in thine eyes this day* (1 Sam. xxvi. 21). David however could not rely on security so long as he remained in Israelitish territory.   He felt himself driven to find refuge with the Philistines.   Achish, king of Gath, gave him a

[1] The two similar narratives of chh. xxiv. and xxvi. may possibly be different versions of the same tradition.

ready welcome, and assigned to him and his followers a settlement in the border-town of Ziklag, lying somewhat north of Gaza. David had now a difficult part to play. He must neither estrange his Hebrew countrymen, nor forfeit the confidence of Achish. Accordingly he made a succession

David among the Philistines: I Sam. xxvii.; xxviii. 1, 2; xxix.; xxx.

of hostile raids upon the Amalekites and other desert tribes, while he feigned to be carrying on warlike operations against the Israelites. Meanwhile the Philistines were preparing for a decisive struggle with David's fellow-countrymen, and Achish summoned his vassal to accompany him to the seat of warfare. Fortunately for David the suspicion of the other Philistine chiefs compelled Achish to dismiss his nominal ally, who was thus saved from taking part in operations directed against his own people. On returning however to Ziklag, he found that the city had been assaulted and sacked by the Amalekites, and its inhabitants, including his own wives, Ahinoam and Abigail, carried captive. David at once started in pursuit, and guided by an Egyptian slave whom he found lying half-dead by the way-side, he fell suddenly on the camp of the Amalekites at dusk, and put nearly all of them to the sword. The captives were recovered together with a great quantity of spoil. Of the captured booty he made a politic use, by sending rich presents to the different towns in Judah which had befriended and sheltered him during his exile.

Meanwhile the Philistines had marched into the plain of Esdraelon. Saul's army was marshalled, and awaited their attack, on the slopes of Mount Gilboa. On the eve of the conflict Saul, who had lost all confidence in himself and was desti-

Saul's last battle and death: I Sam. xxviii.; xxxi.

tute of a single trustworthy adviser, had recourse to a means of ascertaining Jehovah's will which was forbidden alike by the Mosaic law and by his own public decree. He had himself banished all wizards and necromancers from his dominions, but there survived at Endor a witch of whom he resolved to take counsel. Under cover of darkness the king with a few attendants crossed the valley of Jezreel and reached the witch's dwelling. From the lips of Samuel himself, summoned by the woman's art from the grave, Saul learned his approaching doom, and then returned exhausted and dejected to the Israelitish camp. When morning broke the battle began; the Israelites, like the French at Creçy, were overwhelmed by the shower of arrows under which the Philistines advanced to the attack. They gave way and fled in confusion. Saul's three sons, Jonathan, Abinadab and Melchishua, together with his armour-bearer, were slain. The king was sorely wounded, and only saved himself from being captured alive by falling on his own sword. The Hebrews were panic-stricken by the disaster. The neighbouring towns were abandoned by the inhabitants, and for the moment the hateful ascendancy of the Philistines, at least in the fertile valley of Jezreel, was re-established.

The defeat and death of Saul were announced to David at Ziklag two days after his return from *the slaughter of the Amalekites.* The messenger was himself a young Amalekite, who brought Saul's crown and bracelet to David, with the hope of gaining a reward for his tidings. But David with a stern rebuke ordered him to be promptly put to death, for having, by his own admission, *slain the LORD'S anointed.* Then, in a dirge of striking beauty, the 'song of the bow,' as it was afterwards called, David poured forth his generous lament over his kingly foe and his chivalrous friend.

2 Sam. i. 1 foll.

David's lament: 2 Sam. i. 19 foll.

'*Thy glory, O Israel, is slain upon thy high places!*
How are the mighty fallen!

.   .   .   .

Saul and Jonathan were lovely and pleasant in their lives,
And in their death they were not divided.

.   .   ..

How are the mighty fallen,
And the weapons of war perished!'

The Philistines cut off the head of the fallen king, and sent it together with his armour as a trophy to the temple of Astarte. The headless corpse and the bodies of his three sons they fastened to the wall of Beth-shan, a few miles from the battle-field. Thereupon the men of Jabesh, in grateful recollection of Saul's valiant action on their behalf, went under cover of night to Beth-shan, took down the bodies, and brought them to Jabesh, where they were reverently burned and buried.

The position of Israel at Saul's death was practically just what it had been when he was called to the throne. The domination of the Philistines was more securely established than ever. The Hebrews were scattered and disarmed. Saul had in fact proved himself unequal to the task which circumstances had imposed on him. But his fall was not an unmixed calamity for his people. What Israel needed at this crisis of her fortunes was not so much a brave and skilful military leader, as a ruler capable of appreciating her true mission and function in history.

By Saul's death after a reign of probably not more than ten or twelve years a way was opened for David's return to his native territory. With his family and followers he settled at the ancient city of Hebron, situated within the borders of Judah, and here his fellow-tribesmen assembled and solemnly anointed David as their tribal king. The Philistines did not interfere with the arrangement. David continued to be their vassal and collected the tribute due to them; nor apparently was he required to give up the town of Ziklag. Meanwhile Abner, the commander of the Israelitish forces which survived the disaster at Mount Gilboa, had retired to Mahanaim east of the Jordan, and there made Esh-baal[1], the surviving son of Saul, king over

Events after Saul's death: 2 Sam. ii—iv.

---

[1] By later writers called Ish-bosheth. "Later writers changed *Ba'al* into *Bosheth*, 'shame,' in accordance with the custom which grew up when the title of Baal came to signify the god of Phoenicia rather than Jehovah of Israel." Sayce, *EHH*, p. 398.

Gilead, Geshur, Jezreel, Ephraim, Benjamin and *all Israel* (2 Sam. ii. 9). For some time the two rival kingdoms were engaged in desultory warfare. We are told of a conflict at Gibeon in which the Israelites were defeated, but the Judahite Asahel, the youngest brother of Joab and nephew of David, was slain by Abner whom he was hotly pursuing. Then Eshbaal's cause was further weakened by a quarrel with Abner, who thereupon made overtures to David and offered to *bring about all Israel* to his side. David agreed to this proposal, but stipulated that his wife Michal, Saul's daughter, should be restored to him—a step which was perhaps intended to strengthen his claim to be the legitimate successor of Saul. Abner made every effort to win over the northern tribes, especially the late king's own kinsmen of Benjamin: and at length felt himself justified in visiting Hebron to inform David of his success. He was cordially welcomed and entertained by David, but on his departure he was treacherously assassinated

Death of Abner. by Joab in revenge for Asahel's death. Joab's act was indignantly disavowed by David, who caused Abner to be solemnly interred at Hebron, and publicly lamented his death, as that of *a prince and a great man fallen in Israel.* The removal of Abner however was a fatal blow to the hopes of Eshbaal. *His hand became feeble and all the Israelites were troubled,* and at this juncture two Benjamite officers, Rechab and Baanah, resolved to take a desperate and decisive step. They seized an opportunity of

Murder of Eshbaal. murdering Eshbaal during his noon-day sleep, cut off his head and carried it to David. He instantly put the assassins to death, and caused the head of Eshbaal to be honourably interred in Abner's tomb. But having thus cleared himself of all complicity in the deed, David allowed events to take their natural course. For

David king of Israel: 2 Sam. v. 1—5. seven years and a half he had been tribal king of Judah; he was now invited to ascend the throne of Israel as the approved champion of the nation against its Philistine oppressors; for the second time he was anointed at Hebron, and thus became king of a united Israel.

It is worth while at this point to notice the striking parallel presented by early English history to the course of events which brought about the union of the tribes under a single sceptre. The invasion of Britain by the English in the fifth and sixth centuries led to the establishment of a number of small independent kingdoms, which were continually weakened by mutual jealousy and strife. Indeed, the warfare between the Britons and the invaders gradually died down into a warfare of English kingdoms against each other. Then came the invasion of the North-men. The victorious Danes, like the Philistines of Old Testament history, settled down in the midst of the conquered population, which under their domination was gradually welded into a vigorous nation. The need of resistance to a common foe forced the English to recognize a common king; and towards the close of the ninth century, Ælfred, from being the mere chieftain of the West Saxons, became the king and champion of a united English people in its struggle with the stranger.

The elevation of David's house marks the point at which Judah rose to a position of supremacy among the tribes. Since the destruction of the sanctuary at Shiloh the influence of Ephraim had steadily declined, and by the death of Eshbaal the hegemony of this powerful tribe was brought to an end. At a later time indeed Ephraim recovered its independence and became the nucleus of an Israelitish kingdom. But for the present Judah, a tribe of very composite origin[1], became supreme, and bore the brunt of the struggle with the Philistines. David's accession to the

Reign of David: ? 1010—970.

---

[1] In the early stages of the conquest we find the Kenites coalescing with the Judahites, and afterwards the two Kenizzite (Edomitish) clans, Caleb and Othniel. The tribe had also absorbed Canaanitish elements. See Hastings' *DB*, s.v. 'Judah'.

throne of Israel seems to have been regarded by the Philistines as a signal of revolt. They made a determined attempt to capture the new king, and thereby rob the Israelites of their only hope of maintaining independence. David evaded this attempt by retiring to *the hold*, i.e. probably the newly-captured stronghold of Zion. Meanwhile the Philistines overran Judah and even seized Bethlehem[1]. At length however David was able to inflict a defeat on them at Baal-perazim, and this was followed by a more decisive victory in the valley of Rephaim, south-west of Jerusalem. Gradually the Philistines were driven from beyond the borders of Judah, and thus the war was carried into the enemy's country. Gath, 'the mother city[2],' was wrested from the Philistines, and forced to become tributary. For a time at any rate they ceased to be dangerous, though they were occasionally troublesome neighbours to the Israelites. David had not actually subjugated Philistia; but he at least compelled it to acquiesce in Israel's independence; and owing perhaps to David's past connection with the Philistines, more friendly relations were ultimately established between the two nations. David even recruited his body-guard from the ranks of Israel's inveterate foes[3].

From the first it had been a point of policy with the new king to weld into one the tribes which had hitherto been disunited or at variance. An important step in this direction was the capture of the fortress-town of Jebus, from which the Canaanites had never been dislodged, and which was believed by the inhabitants to be impregnable. It was probably while he was still tribal king of Judah that David attacked the

The capture and refounding of Jebus: 2 Sam. v. 4—10.

---

[1] Some heroic incidents of the campaign are mentioned in 2 Sam. xxiii. 8 foll.; xxi. 15 foll.

[2] See 2 Sam. viii. 1 R.V. and cp. 1 Chron. xviii. 1.

[3] The *Krethî* and *Plethî* of 2 Sam. viii. 18, xv. 18 foll., 1 K. i. 8, 10, 38 seem to be two Philistine tribes. In 2 Sam. xv. 18 the Gittites are coupled with them.

place.   He first captured the stronghold of Zion, the fortress
which protected the upper city; this having fallen, the remaining portion was taken by assault, Joab being the first to scale
the walls.   The inhabitants were spared, and new settlers were
introduced from Judah and Benjamin.   The city was newly
fortified, and a palace was built for the king on the western
slope of Mount Zion[1].   The 'city of David' thus re-founded,
was in every respect the most suitable capital for the united
kingdoms of Israel and Judah.   The position of Jerusalem, on
or even within the borders of both Benjamin and Judah, served
to bind together the two royal families and the two most
powerful tribes; from its strong situation it derived important
military advantages, while its high elevation and its seclusion,
alike from the sea and from the great thoroughfares of commerce, fitted the city in a peculiar manner for its future function
as the spiritual metropolis of the world.   The very mixture of
population which was a feature of the new city "was a symbol
and visible token of that unification of races and interests in
Palestine which it was the work of David's reign to effect[2]."
But the king was bent on making Jerusalem the religious
capital of the nation, as well as its political
centre.   Accordingly the ark was solemnly
fetched by David in person from Kirjath-jearim,
where it had rested for many years.   A further
delay was caused by the fate of Uzzah who, when the oxen that
drew the cart containing the ark stumbled, rashly *put forth his
hand and took hold of it,* and was killed on the spot[3].   The ark
remained for three months in the house of Obed-Edom the

*The ark
brought to
Jerusalem:
2 Sam. vi.*

---

[1] On the difficult questions connected with the topography of Jerusalem
see note in Prof. Kirkpatrick's *Second Book of Samuel* (Camb. Bible for
Schools), Appendix, p. 239; and art. 'Jerusalem' in Hastings' *Dict. of the
Bible.*

[2] Sayce, *EHH.*, p. 411.

[3] It has been surmised that Uzzah was crushed by a sudden and violent
movement of the waggon bearing the ark.

Gittite, but was finally brought up to 'the city of David' and deposited in a sacred tent erected within the citadel. The occasion was one of great rejoicing; the king himself, clad in a priestly vestment, led the sacred procession, *leaping and dancing before Jehovah*; numerous sacrifices were offered, and at the close of the ceremony David dismissed the assembled multitude with a benediction and with gifts of food. The only discordant note that marred the general festivity was Michal's contemptuous greeting of the king when he returned to his house. Had a son been born to Michal, Saul's grandson would have succeeded David on the throne of Israel; but as a punishment for her irreverence, she was doomed to remain childless till her death.

The ark of God had thus found a temporary resting-place on Mount Zion, but David was not content himself to dwell in *a house of cedar* while the ark dwelt *within curtains*. He was anxious to erect a permanent sanctuary, but Nathan the prophet, of whom he enquired concerning the divine will, bade him abandon his design and leave to his successor the work of building the Temple. The time indeed was hardly ripe for the centralization of worship at a single fixed sanctuary. David's

Campaigns of David: 2 Sam. viii., x., xii. 26—31. primary task was that of organizing the kingdom and prosecuting the wars which were necessary for its defence and consolidation. The Philistine yoke was, as we have seen, speedily broken, and this may be regarded as the most signal achievement of David's reign. He next directed his arms against the neighbouring Semitic peoples, who menaced the eastern borders of his territory, Moab, Ammon and Edom. Doubtless all these petty states viewed with apprehension the union of the Hebrew tribes under the sceptre of an energetic warrior like David. Their suspicions soon led to open hostilities, but only scanty notices of the different campaigns are preserved. Apparently David first subdued the Moabites, and treated his vanquished foes with merciless severity. The Ammonites, whose

new king Hanun had requited David's courtesy in sending a
friendly embassy by scandalous treatment of his messengers, endeavoured to form a coalition of small Aramaean states, Zobah,
Beth-rehob, Maacah and Tob, to check the growing power of
the Hebrew monarch.   Joab, the commander of David's army,
marched upon Rabbah, the capital of Ammon.   Dividing his
forces, he left to his brother Abishai the conduct of the
operations at Rabbah, while he himself prepared with a picked
detachment to meet the Syrians, who were advancing from the
north to the aid of the Ammonites.   The Syrians were successfully routed, and the Ammonites were driven within the walls
of Rabbah.   In the following year the campaign was renewed
by David himself.   The Syrians, led by Shobach, the general
of Hadadezer, king of Zobah, were defeated at a place called
Helem with immense loss.   Another victory enabled David to
carry his conquests as far northward as Damascus, where he
placed a garrison, and finally returned with large spoil to
Jerusalem ; at the same time Toi, the king of Hamath on the
Orontes, sent his son with presents to David's court.   The war
with Ammon was now vigorously renewed.   After a somewhat
prolonged siege Joab succeeded in forcing an entrance into
Rabbah, though the citadel remained for a while unsubdued.
Joab chivalrously allowed David himself to complete the conquest.   On the arrival of the king with fresh troops, the city
was easily taken, and the captives were put to death with cruel
tortures after the barbarous fashion of that age[1].   Among the
spoils was a golden crown which may have adorned the head
of the Ammonite idol *Milcom*[2].   The subjugation of the
Ammonites seems to have been followed by an expedition
against the Edomites in the valley of Salt.   The success of this

---

[1] The meaning of 2 Sam. xii. 31 is not perfectly certain.   Prof. H. P.
Smith, *ad loc.*, following the LXX, thinks the most probable interpretation
is, *He brought out the people and set them at the saws and the picks and the
axes and made them work at the brick-kilns.*

[2] See 2 Sam. xii. 30, R.V. marg.

campaign gave David command of harbours on the Red Sea.
Joab remained in the district for six months carrying on a war
of extermination[1].

The kingdom of David was now secure from the pressure
of external enemies, but new dangers threatened

The dark side of the picture: 2 Sam. xi.
it from within. Troubles arose in the king's
family,—troubles which were unhappily due to
David's own sin and weakness. He, like other
Oriental despots, had gradually gathered round him a numerous
harem, thereby introducing into his capital the usual abuses of
an Eastern court. Luxury and self-indulgence lured David on
to the commission of a terrible crime. He committed adultery
with Bathsheba the wife of Uriah the Hittite, an officer in his
army, and to conceal his guilt procured the death of her husband.
Though the repentance of the king, when he was denounced
by the prophet Nathan, was deep and sincere, the long train of
miseries which resulted from David's evil example forms a kind
of divine commentary on the heinous character of his crime.
Amnon, his firstborn son, was murdered by his half-brother
Absalom in revenge for an outrage done to his sister Tamar.
Absalom was his father's favourite, but his fratricidal act compelled him to seek refuge with his grandfather, the king of
Geshur, a small principality on the western border of Bashan.
For three years he remained in exile till at last the inter-
vention of Joab procured his recall.

Two years more however elapsed before Absalom was
admitted to his father's presence. He was in

The rebellion of Absalom: 2 Sam. xv. 1— xix. 8.
fact already estranged in heart from David, and
secretly used every art to supplant him. Meanwhile the king's fellow-tribesmen of Judah had
become disaffected. It is probable that the choice of Jerusalem
as capital instead of the ancient and sacred city of Hebron was
a cause of discontent. On the other hand the conduct of
Shimei shows how deep was the resentment felt by the Ben-

---

[1] Cp. 1 Kings xi. 15 foll.

jaminites against a king who owed his elevation to the ruin of Saul's house. Absalom did not fail to take advantage of the wide-spread sense of grievance which David's *régime* had excited. After four years' residence at the court, during which by his handsome presence and affable manners he *stole away the hearts of the men of Israel*, he visited Hebron under pretence of fulfilling a vow. Here he was joined by Ahithophel of Giloh, his father's most trusted counsellor, and Hebron instantly became the centre of a formidable revolt. *The conspiracy was strong; for the people increased continually with Absalom.* It seems indeed that David could only count upon the loyalty of the district east of Jordan, and he resolved to withdraw thither without delay. He had been taken completely by surprise, and his only safety lay in anticipating by flight an attack upon Jerusalem.

The historian draws a graphic picture of the king's hasty departure: his crossing of the Kidron, accompanied by his household and body-guard in the garb of mourning and amid the lamentations of his followers. A few trusty adherents remained at his side: Joab, the devoted commander-in-chief of his army, the warrior Ittai of Gath, and the counsellor Hushai, who willingly undertook to ingratiate himself with Absalom, with a view to frustrating the plans of Ahithophel. The priests Zadok and Abiathar were anxious to accompany David and to bring with them the sacred ark, but the king insisted upon their remaining in Jerusalem. *Carry back the ark of God*, he said, *into the city: if I shall find favour in the eyes of Jehovah, he will bring me again and shew me both it and his habitation.* The priests were in fact able to assist David's cause most effectually by remaining in Jerusalem, where they could be in constant communication with Hushai, and thus keep the king informed of the progress of the revolt.

Meanwhile Absalom made a triumphal entry into Jerusalem, and took formal possession of the royal palace and harem.

David's flight from Jerusalem.

This step destroyed the last chance of a reconciliation between the king and his son.   The usurper however had not the wisdom to use his advantage effectively.   By yielding to the crafty advice of Hushai and delaying an attack, Absalom gave David time to concentrate his loyal followers at Mahanaim, the former capital of Eshbaal.   Ahithophel, who instantly realized that this policy of inaction would be fatal to Absalom's hopes, forthwith destroyed himself.   The decisive battle between the loyalists and the rebels was fought shortly afterwards near Mahanaim.   Amasa, who had espoused the cause of Absalom, led the rebel army to an attack upon David's forces, which occupied a strong position in the forest of Ephraim.   The attack completely failed; twenty thousand of Absalom's men fell, and he himself fled from the field.   As he

Death of Absalom.

hung suspended by his hair from the branches of a terebinth, which caught him in his flight, he was pitilessly slain by Joab.   His body was thrown into a ditch and covered with a heap of stones.   Messengers ran to bring the news to David, but in his grief for the loss of his favourite son, the king forgot the debt which he owed to the devotion of his followers, and it was only the rough rebuke of Joab which recalled him to a sense of his duty.

A revulsion of feeling among the northern tribes was the

David's return:
2 Sam. xix. 11
xx. 23.

immediate consequence of Absalom's defeat and death, and measures were promptly taken for the restoration of the king.   His own tribe of Judah however still held proudly aloof, and the tribesmen were only won over by an appeal to their loyalty which the priests Zadok and Abiathar made on David's behalf, and by the distinction promised to the Judahite Amasa, of superseding Joab as commander-in-chief.   The return of the king to Jerusalem was a triumphal progress; on crossing the Jordan he was welcomed by a multitude of his fellow-tribesmen at Gilgal.   Shimei the Benjamite, who had assailed David with bitter taunts and insults during his hasty flight towards the

Jordan, came down with a thousand clansmen to meet him and implore his pardon. Among those who welcomed David at Jerusalem was Meribaal (Mephibosheth), the crippled grandson of Saul, whom David had treated with marked generosity ever since his accession to the throne, and who on the strength of a false charge of disloyalty brought against him by his servant Ziba, had been deprived of his whole estate. David accepted Meribaal's protestation and restored to him half of his possessions. The jealousy however of the northern Revolt of tribes was excited by the overtures which the Sheba: 2 Sam. king had made to conciliate the Judahites. The xx. signal for a fresh revolt was raised by a Benjamite, named Sheba. The fickle Israelites at once forsook their allegiance, and the tribe of Judah alone remained faithful. The delay of Amasa in collecting and organizing the forces of Judah obliged David to entrust Abishai and Joab with the task of suppressing the revolt. Joab pursued Sheba northwards, and finally besieged him in Abel of Beth-maacah, a town in the neighbourhood of Laish or Dan. The townsmen were induced to put the rebel to death and so extinguished the flames of revolt. An incident of this expedition was the treacherous Murder of murder of Amasa by Joab, who thus forcibly re- Amasa. covered his position as *generalissimo* of David's army.

One or two incidents in David's reign, the date of which is uncertain, may be mentioned by way of illustrating the king's character, and the temper and condition of the people over whom he ruled.

In some respects he followed the example of other Oriental monarchs. Thus he maintained a numerous harem[1], to the influences of which, as we have noticed, many of his later troubles may be traced. That there was an element of moral weakness in his character was proved by at least one terrible crime, and by the outbreak of disorders in his own family which he was powerless to control. Again, he instituted

[1] Cp. 2 Sam. v. 13.

a body-guard which formed the nucleus of a standing army, and included all the most valiant and distinguished warriors of the kingdom.   Benaiah the son of Jehoiada was their captain[1]. He also employed a body of Philistine mercenaries who are said to have followed him from Gath[2] and were apparently under the command of Ittai.   In the direct administration of justice David took a leading part, nor does there seem to have been truth in Absalom's implied complaint that the king neglected this branch of his duty[3].   Of his great officers of state various lists are given.   They include a commander-in-chief of the army; a recorder or chronicler who registered all important acts, decrees and events ; two priests (or high priests), one of whom probably officiated in the tabernacle at Gibeon, the other at Jerusalem before the ark; a scribe or 'secretary of state'; a captain of the royal body-guard, and other ministers who may have formed the king's council of state[4].   This system of organization seems to have become permanent, and on the whole worked satisfactorily.   Nevertheless the tribal jealousies of Israel and Judah were a constant source of danger to the monarchy and some customs of a ruder age were still tolerated, for instance the law of blood-revenge.   The king himself

Blood revenge: 2 Sam. xxi. — allowed it to be enforced in one notable instance.   The land, we are told, was distressed by a three years' famine, the cause of which was declared by the oracle to be the slaughter of the Gibeonites by Saul[5].   The only atonement for this bloodshed which the Gibeonites would accept was the execution of seven of Saul's

[1] A list of David's heroes or 'mighty men' (*Gibbôrim*) is given in 2 Sam. xxiii.

[2] 2 Sam. xv. 18.   These are probably identical with the *Krêthi* and *Plêthi* of 2 Sam. xx. 7 etc.

[3] 2 Sam. xv. 3.   See 2 Sam. viii. 15.

[4] See 2 Sam. viii. 16—18 with Kirkpatrick's notes.

[5] The occasion mentioned in 2 Sam. xxi. 2 is uncertain.   Possibly, as Prof. Sayce suggests, some Gibeonite temple-servants were involved in the wholesale massacre of the priests at Nob (1 Sam. xxii. 19).

sons. David spared Meribaal for Jonathan's sake, but the two sons of Rizpah, the daughter of Aiah, and the five sons of Merab[1] were put to death ; their bodies were left hanging *in the mountain before the Lord*, and were watched with pathetic devotion by Rizpah till the autumn rains began to fall. The remains were then interred, together with the bodies of Saul and Jonathan, which David had removed from Jabesh-Gilead.

It was probably in the later period of David's reign that he made an attempt to number the people. The unpopularity of the census was perhaps due to a widespread belief that the king contemplated a scheme of universal conscription. The severe visitation which followed was regarded as a manifest proof of Jehovah's displeasure. For three days a pestilence devastated the whole country. It was about to attack Jerusalem when the hand of the destroying angel was arrested. At the threshing-floor of Araunah the Jebusite, on the summit of Mount Moriah, David beheld the angel standing with hand outstretched to smite the city. The king at once marked the sanctity of the spot by the erection of an altar and the offering of sacrifice. He purchased the place from its owner, and it became the site afterwards chosen for the Temple.

> Attempt to number the people : 2 Sam. xxiv.

The closing years of David's life were disturbed by troubles connected with the succession to the throne. The faculties of the king, who had now reached his seventieth year, gradually failed and he became little more than a helpless puppet in the hands of his ministers and of his wife Bathsheba. David's eldest surviving son was Adonijah the son of Haggith, who was generally regarded as David's heir[2]. But the ambition of Bathsheba designed the succession for her son Solomon, whose claims were supported by Nathan and other influential persons. As his father's end now seemed to be close at hand Adonijah

> David's successor : 1 Kings i.

[1] Reading *Merab* for *Michal* in 2 Sam. xxi. 8. Cp. 1 Sam. xviii. 19.
[2] 1 Kings ii. 15.

resolved to assert his rights without delay; he invited his supporters, among whom were Joab and Abiathar, to a sacrificial feast at En-rogel, a sacred spot near Jerusalem, and actually allowed them to salute him as king. Acting on the prophet Nathan's urgent advice, Bathsheba at once approached David and begged him to confirm his promise of the succession to Solomon. David accordingly ordered Nathan, Zadok, and Benaiah, the captain of the royal body-guard, to proclaim Solomon king at Gihon, a sacred spot in the valley of the Kidron; he was anointed forthwith and greeted by the acclamations of the populace. The sounds of jubilation reached the ears of Adonijah. His adherents dispersed in consternation while he himself fled for refuge to the sanctuary. His life however was spared on his doing obeisance to the new monarch.

The closing scenes of David's life are not wholly in accord with the nobler side of his character. He secretly advised Solomon to take measures for ridding himself of his most dangerous antagonists, Joab and Shimei; on the other hand he commended the aged Barzillai of Gilead to his kindness. Tradition also ascribes to David a last prophetic utterance concerning the future fulfilment of the *everlasting covenant* which Jehovah had made with his house[1]. At length he passed away *in a good old age* after a reign of about forty years. In a later age the memory of David's sins and weaknesses faded away in the light of the high hopes which rested on his house. By the force of his personal ascendancy he had welded together the different tribes of Israel into a vigorous and united nation, which he had inspired with a strong consciousness both of its military strength and of its peculiar vocation. It can scarcely be a matter of wonder that the figure of the generous, impulsive and heroic warrior-king was in process of time idealized and invested with the glories of a saint. There is no

---

[1] 2 Sam. xxiii. 1—7.

reason to deny his claim to be in some sense *the sweet psalmist of Israel*[1], the founder of the art of sacred song and an organizer of worship; moreover his religious faith, however defective from a Christian standpoint, was deeply-rooted and sincere. In dark days of disaster and perplexity the thoughts of patriotic Israelites often reverted to the reign of David, and anticipated an era when the hopes and longings which it had kindled in men's hearts should be gloriously fulfilled. *Behold, the days come, saith the Lord, that I will raise unto David a righteous Branch, and he shall reign as king and deal wisely, and shall execute judgment and justice in the land. In his days Judah shall be saved, and Israel shall dwell safely: and this is his name whereby he shall be called, The Lord is our righteousness*[2].

---

[1] 2 Sam. xxiii. 1. Am. vi. 5 suggests that the music for which David was famed was chiefly of a secular kind, but the passage is quite consistent with the tradition that he was "the father and great master" of Israel's sacred music. See Robertson Smith, *OTJC.*, p. 223 foll.

[2] Jerem. xxiii. 5, 6.

CHAPTER VII.

SOLOMON AND THE DIVISION OF THE KINGDOM.

THE exact limits of the kingdom which David bequeathed
to his successor cannot now be determined; but
there is little reason for doubting that the traditional account of its dimensions is well-founded.
It is said to have extended from the borders of Egypt to the
river Euphrates, its northern boundary being Kadesh on the
Orontes—a city which during the reigns of David and Solomon
seems to have belonged to the Hittites. The condition of the
surrounding nations was not such as to hinder the growth
and expansion of an Israelitish kingdom. Owing to certain
elements of internal weakness the Assyrian empire was not at
this time able to adopt an aggressive policy. The Syrians
(Aramaeans) indeed were beginning to press westward, but the
petty kingdom of Zobah was, as we have seen, practically overthrown by the conquests of David, and even Damascus itself
had been made tributary. With the Phoenician king both
David and Solomon were on terms of cordial friendship[1].

Solomon, however, was not slow to recognize the dangers
which rendered his widely extended dominion
unstable, and as time went on he turned his
attention to the task of defending his possessions in Palestine itself by a chain of strong

The reign of
Solomon ? 970
—930.

Solomon's
internal ad-
ministration:
1 Kings iv.

---

[1] The ally of David was probably Abibal, the father of Hiram; Hiram
himself was the friend of Solomon.

fortresses (1 Kings ix. 15 foll.). He also fortified Jerusalem, increased the numbers of his army, and raised for the first time a large force of cavalry. Nevertheless the dissolution of the Israelitish empire began even before Solomon's death; the Syrian kingdom of Damascus recovered its strength; Edom regained its independence, and in all probability even Moab and Ammon ceased to be tributary. Solomon's gifts indeed lay in the direction of administration rather than of warfare. He needed large resources to maintain his own magnificent state, and to enable him to carry out his schemes for making Jerusalem the worthy metropolis of his empire. The revenue which Solomon derived from commerce was of course considerable. He collected tolls from the caravans which were constantly traversing his territory; he made a large profit by carrying on a traffic in horses, which he procured from Egypt and sold again to the kings of the Hittites and other peoples of western Asia. He even seems to have borrowed heavily from the neighbouring kingdom of Tyre, and the repayment of the loan ultimately involved the cession to Hiram of a district in Galilee which included twenty cities (1 Kings ix. 11 foll.). But naturally he relied chiefly on the supplies raised by taxation of his own subjects. Accordingly Palestine was divided, without regard to any distinction between Canaanites and Israelites, into twelve fiscal districts, each controlled by an overseer who was charged with the duty of providing during one month of the year for the expenses of the royal household. Apparently the Judahites were exempted from the burden of taxation, doubtless with the object of attaching the tribe more closely to the Davidic dynasty. The other tribes naturally resented a system which pressed so heavily on themselves and which practically ministered to the strength and importance of Judah and Jerusalem alone. The old tribal jealousies were fanned into flame by discontent with the king's oppressive *régime*, for Solomon in spite of his wisdom and skill in the art of government soon betrayed the characteristic failings of an oriental despot. "He was more interested in the privileges of the throne and its comforts than in its lofty duties and mission....His chief interest was in costly buildings, foreign wives, and gorgeous display[1]."

Solomon's first act was to strengthen his position by putting Adonijah, Joab and Shimei to death, a step for which various pretexts were speedily found. He also banished to the city of Anathoth the high-priest Abiathar, who was superseded in his office by Zadok. The priesthood thus passed out of the line of Eli's direct descendants, and they were never reinstated. Solomon next allied himself, by a marriage with Pharaoh's daughter, to the reigning house of Egypt, while he cemented his friendship with Hiram of Tyre by concluding a formal alliance[2]. Thus Israel entered into relationship with the heathen kingdoms which lay beyond its borders. This closer intercourse led to important results : on the one hand a great development of commerce and an inevitable interchange of customs and ideas ; on the other the enlargement of Israel's spiritual horizon. Israelitish caravans traversed the eastern deserts, and followed the trade-route which led southwards into Egypt; the merchant-ships of Solomon carried the wares of Palestine from Elath and Ezion-Geber on the gulf of Akabah to the ports of Arabia, India, and possibly even of Spain[3]. Indeed the contrast between the conditions of life

1 Kings ii. 12 foll.

Alliance with Hiram, etc. 1 Kings v. ix. 26 foll., x.

---

[1] Kittel, *History of the Hebrews* [Eng. tr.], vol. ii., p. 186.

[2] There was no real cause of antagonism between Phoenicia and Israel. The Hebrews never entertained the idea of assailing the powerfully fortified cities of the Phoenician coast; the Phoenicians on the other hand had no interest in extending their territory eastwards into Syria. So long as their caravans could travel securely and they could find a profitable market for their wares among the cities of the interior they were content. In exchange they provided an open market for the agricultural produce and cattle of the Israelites.

[3] The phrase 'navy of Tarshish' (1 Kings x. 22) does not necessarily imply that the ships visited Tarshish (Tartessus in Spain). Like our 'East

during the reign of Solomon and those of the age of Saul is almost startling. Under Saul the Hebrews were for the most part a nation of peasants, to whom the comforts and conveniences of highly civilized life were unknown. The first king himself, when not engaged in warfare, lived the simple life of an ordinary yeoman ; when Jesse sends David to the court, he offers for Saul's acceptance a sample of the produce of his farm, loaves of bread, a bottle of wine and a kid (1 Sam. xvi. 20). Yet only seventy-five years elapsed before the royal state of Solomon and the prosperity of his kingdom were the wonder of the East. The magnificent presents of the Queen of Sheba, the wealth of gold, spices and precious stones which she lays at the feet of the Hebrew monarch, significantly mark the change which had resulted from the enormous development of Israel's commerce with surrounding nations, and the consequent growth of luxury. A comparison of the England of Elizabeth with the England of Henry II. supplies an example of a somewhat similar social change, but in Israel the transition was more rapid, and more evidently due to the policy and influence of the new monarchy. Nor do we find in modern history the same kind of social reaction which constantly tended to appear in Israel (Nazaritism, etc.)—reaction in favour of the simplicity of nomadic life, a distaste for life in cities and even for systematic culture of the soil[1]. Among the Israelites the development of wealth was too rapid to be healthy ; and consequently the age of Solomon was a period not only of social advance, but of religious and moral declension.

At the same time it is probable that this period of Israel's national expansion suggested certain religious ideas, which Hebrew prophecy afterwards developed : the conception of a universal empire, Israel being as it were a visible type of the kingdom of God, holding out hands to the wealthy and powerful

Indiaman,' *a ship of Tarshish* denoted simply a ship intended for long voyages.

[1] The Rechabites are an instance in point.

kingdoms of the world; and the idea of a universal religion, embracing all that was sound and noble in the 'wisdom' of heathendom and proclaiming to all nations the knowledge of one true God, the God of Israel.

The narrative of the First Book of Kings represents Solomon

Solomon's wisdom:
1 Kings iii.
iv. 29 foll.

as a monarch specially endowed with 'wisdom' and administrative ability. A famous judicial decision pronounced by him at the beginning of his reign convinced his subjects that *the wisdom of God was with him to do judgment* (1 Kings iii. 28). Posterity credited him with a superhuman knowledge of nature, and reverenced him as the originator of that 'proverbial philosophy' of which the Wisdom literature (*Khokmah*) of the Hebrews is the noblest specimen[1]. *He spake*, we read, *three thousand proverbs, and his songs were a thousand and five* (1 Kings iv. 32). His fame as a sage was spread abroad throughout the east: the Queen of Sheba or Saba in distant Arabia paid him a visit *to prove him with hard questions* (1 Kings x. 1). Indeed, the name of Solomon became a kind of symbol of moral and spiritual wisdom, just as the name of David became connected with the art of sacred music and poetry. Thus although the book of Proverbs is a sacred anthology to which different epochs in Hebrew literature contributed, Jewish tradition ascribed it to Solomon as the earliest and most conspicuous of Israel's sages, and indeed in some parts it reflects the comparatively simple and stable conditions of a peaceful and prosperous age.

But Solomon's wealth and wisdom did not constitute in

Building of the Temple,
1 Kings vi. vii.

the eyes of devout and patriotic Israelites his principal title to honour. His fame rested chiefly on the fact that he was the builder of the

---

[1] The 'Wisdom' or 'sapiential literature' of the Hebrews is represented in the Jewish Canon by the Books of Proverbs, Job, and Ecclesiastes. Other similar books, not included in the Canon, are 'The Wisdom of Solomon,' and 'The Wisdom of Jesus the Son of Sirach' (Ecclesiasticus).

Temple at Jerusalem, that visible monument and token of the national and religious unity of the tribes. He did not directly aim, as did some kings of a later period, at the abolition of the various local sanctuaries, which had become hallowed by long-established use. But owing to the presence of the ark, Jerusalem was already regarded as a holy city, and the erection of a splendid permanent shrine was a task for which David had made provision, and which he had expressly bequeathed to his successor. Like the other magnificent designs of Solomon, the building of the Temple could only be carried on by means of forced labour on a large scale; while his alliance with Hiram enabled him to procure the most necessary materials, cedar wood and hewn stone from the forests and quarries of Lebanon, together with skilled craftsmen to superintend and execute the work.

The site selected was in all probability that which is now occupied by the 'Dome of the Rock.' An ample space was levelled by means of vast substruc- *The Temple.* tions, portions of which remain standing to this day. The Temple itself was constructed of huge blocks of stone, ready hewn and squared in the quarry. In form, design and ornamentation it naturally bore distinct traces of Phoenician workmanship[1]. Like the Tabernacle, the Sanctuary consisted of two chambers: the Holy Place (40 cubits long by 20 broad), and the Holy of Holies (*Debir*), which formed a perfect cube of 20 cubits, and which was left in perfect darkness as being the dwelling-place of Jehovah Himself (1 Kings viii. 12). The approach to the Holy Place, which lay towards the east, consisted of a porch with two bronze pillars at the entrance, called respectively *Jachin* and *Boaz*[2]. Abutting upon the outer walls

[1] Sayce *EHH*, p. 467, says, "The great temple of Melkarth which Hiram had just completed at Tyre probably served as the model for the temple at Jerusalem."

[2] *i.e. He shall establish* and *In it is strength* (2 Chron. iii. 17, R.V. marg.).

of the Temple were built chambers, rising in three stories, for
the use of the priests and other officials. The place of worship
assigned to the people was the large outer court, containing a
brazen 'sea' or laver intended for the ceremonial ablutions of
the priests, and doubtless also (though it is not expressly mentioned) the great brazen altar of burnt-offering. Access to the
Holy Place was restricted to the priesthood. Within the *Debîr*
was deposited the ark, which was overshadowed by the outstretched wings of two golden cherubim.

  The Temple of Solomon was completed in seven years.
In due course the splendid shrine was dedicated
1 Kings vii. by the king himself with great solemnity, and
the ark was brought by the priests *unto its place.* The Temple
however was in reality not so much a national sanctuary as an
appanage of royalty. It formed part of a series of magnificent
buildings which crowned the ridge east of the city: the 'House
of the forest of Lebanon,' which derived its name from its
massive pillars of cedar,—an edifice originally intended for an
armoury, but suitable also for the holding of assemblies and
other functions of state ; the royal palace of Solomon himself,
which it took thirteen years to complete ; the 'House for
Pharaoh's daughter ;' and the fortress (Millo) protecting the
whole range of buildings. The precise situation of these cannot now be ascertained: but it is clear that the king's palace,
with the *harem* and the 'House of the forest of Lebanon,'
lay to the south of the Temple area. The position of the
fortress (Millo) is however uncertain[1].

  Unhappily the luxury and splendour of Solomon's court
was only kept up at a cost which imperilled the
Decline of integrity both of his kingdom and of the religion
Solomon's which he was pledged to defend. He maintained
power:
1 Kings xi. an immense *harem* of foreign wives, an institution
which violated the spirit if not the letter of the Mosaic Law,
and polygamy led to the toleration of different types of heathen

---

[1] See Hastings' *DB*, s. voc. 'Jerusalem.' Cp. Sayce *EHH*, p. 466.

worship. Solomon permitted the erection on the Mount of Olives of shrines in honour of Ashtoreth the goddess of the Zidonians, of Milcom the deity of the Ammonites, of Chemosh *the abomination of Moab ; and so did he for all his strange wives, which burnt incense and sacrificed unto their gods.* Whether Solomon's encouragement of alien cults was prompted by cosmopolitan tastes and motives of policy, or whether it was the result of a real religious indifference, it marked in any case a disastrous turning-point in Israel's religious history. It familiarized the people with the spectacle of idolatrous rites ; it introduced a condition of things which, until the age of Josiah, it was found impossible or impolitic to abolish. In fact the evil consequences of Solomon's weakness far outweighed the effects of the zeal which he displayed as founder of the Temple. Moreover the oppressive system of forced labour and burdensome taxation by which the king gratified his taste for luxury and for splendid architecture; his heartless disregard for the welfare and even the liberty of his subjects ; his despotic treatment of the northern tribes, coupled with his manifest partiality for his own kinsmen of Judah—all these things sowed broadcast the seeds of discontent and prepared the way for a disruption of the kingdom. Towards the end of Solomon's reign a young Ephraimite, Jeroboam the son of Nebat, whom the king had appointed overseer of the workmen employed in the fortification of Jerusalem, planned a revolt. In this enterprise he was probably acting as the representative of his tribe, and he was further encouraged by the approval of the prophet Ahijah of Shiloh, the ancient sanctuary of Ephraim which had been finally superseded by the Temple at Jerusalem. For the moment the plot failed, and Jeroboam was compelled to take refuge at the court of Shishak, king of Egypt, the founder of a new dynasty, who now filled the throne lately occupied by the father-in-law of Solomon.

Defects of Solomon's régime.

The revolt of Jeroboam: 1 Kings xi. 26.

Meanwhile Hadad, a scion of the royal house of Edom, who had returned from a long exile in Egypt after David's death, was doing his utmost to injure the interests and weaken the power of Solomon ; and in the north a new kingdom had been established at Damascus by Rezon of Zobah, in whose person the long-standing enmity between Syria and Israel was perpetuated. Accordingly, though Solomon's empire was not actually impaired during his own lifetime, the symptoms of decline and disruption already began to appear. After his death, the spirit of discontent and bitterness which his foreign tastes and his oppressive *régime* had excited, burst into flame. As the result of a popular assembly held at Shechem a solemn appeal was made by the northern tribes to Rehoboam, Solomon's son and successor, beseeching him to lighten the burdens which pressed on them so unfairly. After due deliberation the ill-advised monarch *answered the people roughly*, and precipitated the disaster which a soft answer might have averted. The ten tribes openly revolted, and having sent for Jeroboam, their champion and spokesman, elected him as their king. Two tribes only, Judah and Benjamin[1], remained faithful in their allegiance to the house of David. The union of the tribes under one sceptre was an object which David had by means of tact and patience successfully achieved : but the hopes to which his reign had given birth were shattered for ever by the short-sighted policy of his son and grandson. The consequences of the disruption affected the two kingdoms differently. On the one hand, the burden of prolonged defensive warfare against the growing power of Syria was destined to fall almost exclusively upon the northern tribes (Israel). On the other, the

Rehoboam king (c. 930): 1 Kings xii.

The disruption of the kingdom.

----

[1] Probably, however, a considerable number of the Benjamites attached themselves to the northern kingdom. Both Jericho and Gilgal seem to have been included within its border. Cp. 1 Kings xvi. 34; 2 Kings ii. 1 foll.

comparative tranquillity enjoyed by the southern kingdom (Judah) was conducive both to the stability of the monarchy and to the maintenance of a type of religious life and worship purer on the whole than that which prevailed in the rival kingdom.

Rehoboam made one attempt to win back the ten tribes to their allegiance, the only result of which was that the king's emissary Adoram *who was over the levy* lost his life. *All Israel stoned him with stones that he died* (1 Kings xii. 18). Rehoboam was preparing to recover the lost territory by force of arms, but he was forbidden to make the attempt by the prophet Shemaiah. Nevertheless, in spite of this admonition, hostilities seem to have been carried on between the two kingdoms for some time (1 Kings xiv. 30). But Rehoboam was crippled by the lack of resources. Judah was invaded shortly after Jeroboam's revolt by the forces of Shishak, king of Egypt, who captured some of the recently fortified cities and carried off the bulk of the treasure which Solomon had accumulated in the capital[1]. The war with the northern tribes was continued by Rehoboam's successors, Abijam and Asa. The latter king had raised the army of Judah to a high state of efficiency, and early in his reign is said by the Chronicler to have won a decisive victory over Zerah, the king of Ethiopia (2 Chron. xiv. 9 foll.) ; but he was so hardly pressed by Baasha of Israel, who established at Ramah (six miles north of Jerusalem) a close blockade of Asa's northern border, that he applied to Benhadad I. king of Syria for aid, using the treasures of the Temple and the palace as means to purchase his alliance. This stroke of policy

> Invasion of Judah by Shishak: 1 Kings xiv. 25 foll.

---

[1] Shishak's expedition (according to the evidence of an inscription discovered at Karnak) was directed against *both* kingdoms. Some cities of Northern Israel, *e.g.* Mahanaim, Bethhoron, and Megiddo, were actually conquered and plundered.

[2] Cp. the mention (1 Kings xv. 23) of *the acts of Asa and all his might,* i.e. *all his warlike deeds.*

was successful for its immediate purpose. Baasha was compelled to abandon the stronghold of Ramah which he was engaged in fortifying when the rupture with Syria took place. But Asa's request for the intervention of a foreign power was a dangerous precedent, and the price which he paid for the Syrian alliance was ruinous. According to the Chronicler (2 Chr. xvi. 7) the king was sternly reproved for his faithless policy by the prophet Hanani, in spite of the zeal and determination which he had displayed in the religious reformation of Judah.

It was probably the severe pressure on Israel of the war with Syria that afterwards compelled the two kingdoms to come to terms and to combine their forces. Jehoshaphat, the successor of Asa, concluded an alliance with Israel, which was sealed by the marriage of his son Jehoram to Athaliah, the daughter of Ahab. For rather more than a century the mutual relations of the two kingdoms continued to be peaceful.

Alliance between the two kingdoms: 1 Kings xxii. 44; 2 Chron. xviii. 1.

We must now briefly trace the history of the northern kingdom from the disruption to the death of Ahab (circ. 930—853).

Jeroboam was virtually the leader of a democratic movement, inspired partly by jealousy of the predominance of Judah among the tribes, partly by unwillingness to accept the principle of a non-elective and hereditary monarchy. He seems also to have been the champion of that popular religious system which was connected with the worship of the local sanctuaries, and which seemed to be threatened by the inauguration of the Temple at Jerusalem. Jeroboam accordingly fixed on two of the traditional holy places of northern Israel, Dan and Beth-el, as the chief centres of tribal worship. At these places there already existed altars and other sacred objects. Jeroboam now set up at each of them a metal image

The reign and policy of Jeroboam: 1 Kings xii. 25 —xiv. 21.

of Jehovah, in the form of a bull; he instituted a new (non-levitical) priesthood, and festivals that might serve as a counter-attraction to the religious feasts periodically celebrated at Jerusalem. The real offence of this schismatic worship in the eyes of the prophets lay in its reactionary character. It gave permanence and prestige to a popular system, which the higher and more elaborate *cultus* established by Solomon at Jerusalem would ultimately have superseded. The establishment of the bull-worship was specially disastrous; it involved a practical abandonment of the Mosaic ideal; the simple and imageless service of Jehovah was debased to the level of a heathen ceremony. We can scarcely be surprised therefore that the prophets and the compilers of the historical books uniformly regard Jeroboam with horror and aversion as the man *who made Israel to sin.* Indeed on the occasion when the altar at Bethel was inaugurated by Jeroboam himself, *a man of God out of Judah* openly denounced the sacrilegious service. The king's hand outstretched to seize the prophet was suddenly withered: *the altar also was rent and the ashes poured out from the altar* (1 Kings xiii. 5). At a later time the consequences of Jeroboam's policy were predicted by the aged prophet Ahijah. He announced to Jeroboam's queen that her son, who lay sick at the royal palace of Tirzah, should die; that Jeroboam's house should be swept away, and that the people whom he had seduced into idolatry should be uprooted from their *good land* and scattered *beyond the river.* It is certain that Jeroboam's personal career was inglorious; he founded no lasting dynasty, and could lay claim to no distinguished success in war. Nor did he derive any advantage from the invasion of the rival kingdom by Shishak, his former protector. From the first, the curse of instability rested upon a throne which had been founded in rebellion. The history of the northern kingdom was marked by a series of revolutions, while in Judah the regular succession of Davidic kings was uninterrupted till the Captivity.

Nadab, the son of Jeroboam, was murdered after a reign
of two years by Baasha, while he was engaged in
besieging the Philistine town of Gibbethon.
Baasha, a man of mean origin[1], was probably a
captain in the Israelitish army, and owed his
elevation to a military revolution. His energetic prosecution
of the war with Judah has been already mentioned. The invasion, however, of the Israelitish territory by Benhadad of Syria
forced Baasha to abandon his outpost at Ramah, and brought
his offensive operations against the southern kingdom to an
abrupt end. His maintenance of the bull-worship at Dan and
Bethel was denounced by the prophet Jehu, son of Hanani,
and a fate similar to that incurred by Jeroboam's house was
predicted for Baasha and his descendants. His son Elah, a
worthless and dissolute prince, fell a victim to conspiracy after
a reign of two years. Zimri, one of his officers,
murdered the king and seized the palace at
Tirzah; but he had neglected to secure the
support of the army, which was still encamped before Gibbethon. Accordingly Omri, the commander of the Israelitish
forces, was saluted as king by the soldiers, and without an
hour's delay marched upon Tirzah. The efforts of Zimri to
hold the town were futile; the usurper perished amid the
flames of his palace after a reign of only seven days. Another
pretender to the throne, Tibni the son of Ginath, was speedily
crushed and Omri found himself in secure possession of the
throne.

Nadab, Baasha, and Elah: 1 Kings xv. 25—xvi. 14.

Zimri and Omri: 1 Kings xvi. 8—28.

The new king fixed his capital not at Shechem, but at
Samaria, which lay nearer to the coast. The
situation of the city built by Omri had great
military and political advantages. Its very name
'watch-tower' is significant. It was within sight and easy reach
of the sea—an important consideration for a dynasty which

The reign of Omri, c. 890.

---

[1] Cp. 1 Kings xvi. 2.

depended to a great extent on the support of Phoenicia[1]. The new city stood on an eminence overlooking a broad and fertile valley, and though surrounded by hills of greater height, it was capable of being strongly fortified, and rendered under the conditions of ancient warfare almost impregnable. On the other hand, the position of Samaria was less central than that of Shechem; the latter place moreover derived prestige from its religious associations which reached back to patriarchal times[2].

The Books of Kings contain only a short notice of Omri's career. He was evidently a capable and energetic warrior, and his military successes in the land of Moab are recorded on the so-called 'Moabite stone' erected at Dibon by Mesha king of Moab. This monument shows that for about forty years the Moabites were tributary to Israel[3]. But there are two circumstances which make Omri's reign specially noteworthy. In the first place, he was the founder of a dynasty—the first that can be properly so called in the history of the northern kingdom—which flourished for nearly half a century. Secondly, Omri's name is mentioned in the Assyrian inscriptions, "the land Omri" or "the land of the house of Omri" being in fact the ordinary terms employed by the Assyrians to denote Israel. The first appearance of Assyria within the limits of Israel's horizon constitutes a momentous epoch in her history. For about two centuries (*circ.* 1050— 858) the great empire, which Tiglath-Pileser I. had extended westward to the Euphrates, had suffered from internal weakness sufficient to hinder its further expansion. It was during this period that the Syrian monarchy became powerful, and that favourable circumstances enabled the earliest kings of Israel, David and Solomon, to extend their sway over a region

Movements of Assyria.

---

[1] Cp. G. A. Smith, *HGHL*, p. 346 foll.

[2] Gen. xii. 6, xxxiii. 18.

[3] Sayce, *Fresh light from the ancient monuments*, ch. iv. Cp. *The higher criticism and the monuments*, pp. 366 foll.

extending from the Euphrates to the borders of Egypt. Under Assur-nazir-pal III. (884—860) and his successor Shalmaneser II. (860—825), Assyria entered on a new career of conquest in a westward direction. The former of these two monarchs even advanced to the coasts of the Mediterranean, and exacted tribute from Tyre, Sidon, and other cities of Phoenicia and Syria. Apparently little or no resistance was offered to the advance of Assur-nazir-pal, and it is possible, though not certain, that Omri was among the kings who paid tribute to the Assyrian invader. As yet however Israel was too insignificant a power to be really formidable to such an empire as that of Assyria. The only serious obstacle to its expansion was presented by the newly-organised kingdom of Syria.

The mention of Syria brings us back to the history of Israel. Since the seizure of Damascus by Rezon[1], the growing strength of Syria was a source of constant danger and annoyance to the kings of Israel. Omri and Ahab succeeded in keeping the Syrians in check, mainly by forming a close alliance first with Phoenicia (1 Kings xvi. 31) and afterwards with Judah (1 Kings xxii. 2 foll.). Ahab, who succeeded his

Ahab and the Syrian war: 1 Kings xx. father about 875 B.C., inherited a considerable measure of his military skill, but from the fragmentary narrative of 1 Kings it appears that his conduct of the war with Syria was for some time unsuccessful. It is evident that the Israelites were hard pressed, and even Samaria was closely besieged by Benhadad II. The desperate position of the city, however, threw the Syrians off their guard, and nerved Ahab for a fresh effort. While Benhadad was giving himself up to voluptuous ease in his camp, Ahab at the head of seven thousand men suddenly attacked the Syrians and completely discomfited them. In the following year Benhadad renewed the campaign. He attributed his recent defeat to the difficult nature of the hill-country which surrounded Samaria. The god of Israel, his

[1] 1 Kings xi. 23—25.

officers told him, was *a god of the hills; but let us,* they said, *fight against them in the plain and surely we shall be stronger than they.* The Syrian king accordingly pitched his camp in the open valley near Aphek. After an interval of seven days a battle took place, and again the Syrians were routed with heavy loss. After this victory, however, for some reason unknown to us, Ahab completely changed his policy. He received Benhadad and his followers, who abjectly sued for their lives, with marked friendliness, and he was even induced to conclude a treaty with Syria. Benhadad promised to restore to Israel the cities which had been captured by his father, and conceded certain 'streets' in Damascus as a quarter for Israelitish residents[1] (1 Kings xx. 34). Whatever may have been Ahab's motives, his action gave great offence to the prophets, one of whom expressed by a symbolic action the divine displeasure which the king had incurred (1 Kings xx. 35—43). It is probable however that both Ahab and Benhadad recognized at length the necessity of bringing to a conclusion hostilities which weakened their power of joint resistance to Assyria. In the sixth year of his reign (854) Shalmaneser II. advanced into Syria and captured several cities. At a place called Karkar, between Hamath and Aleppo, he found himself opposed by the combined forces of Hamath, Damascus, and other allied states. An Israelitish contingent seems to have been sent by Ahab, who, according to the Assyrian inscription which records Shalmaneser's success, contributed a force of 2000 chariots and 10,000 men[2]. The confederacy however was utterly overthrown; more than 20,000 men perished, and the temporary alliance between Israel and Syria came abruptly to an end[3]. Indeed, towards the close of Ahab's reign, hostilities

The battle of Karkar: 854 B.C.

---

[1] The Syrians already enjoyed a similar privilege in Samaria.

[2] See Driver in *Authority and Archaeology*, etc. p. 93; cp. Sayce, *Fresh light from the ancient monuments*, ch. vi.

[3] Probably the Assyrian losses were very heavy, for the victory was

between the two kingdoms were renewed, and Ahab made an attempt to recover Ramoth-Gilead which cost him his life.

As we have seen, Ahab was compelled by the pressure of the Syrian wars in the early part of his reign to strengthen the alliance with Phoenicia, which had been a point of policy with Solomon and afterwards with Omri. He accordingly married Jezebel, daughter of Eth-baal king of Tyre and priest of Astarte. This union brought with it certain commercial advantages, but it could not fail to exercise a disastrous influence on the religion of the northern kingdom. The worship of the Tyrian Baal was formally established by Ahab in Samaria: and beside the temple of Baal was erected an *ashêrah*[1]. We have already observed that this latter symbol, as well as the name *Ba'al* ('lord' or 'owner'), by which Jehovah was habitually addressed, were already familiar to the Israelites, nor perhaps did the average worshipper recognize any clear distinction between the *cultus* offered to Jehovah at the 'high places' and the rites practised by the heathen Canaanites. But the higher conscience of the people was now at length roused by the fiery preaching of the great prophet Elijah, whose abrupt and mysterious appearance as a messenger of divine judgment was occasioned by the religious policy of Ahab and Jezebel. Ahab's imperious and fanatical consort speedily gained a complete ascendancy over him. Under her influence he not only introduced into his realm a multitude of heathen *Nebiim*[2], but even sanctioned a rigorous persecution of those who remained faithful to Jehovah. Thereupon the stern ascetic Elijah suddenly emerged from the solitudes of Gilead as the 'personified conscience' of the nation. After

Ahab's re-ligious policy: 1 Kings xvi. 29 foll.

Elijah: 1 Kings xvii.— xix.

apparently followed by the retreat of the invading army, and five years elapsed before the attack was renewed.

[1] Cp. Judg. vi. 25 for a similar combination.

[2] 1 Kings xviii. 19.

publicly predicting that Jehovah would chastise the apostasy of Israel by a prolonged drought, he vanished as suddenly as he had appeared. An interval of three years elapsed, during which Ahab made fruitless efforts to lay hands on the prophet, and the land was utterly wasted with famine. At length Elijah resolved to confront the king once more. When they met, Ahab bitterly upbraided the prophet as the *troubler of Israel. I have not troubled Israel*, was Elijah's reply, *but thou and thy father's house, in that ye have forsaken the commandments of the Lord and thou hast followed the Baalim* (1 Kings xviii. 18). The silence with which Ahab received this rebuke implies that Elijah had brought home to him the true significance of his recent religious policy[1]. He did not reject Elijah's proposal that the contest between Jehovah and Baal should be brought to a decisive issue.

He summoned to Mount Carmel all the heathen prophets, and a great concourse of the common people, in whose presence the ordeal took place. *How long*, cried Elijah to the assembled multitude, *halt ye between two opinions? if Jehovah be God follow him: but if Baal, then follow him.* He then bade the heathen prophets call on the name of their god; he himself would *call on the name of Jehovah*, and the god that should answer by fire, *let him be God.* An altar was reared by the prophets, but their wild cries, passionate gestures and self-mutilations availed nothing. From dawn till evening they invoked the name of Baal: *but there was no voice nor any that answered.* Then came Elijah's turn. He called the people near to him, and having repaired the ruined altar of Jehovah, ordered the wood and the offering upon it to be drenched with water. Then in answer to his earnest prayer, *the fire of Jehovah* fell from heaven and *consumed the burnt offering and the wood and the stones and*

The ordeal on Carmel: 1 Kings xviii.

---

[1] That Ahab did not intend personally to abandon the national religion is proved by the names which he gave to his sons, Ahaziah ('Jehovah holds'), and Jehoram ('Jehovah is high ').

the dust and licked up the water that was in the trench. The momentous issue was decided. In an access of zealous fury the people fell upon the false prophets at Elijah's bidding, and slaughtered them mercilessly at the brook Kishon. Immediately afterwards the long-delayed rain began to fall, and Ahab, who had apparently been present at the scene on Carmel, hastened back, preceded by Elijah, to Jezreel, and informed the queen of all that had passed.

The angry threats of Jezebel compelled Elijah to flee

Elijah at Horeb: 1 Kings xix.

without delay. Broken-spirited and despondent he traversed the southern wilderness and reached the sanctuary of Mount Horeb. There in profound solitude he poured out his complaint to Jehovah, and was strengthened by a revelation which assured him of the divine presence and support. At the same time he was charged to return by way of Syria, and to appoint both his own successor, Elisha, and two instruments of the vengeance which was shortly to descend on Ahab and his kingdom, namely Hazael and Jehu. An occasion for announcing to Ahab his

The murder of Naboth: 1 Kings xxi.

impending doom quickly presented itself. The popular sense of justice was no doubt violently outraged by the judicial murder of Naboth—a high-handed crime which Jezebel deliberately planned in order to gratify Ahab's whim for improving his property at Jezreel. While walking in his ill-gotten estate, Ahab was confronted by Elijah, who in denouncing the king's conduct acted as the champion of the people's liberties and of social order. Ahab was for the moment conscience-stricken, and in view of the sincerity of his remorse, the threatened ruin of his house was delayed.

It seems to have been shortly after this occurrence that the

The war with Syria renewed: 1 Kings xxii.

war between Syria and Israel broke out afresh. Ahab· determined to recover the important border-fortress of Ramoth-Gilead, and invited Jehoshaphat king of Judah, who was now his ally and connected with his house by marriage, to cooperate with him. Jehoshaphat hesitated to comply without prophetic sanction. Among the crowd of obscure *Nebiim* who loudly applauded Ahab's cherished design, was found one, Micaiah by name, who had the courage to prophesy disaster. His outspokenness cost him his liberty. He was thrown into prison, and Ahab, disregarding his warning, set forth on his expedition. In the battle that ensued, Ahab disguised himself, probably because he was aware how highly Benhadad rated the importance of his capture or death, but a chance arrow pierced his armour. The king fell back in his chariot mortally wounded, and though by a superhuman effort he held himself erect in his chariot till evening in order not to discourage his troops, his strength gradually failed and he died before reaching Samaria. At the tidings of the king's death a panic seized the army, which quickly dispersed. Thus the attempt to recover Ramoth-Gilead failed, nor was this the only reverse which the northern kingdom sustained.

Death of Ahab: c. 853.

In the second book of Kings (i. 1) it is stated that Moab *rebelled against Israel after the death of Ahab*. But from the Moabite stone discovered at Dhibân (the ancient Dibon) in 1868, it appears that the revolt of Mesha king of Moab had already taken place some years before Ahab's death[1]. In the course of a long and obstinate struggle Mesha forced the Hebrews to evacuate the cities which they had occupied since the days of Omri; large numbers of the Israelitish inhabitants were put to death, and the towns themselves were rebuilt and fortified as a precaution against future attempts to recover them on the part of the kings of Israel. Ahab's feeble successor Ahaziah died after a reign of two years. The only incident recorded of him is the fact that, having been severely injured by a fall, he sent messengers to

Ahaziah.

---

[1] The revolt had probably taken place before the middle of Ahab's reign. See Driver in *Authority and Archaeology*, etc., pp. 88—92.

enquire of Baal-zebub, the god of Ekron, whether he should
recover—a proceeding which brought upon him
a scathing rebuke from Elijah. Jehoram, the
brother of Ahaziah, resolved to recover the allegiance of the Moabites, and called to his aid Jehoshaphat
the king of Judah. At first the expedition was successful.
Mesha was driven from the field and besieged in his capital,
and was presently reduced to such extremities that he sacrificed his son for a burnt-offering to Chemosh upon the wall.
Apparently the Moabites having thus assured themselves of
the aid of their national deity, made a supreme effort, and
forced the allied armies of Israel and Judah to raise the
siege. It is doubtful whether Moab ever again became tributary to the kings of Israel.

Jehoram:
2 Kings iii.

CHAPTER VIII.

THE PROPHETS AND THE KINGS OF ISRAEL
AND JUDAH.

A POLITICAL revolution, which was expressly sanctioned and actively supported by the prophets, was the means of extirpating Baal-worship from the northern kingdom. It will be useful at this point to enquire briefly into the precise nature and extent of the influence exercised by the prophets.

The *Nebîim*, as we have already stated, first rose to prominence in connection with that national and patriotic movement which elevated Saul to the throne of Israel, and consolidated the tribes into a united people. The wild and ecstatic companies of enthusiasts, who traversed the land preaching a holy war against the Philistines, were to some extent organized and disciplined by the efforts of Samuel, the founder of the prophetic 'schools.' At the time of Ahab's accession, a great change had passed over these communities. Schools of prophets existed at certain centres such as Bethel, Gilgal and Jericho. In these the sacred gift of prophecy was regularly cultivated by means of a system of instruction and devotion; *the spirits of the prophets* were thus trained to become *subject to the prophets* (1 Cor. xiv. 32). The *Nebîim* in fact gradually became a professional order, having a recognised place and function, alongside of the priesthood, in the religious life of the nation[1]. Occasionally there arose among them, and sometimes outside of their communities, an individual of exceptional power (Amos for example), qualified to be the public champion of Israel's traditional faith, and claiming the right to control and judge in Jehovah's name the conduct of statesmen and kings. During the earlier period of the monarchy prophets were the most prominent supporters of the throne. On occasion, however, they did not shrink from fearlessly rebuking unrighteousness even in the person of the monarch himself. Thus, for instance, Samuel reproved the wilfulness and foretold the impending doom of Saul; Nathan and Gad rebuked David; Ahijah the Shilonite denounced the sins of Jeroboam and predicted the overthrow of his house. A prophet of this exceptional type was the great Elijah, the divinely-commissioned scourge of Ahab's dynasty and the sleepless foe of Phoenician Baal-worship. It is true that Elijah, in spite of his own misgivings (I Kings xix. 14), was actually supported to some extent by the better and higher instincts of the people, who were evidently not prepared for anything like a formal apostasy from Jehovah. But as time went on the religious degeneracy of the northern kingdom became a patent fact, and the prophets found themselves placed in a position of antagonism not merely to the rulers of Israel, but also to the down-grade tendencies, beliefs and customs of the nation at large. Indeed the truths which they proclaimed struck at the very root of certain elements in the popular religion of their countrymen. In particular they taught that the nature and requirements of Israel's God were quite other than they were popularly supposed to be. They made it their principal business to root out false conceptions of Jehovah, and to awaken the national conscience to the true moral conditions of His original covenant with Israel. It should be added that the first attempts to collect the earliest specimens of Hebrew literature,—the ancient songs and ballads

---

[1] In the earlier period the prophets themselves exercised sacerdotal functions. Such was the case with Moses, Samuel, and Elijah.

of which fragments still survive in the historical books,—probably originated in the schools of the prophets; and we may reasonably trace to the same source the two connected versions of Israel's past history, which are respectively styled by critics the 'Jehovistic' (J) and the 'Elohistic' (E) narratives. These two documents appear to have been compiled independently some time during the ninth or eighth century B.C. At a later period they were skilfully combined so as to form one continuous narrative, which was repeatedly revised and re-edited under prophetic influence. Thus before the appearance of the earliest of the eighth-century prophets (Amos, *c.* 760), a mass of literary materials was already in existence—poems, ballads, prose narratives, maxims and written ordinances—out of which some attempt had already been made to construct an authoritative national history.

The purely political influence of the prophets was at certain epochs very great. Samuel had virtually established the monarchy. Ahijah had encouraged the revolt of Jeroboam. The power which they were enabled to exercise at critical turning-points of Israel's history is illustrated by the part played by Elisha in the subversion of Omri's dynasty. Elisha was originally the servant and afterwards the successor of Elijah: he was the inheritor of his great master's thoughts and purposes, and was commonly believed to be endued with *a double portion* of his spirit. At the beginning of Jehoram's reign he already enjoyed a position of recognized eminence and authority. He was consulted by the confederate kings of Israel (Jehoram), Judah (Jehoshaphat) and Edom, respecting the conduct of the campaign directed after Ahab's death against Mesha king of Moab. It is noteworthy however that on this occasion the prophet sternly declined to have any personal dealings with Jehoram (2 Kings iii. 14). The issue of the expedition against Moab has been already noticed. During the prolonged and desultory

Elisha:
2 Kings ii.—viii.

Elisha during the Syrian wars: 2 Kings iv.—vii.

warfare with Syria, Elisha's prophetic insight made him an indispensable adviser of the Israelites, and seriously thwarted the designs of the Syrians. The history of the campaign is obscure, and only a few incidents are recorded, the exact period of which can only be a matter of conjecture. We hear of a Syrian force penetrating westward across the plain of Esdraelon as far as Dothan, and being guided by Elisha himself to Samaria. The prophet, we are told, dissuaded the king of Israel (presumably Jehoram) from putting to death the captives, thus unexpectedly thrown into his power. The story of Naaman, the Syrian officer, whom Elisha healed of his leprosy by persuading him to bathe in the waters of Jordan, may also belong to Jehoram's reign[1]. So far as we know however the war with Syria was barren of result. It may have been Benhadad's death that encouraged Jehoram to renew the attempt to recover Ramoth-Gilead. The city was ultimately taken, but Jehoram was compelled by an injury received in battle to return to Jezreel.

At a later time we hear of Elisha as visiting Damascus where, in pursuance of the commission originally given to Elijah[2], he designated Hazael as Benhadad's successor and the destined scourge of Israel. But the chief task assigned to Elisha was that of bringing about the downfall of Omri's dynasty, by the anointing of Jehu. Of this momentous act the prophet took the responsibility upon himself, but employed as his instrument one of 'the sons of the prophets.' In obedience to his superior's injunctions the young man sought out Jehu, an officer of the army, which was at that time engaged in operations against the Syrians at Ramoth-Gilead, and privately anointed him king. Jehu was a restless and ambitious soldier. He had been present at the memorable scene when Elijah denounced Ahab for the murder of Naboth

---

[1] As Elisha survived Jehoram some forty years, it is possible that some other king of Israel is intended in some passages of 2 Kings, chh. iv.—vii.

[2] 1 Kings xix. 15; 2 Kings viii. 7 foll.

and predicted his coming doom. He recognized at once that the moment was favourable for open revolt, Jehoram having, as we have seen, recently withdrawn to Jezreel. Accordingly the usurper lost not a moment; he made known to his fellow-officers the nature of the prophet's communication, and was forthwith hailed as king by the army. Then, forbidding anyone to leave the camp, he mounted his chariot and rode at full speed towards Jezreel, attended only by an armed retinue. The rapid approach of the cavalcade, as it was observed mounting the ascent from the Jordan valley, aroused Jehoram's suspicions. He sent two messengers to meet Jehu with the enquiry *Is it peace?* but both were forcibly detained. Jehoram himself thereupon set forth in his chariot, accompanied by his nephew Ahaziah, king of Judah, who chanced to be his visitor at Jezreel. Close to the fatal plot of ground, which Ahab had acquired by the murder of Naboth, the two kings met the insurgent captain. An arrow from Jehu's bow smote Jehoram, who instantly *sunk down in his chariot.* Ahaziah attempted to fly, but was overtaken and mortally wounded before he could reach Megiddo. Entering Jezreel in triumph, Jehu was greeted by Jezebel the queen mother, who, leaning from a window of the palace, taunted him with his treachery. *Is it peace, thou Zimri, his master's murderer?* His only reply was an order given to the queen's attendants to *throw her down.* Her blood sprinkled the wall of the palace and Jehu's horses trode her underfoot. He presently gave directions that Jezebel should be buried in a manner befitting a king's daughter, but it was found that her flesh had already been devoured by the dogs, as Elijah had foretold. *They went to bury her: but they found no more of her than the skull and the feet and the palms of her hands.* The extermination of Ahab's family was completed by the elders of Samaria, who, in obedience to a grim and significant hint from Jehu, and trembling for their own safety, promptly put to death seventy

Revolt of Jehu: 2 Kings ix.

Death of Jezebel: 2 Kings ix. 30 foll.

princes of the royal house. Forty-two of Ahaziah's kinsmen, who accidentally fell into Jehu's hands as he was travelling from Jezreel to Samaria, were also ruthlessly slain.

Jehu was resolved to signalise his accession by dealing a fatal blow to the popular worship of Baal, at least to that gross and licentious form of it which the late queen had introduced from Phoenicia. He does not seem to have discountenanced the more primitive type of worship which was still carried on at the local sanctuaries; but at Samaria there stood an imposing heathen temple, which in the eyes of zealous puritans like Jehonadab the Rechabite, whom Jehu invited to *come and see* his *zeal for Jehovah*, was an intolerable abomination. In this sanctuary, under pretext of special zeal for the service of the Tyrian deity, Jehu collected the devotees of Baal. Then by his directions, while they were intent on their worship, they were surrounded by soldiery and butchered. The temple was desecrated and the sacred pillars (*mazzeboth*) which it contained were burned (2 Kings x. 26). Thus by fire and sword the worship of Baal was rooted out; Jehu had indeed 'made a solitude and called it peace'; but that these wholesale massacres deeply outraged the conscience of the nation is proved by the language of the prophet Hosea, writing a century later: *Yet a little while and I will avenge the blood of Jezreel upon the house of Jehu* (Hos. i. 4). It is evident that no lasting reformation of religion was effected by Jehu's violent and unscrupulous action. The bulls erected by Jeroboam were left unmolested, while idolatrous emblems and usages were still allowed to find a place in the worship of Jehovah.

Jehu had now secured his position, but he inherited from the dynasty of Omri the burdensome task of defending his realm against the constant aggression of Syria, the temporary alliance of Ahab with the Syrians having been abruptly dissolved by the disastrous

Marginal notes:

Extirpation of Baal-worship: 2 Kings x. 15 foll.

Reign of Jehu, c. 843—815.

battle of Karkar. Further, Jehu's religious policy quickly severed the ties which had formerly connected Israel with Phoenicia. He accordingly found himself driven to make terms with Shalmaneser II. of Assyria[1], who early in Jehu's reign again invaded Syria and inflicted heavy losses on Hazael of Damascus (842). For about three years Israel was protected from aggression; but the Syrian kingdom presently recovered its strength and again took the offensive.

Israel suffered severely from hostile invasions during the remainder of Jehu's reign, and throughout that of his son Jehoahaz (2 Kings x. 32 foll.; cp. 2 Kings viii. 12). The entire district east of

Jehoahaz, c. 815—802.

Jordan that lay to the north of the river Arnon fell into the possession of the Syrians, and even Judah was exposed to their inroads. Hazael actually attacked and captured the town of Gath, and was only induced by the payment of a heavy ransom to spare Jerusalem itself (2 Kings xii. 17, 18). Certain it is that at this time the military strength of the northern kingdom reached its lowest point. Hazael's son, Benhadad III, we are told, left to Jehoahaz only ten chariots, fifty horsemen, and ten thousand foot-soldiers; *for the king of Syria destroyed them and made them like the dust in threshing.* There are accordingly some grounds for supposing that the narrative of the siege of Samaria in 2 Kings vi. 24—vii. 20 with its terrible incidents, describes an event belonging to the reign of Jehoahaz. The sudden

Siege of Samaria.

break-up of the siege may have been occasioned by some rumour of the approach of an Assyrian army, which obliged the Syrians hastily to retreat[2]. The statement of 2 Kings

[1] An obelisk of black marble (now preserved at the British Museum), on which the annals of Shalmaneser's reign are recorded, gives a representation of Jehu's ambassadors bringing offerings to the Assyrian monarch.

[2] Such an inroad may have taken place in the reign of Rammannirârî III. (812—783). See Driver in *Authority and Archaeology,* etc., p. 96.

O. H. 12

xiii. 5, *Jehovah gave Israel a saviour so that they went out from under the hand of the Syrians,* may refer to this sudden and unexplained deliverance.   The tide of disaster turned at last during the reign of Jehoash.   We are told that he thrice defeated the Syrians and recovered the cities which Hazael had captured, probably those of the trans-Jordanic region.   These successes were in great measure due to the influence of Elisha, whose patriotic energy and foresight made him the mainstay of his country during this period of misery and depression.   On his death bed[1] the pro-phet was visited by Jehoash, who wept over him and called him *the chariots of Israel and the horsemen thereof.*   Elisha directed the king to take his bow and shoot an arrow eastward toward Syria.   *And he said, Jehovah's arrow of victory, even the arrow of victory over Syria ; for thou shalt smite the Syrians in Aphek till thou have consumed them.*   Thrice at the prophet's bidding Jehoash smote the ground with his arrows, and then paused.   Elisha *was wroth with him and said, Thou shouldest have smitten five or six times, then hadst thou smitten Syria till thou hadst con-sumed it: whereas now thou shalt smite Syria but thrice.*   What-ever may have been the actual extent of his successes, Jehoash effectually delivered Israel from the yoke of Syrian oppression. His attention was next turned to a danger that threatened him from another quarter.   Possibly the recovery of the northern kingdom under Jehoash had excited the fears or the jealousy of Amaziah king of Judah ; at any rate he suddenly resolved to declare war against Israel, a step which only involved his own kingdom in disaster.   Jehoash advanced into Judah, met the forces of Amaziah at Beth-shemesh and completely defeated them. The king himself was taken prisoner, Jerusalem

*Jehoash,
c. 802—790.*

Death of
Elisha, 2 Kings
xiii. 14 foll.

Conflict of
Jehoash with
Amaziah,
2 Kings xiv.
8—14.

---

[1] Elisha probably died at the opening of the eighth century B C., *circ.* 798 or 797.

was compelled to open its gates to the victor, a portion of its walls was destroyed; the gold and silver contained in the temple treasury were confiscated, and Jehoash returned in triumph, followed by a train of hostages, to Samaria.

Under Jeroboam II., the son of Jehoash and the last king of Jehu's dynasty, Israel rose to a height of prosperity which recalled the palmy days of Solomon's reign.   The Syrian kingdom was reduced to impotence by the repeated attacks of Assyria, so that Israel had little more to fear from its inveterate foes.   Jeroboam was thus enabled to recover what previous kings had lost, and the border of Israel was once more restored from *the entering in of Hamath unto the sea of the Arabah* (2 Kings xiv. 25 ; Amos vi. 14).   The desultory war with Syria, which had lasted for a century, was finally at an end, and the northern kingdom entered on a new career of prosperity and peace.

Jeroboam II.
c. 782—743.

Meanwhile the history of the southern kingdom, during the century which followed the accession of Jehoshaphat, had been comparatively uneventful.   We have seen that the alliance of Jehoshaphat with Ahab, cemented by the marriage of the former king's son Jehoram to Ahab's daughter Athaliah, inaugurated a new era in the relations between the two kingdoms.   The policy of fraternization was however denounced by the prophets, and a disaster which wrecked the navy of Jehoshaphat was regarded by them as a manifest token of Jehovah's displeasure[1].   The king devoted his energies mainly to the internal organization of his kingdom, and to the abolition of some flagrant religious abuses.   The brief reign of his successor, Jehoram, brought to light some of the baneful consequences of the mar-

History of Judah, B.C. 874—778.
Jehoshaphat, c. 874.

Jehoram, c. 849—844.

---

[1] 2 Chron. xx. 35—37.   The fact that Jehoshaphat had access to the harbour of Ebion-Gezer shows that Edom was for the time in a state of subjection to Judah (cp. 2 Kings iii. 9).

riage which had united the fortunes of the two kingdoms. The queen Athaliah used her influence to introduce into the southern kingdom the heathenism and profligacy of Ahab's house[1]. Jehoram, we read, *walked in the way of the kings of Israel as did the house of Ahab* (2 Kings viii. 18). The chief incident of his reign was the final revolt of the Edomites, after an unsuccessful attempt on Jehoram's part to recover their allegiance. The revolt of Libnah about the same time probably encouraged the Philistines to assume the offensive. The Chronicler mentions a joint invasion of Judah by the Philistines and Arabians, in the course of which Jerusalem itself was attacked. The royal palace was sacked, and all the king's sons, except the youngest, were carried off as hostages[2]. Jehoram himself died prematurely of a painful disease. His successor

Ahaziah, c. 844—842.

Ahaziah took part with Jehoram of Israel in operations against Syria, but his reign was brief; his connection with Ahab's son involved him, as we have already seen, in the ruin of Omri's dynasty, and he fell by the hand of Jehu. The ambitious queen-mother Athaliah thereupon usurped the throne, and put to death all surviving members of the royal house of Judah, the child Joash alone being rescued from her frenzy by the care of his aunt Jehosheba. Athaliah occupied the throne for six years, during which time Joash was kept concealed in the temple precincts by Jehoiada the high-priest. Meanwhile Athaliah seems to have established in Jerusalem the foreign cult which Jehu had extirpated in Samaria; she even erected a temple of Baal, served by a priest of her own appointment (2 Chr. xxiii. 17). In the seventh year Jehoiada organized an insurrection; he seized the opportunity offered by the customary attendance of the royal

[1] 2 Chron. xxiv. 7 (cp. xxi. 6, 13).

[2] 2 Chron. xxi. 16 foll. The occasion of the great victory of Jehoshaphat described in 2 Chron. xx. is quite uncertain. If, as is probable, it took place early in his reign, it may have led to the temporary subjugation of Edom implied in 1 Kings xxii. 47.

body-guard at the temple on the sabbath day, to present Joash
to the troops and solemnly crown him in their
presence.   Startled by the sound of acclamation
Athaliah hastened to the temple unattended,
only to find that the revolt was a *fait accompli.*

Accession of
Joash, c. 836
—797 : 2 Kings
xi. and xii.

Having no troops at her command, she was arrested and slain
at the palace gate.   The accession of the youthful Joash was
the signal for a strong reaction against the worship of the
Phoenician Baal which Athaliah had introduced.   The house
of Baal was destroyed and the priest Mattan fell a victim to
popular fury.   After some difficulty in devising a scheme for
raising the necessary funds, the temple was thoroughly restored.   Indeed, so long as Jehoiada lived, his influence with
the king (his nephew) secured the interests of the priesthood
and of religion.   Nothing was done however to restrict the
custom of sacrifice at the local 'high places,' and after the
high-priest's death Joash himself, according to the Chronicler,
permitted the revival at Jerusalem of idolatrous practices
(2 Chr. xxiv. 17 foll.).   The example of the aristocracy was
followed by the mass of the people.   The warnings of the
prophets were unheeded, and a bold protest publicly uttered
by Zechariah, the son of Jehoiada, even cost him his life.
*They conspired against him and stoned him with stones at the com-
mandment of the king in the court of the temple.*   The calamities
which speedily overtook the southern kingdom were naturally
ascribed by the later Jews to the weakness and apostasy of
Joash.   Hazael of Damascus invaded the territory of Judah,
and an attack on Jerusalem was only averted by an immense
bribe taken from the treasures of the palace and temple.
Joash himself fell a victim to conspiracy and was murdered as
he lay sick within his fortress on Mount Zion.
His successor Amaziah was involved in a fresh
conflict with Edom ; he succeeded in inflicting

Amaziah,
c. 797—778.

on the Edomites a severe defeat in the valley of Salt, and even
captured the stronghold of Sela or Petra.   Thereupon in the

pride of conscious strength he rashly challenged Jehoash, the powerful king of Israel, and the humiliation which this foolish step brought upon the southern kingdom has already been described. The disaster must have excited intense indignation in Judah, and especially in Jerusalem, which bore the brunt of the campaign. Before long a conspiracy was formed against the king's life, and he was assassinated at Lachish whither he had fled for refuge.

The accession of Azariah or Uzziah seems to have taken place a few years after that of Jeroboam II. of Israel, and speaking broadly the two reigns were contemporaneous. The circumstances of both kingdoms were favourable to their internal development and to the tranquil enlargement of their power and resources. The statement that Uzziah built the important harbour of Elath and restored it to Judah (2 Kings xiv. 22), implies that during his reign Judah discovered new openings for its commerce. Indeed, if we may judge from the writings of the prophets[1] and from the Chronicler's detailed account, Judah, like Israel, reached during Uzziah's long reign the very zenith of prosperity. The military strength of both kingdoms was now considerable, and while Jeroboam succeeded in carrying his conquests northwards as far as Hamath, Uzziah secured his territory against Philistine aggression by a chain of fortresses, and even gained a footing on the shore of the Red Sea. Meanwhile the general standard of comfort and luxury in both kingdoms was high; the two capital cities of Samaria and Jerusalem were adorned with splendid buildings and defended by strong fortifications; wealth rapidly increased, and brought about a revival of the arts of peace. The personal prosperity of Uzziah was only marred by the fact that he was afflicted with leprosy during the last few years of his life, during which time his son Jotham administered the kingdom as regent.

Uzziah,
c. 778—740:
2 Kings xv.
1—7.

Jotham,
c. 740—736.

[1] See especially Isai. ii.; cp. 2 Chron. xxvi.

A vivid light is thrown on the history of the eighth century B.C., and on the social and political condition of the two kingdoms, by the writings of the prophets. No period in the career of Israel and Judah was of more critical importance, whether as regards their political fortunes or their religious development. Prophets like Amos and Hosea in the northern kingdom, or Isaiah and Micah in Judah, found themselves brought into sharp collision, not only with the habits and traditions of the governing classes, but also with the temper and tendencies of the people in general. The dominant fact of the political situation was the restless aggressive- General ness of the gigantic empire of Assyria, which aspects of the had already succeeded in crushing the power of eighth century. Damascus and now menaced the borders of western Palestine. Thus at the very moment when the material strength of both kingdoms had reached its highest level, their political independence was imperilled. If they desired to hold their own and to play an active part on the stage of secular history, they could only do so at the expense of forfeiting their ideal vocation. For we must remember that Israel, in so far as she recognized her God-given destiny, was bound to remain an isolated people[1]. She could not compete with other nations for the prizes of the world, nor could she consistently employ its weapons. Accordingly the great prophets of the eighth century found themselves constrained Function to take a prominent part in the sphere of social of prophecy. and political life. Their voices were uplifted in the hope of recalling the chosen people to a sense of its mission to the nations, and they advocated such courses of policy as were demanded not by considerations of worldly interest, but by the essential principles of Jehovah's religion.

A short account of the social and religious condition of Israel and Judah during the middle period of Judah and Israel in the the eighth century B.C. (circ. 780—740) may 8th century.

[1] Cp. Num. xxiii. 9; Deut. xxxiii. 28.

be regarded as a necessary introduction to the study of their external history.

In the first place it should be noticed that the material splendour and prosperity of the two kingdoms was mainly due to the cessation of the harassing wars with Syria. A state of long-continued hostilities had produced its usual economic effects: the free practice of agriculture had given way before the exigencies of military organization; the insecurity of life in unwalled villages and the stern pressure of poverty had fostered the growth of cities; the simple manners and customs of a pastoral community had gradually been replaced by the habits of town life, with its sharp contrasts between wealth and poverty, its vices and luxuries, its artificial wants, its deterioration of character. The change from agricultural to mercantile and civil pursuits was obviously fraught with moral danger. "There was the closer intercourse with foreign nations and their cults. There were all the temptations of rapid wealth, all the dangers of an equally increasing poverty. The growth of comfort among the rulers meant the growth of thoughtlessness. Cruelty multiplied with refinement. The upper classes were lifted away from feeling the real woes of the people. There was a well-fed and sanguine patriotism, but at the expense of indifference to social sin and want[1]." Moreover the opening of new avenues for trade and commerce led to the rise of a mercantile community, tainted with the characteristic vices of a middle class: the passion for quickly making money, unscrupulous greed, dishonest trading, and callous harshness in the exaction of debt. The gulf between rich and poor grew daily wider, while the inveterate curse of Oriental life, corruption and partiality in the administration of justice, aggravated the burdens of the oppressed and helpless classes. The northern kingdom in particular, owing to the strain of long-continued warfare and the frequent and violent changes of

---

[1] Prof. G. A. Smith, *The Book of the Twelve Prophets*, vol. i. pp. 33, 34.

dynasty, had lost the tradition of good and stable government. Though a multitude of social problems pressed for solution, the statesmen of Samaria were neither willing nor qualified to give them serious attention.

The outwardly flourishing state of religion was a circumstance which only embittered the evils of the time. It is true that the worship of the Tyrian Baal had been practically extirpated in both kingdoms, but gross abuses and corruptions were still rife which defied the spirit of reform. Meanwhile the nation was proud of its devotion to *Jehovah, the God of Israel,* and hailed the prosperous issue of the Syrian wars as a sure pledge of the divine favour and protection. The numerous sanctuaries, among which those of Bethel, Gilgal and Dan were perhaps the most popular, were thronged on the stated feast-days by crowds of zealous worshippers, and were constantly enriched by the regular payment of tithes and free-will offerings. The ceremonial usually observed at these 'holy places' was of the type which had now become traditional: Jehovah was worshipped under the form of a metal bull; beside the altar stood emblems borrowed from Canaanitish heathenism, the *ashêrah* and the *mazzeboth*[1]; sabbaths and new-moons were punctiliously observed, and the sacred festivals were looked upon as legitimate occasions for tumultuous revelry and excess. Nor did the form of worship practised in Judah remain for long pure and untainted, in spite of its comparative seclusion and its possession of the royal temple at Jerusalem. Isaiah complains in the early chapters of his book of the many abuses which corrupted the religion of Judah: the *cultus* of images and *ashêrim,* the use of pagan customs and emblems, the practice of magic, necromancy and other superstitious rites. But it was the condition of the northern kingdom that first challenged the attention and roused the indignation of the prophets. Indeed,

Condition of religion.

---

[1] Cp. G. A. Smith, *op. cit.* p. 38, note 4.

religion in Israel had become not only the occasion of popular delusion, but the cloke of grievous social iniquities. The favourite watchword of the time was *Jehovah God of hosts is with us*[1]. Predictions of national disaster or calamity were repudiated as absurd and even blasphemous, for Jehovah was popularly regarded as Israel's national deity and therefore as pledged under all circumstances to protect and befriend the people of His choice. The ancient Mosaic conception of Jehovah as a God of righteousness, punishing the guilty and avenging the oppressed, was forgotten. The claims of morality and justice, of mercy and good faith between man and man, of personal integrity, honesty and temperance, were ignored. The richly-appointed *cultus* of the local sanctuaries was supposed to be a sufficient guarantee of the divine favour. Indeed "to the mass of the people, to their governors, their priests and most of their prophets, Jehovah was but the characteristic Semitic deity —patron of His people and caring for them alone—who had helped them in the past and was bound to help them still— very jealous as to the correctness of His ritual and the amount of His sacrifices, but indifferent about real morality[2]."

Such was the religious state of Israel. On the other hand Amos and Hosea draw a very dark picture of the various forms of iniquity that flourished under the cloke of religion. Brutish luxury prevailed in the palaces of the rich; shameless sensuality was practised at the sanctuaries. The ruling classes enriched themselves by cruel deeds of spoliation and violence; the poor were at the mercy of harsh creditors, corrupt judges, and avaricious traders. Hosea in particular describes the priests as leading the way in lawless wickedness, as actually anxious for the multiplication of legal offences, as even guilty of highway robbery and murder[3]. We cannot wonder that the message proclaimed by these two prophets is a gloomy one,

[1] Cp. Amos v. 14.
[2] G. A. Smith, *op. cit.* p. 40.
[3] See Amos ii. 7, iii. 9, 10, vi. 4—11; Hos. iv. 8—14, vi. 9.

and that in an age like theirs "the divine purpose could not be one of peace[1]." The note of judgment rang out with startling suddenness. It was apparently during the celebration of a religious festival at the popular sanctuary of Bethel, that Amos, a native of Tekoa in South Judah, unexpectedly appeared in the midst of the joyous throng of worshippers and raised the discordant cry of warning and lamentation. Amos was not one of the professional *Nebîim.* He was engaged in the humble tasks of a shepherd and dresser of sycomore trees in the wilderness of Judah, when the voice of Jehovah summoned him to be the bearer of a prophetic message to Israel (Am. vii. 15). We can but faintly imagine the dismay and indignation with which the festal crowd listened to the fateful cry of the obscure stranger from Judah : *The virgin of Israel is fallen, she shall no more rise: she is cast down upon her land: there is none to raise her up* (Am. v. 2). The prediction of judgment to come was equally unwelcome and incredible. But in spite of the incredulity with which it was received, Amos persisted in his warning. He foretold the speedy downfall of the reigning dynasty, the total destruction of the national sanctuaries, the impending invasion of Israel's territory, the captivity and exile of its population. Neither the people nor their accepted rulers and guides were capable of comprehending the real significance of that steady westward movement of Assyria which has rightly been described as "by far the greatest event in the eighth century before Christ." Nevertheless, in the mighty empire beyond the Euphrates, the prophets discerned the scourge which the divine Providence was preparing for the overthrow of Israel's prosperity as a secular state, and the purification of its faith. They understood that their nation's high destiny could only be fulfilled through the destruction of its illusions and the overthrow of its false hopes and ideals.

Amos:
c. 760.

[1] See *Encyclopaedia Biblica*, s.v. ' Amos.'

Shortly after Amos appeared Hosea, the prophet of Israel's

'decline and fall.' His ministry probably covered the disastrous period between the death of Jeroboam II. and the accession of Pekah (735). More explicitly than Amos, Hosea denounces the short-sighted foreign policy which was hurrying the northern kingdom to destruction. *Ephraim*, the prophet complains, *hath hired lovers* (Hos. viii. 9). He means that Israel's rulers, instead of relying on Jehovah, their *God from the land of Egypt*, were vainly seeking to strengthen themselves by forming alliances with foreign powers. One faction looked to Egypt for help, another to Assyria, blind to the fact that overtures made to either of these secular empires must eventually lead to expatriation. Israel would return to its former bondage in Egypt, or else would pass under the cruel yoke of Assyria[1]. In either case a faithless policy would defeat its own end, and bring not safety but ruin.

Such was the burden of Hosea's warning, but it was uttered too late to avert the approaching downfall of his country. The closing scene of Israel's history as a nation was already at hand. Here and there individuals might obey the prophet's urgent call to repentance and *seek Jehovah* (Hos. x. 12 ; cp. Am. v. 6), but the unthinking mass of the people, led by worthless kings, false prophets, corrupt statesmen, and unscrupulous priests, was irrevocably doomed[2]. The Assyrian army, the instrument of Jehovah's righteous vengeance, was already on its way.

In order to understand the situation of Israel at the time

of Hosea's ministry we must glance back a few years. After an interval of nearly forty years, during which the Assyrians had been comparatively inactive, they again advanced into Syria (803) and in 797 finally besieged and captured Damascus. The power of

---

[1] See Hos. xi. 5 with Cheyne's note.

[2] Hos. x. 13.

Syria was at last effectually broken, and the respite thus gained enabled Israel, as we have seen, to recover from the disastrous effects of the recent wars, and presently, under the leadership of Jeroboam II., to regain a footing in eastern Palestine. The successes of Jeroboam were really due to the repeated intervention of Assyria, which crippled the energies of Syria for more than half a century. But the long immunity from invasion which Israel enjoyed throughout Jeroboam's reign came to an end at its close. In 745 Pul or Tiglath-Pileser III. ascended the throne of Assyria, and renewed the campaign against the western kingdoms. The siege of Arpad delayed his advance for three years, the conquest of Babylonia for another two years; but in 738 he marched westward, annexed to his empire a large part of the land of Hamath, and forced the independent kings of Syria to pay tribute. Meanwhile a series of puppet-kings occupied in rapid succession the throne of Israel. After a reign of six months Zechariah the son of Jeroboam (743) was murdered by a conspirator named Shallum, the son of Jabesh. Only a month passed before Shallum himself was dethroned and slain by Menahem, a rough and unscrupulous soldier, who purchased at the cost of an immense bribe, raised by the imposition of a poll-tax on the wealthier citizens, the support of the Assyrian monarch *that his hand might be with him to confirm the kingdom in his hand*[1]. Menahem was succeeded by his son Pekahiah (738), but he also after a two years' reign fell a victim to a military plot. Pekah, the son of Remaliah, a captain of the army, with fifty Gileadite followers, broke into the palace at Samaria, slew Pekahiah and seized the throne (735). It is perhaps in allusion to these swift and tragic vicissitudes that Hosea says (x. 7), *As*

Successors of Jeroboam. Zechariah, Shallum, Menahem (c. 741—737), 2 Kings xv. 8—22.

Pekahiah, Pekah, c. 737—736.

---

[1] Hosea v. 13 seems to refer to the tribute sent by Menahem to the king of Assyria in 738. On the identification of Pul (2 Kings xv. 19) with Tiglath-Pileser, see Driver in *op. cit.*, p. 97.

for Samaria, her king is cut off as foam upon the water. Pekah may have been the representative of a strong national sentiment.   Doubtless Menahem's subservience to Assyria was costly and provoked deep resentment, and it is likely that Pekah was supported by popular opinion in his endeavour to form an anti-Assyrian league.   He accordingly entered into an alliance with Rezin of Damascus, and conceived the project of forcing Ahaz, who had recently ascended the throne of Judah (736), to join the coalition.   Preparations were made for an invasion of Judah by the Syro-Ephraimitish army; but Ahaz, in spite of the urgent warnings of Isaiah[1], appealed for aid to Tiglath-Pileser.   The Assyrian monarch instantly marched westward, and advanced as far as Gaza, which he captured (734).   He also took a number of towns in the districts of Gilead and Naphtali, and exacted a heavy tribute from Israel.   Meanwhile a conspiracy removed Pekah himself: he was slain by Hoshea the son of Elah, who owed his elevation to the support of Assyria, and who was content to reign as the vassal of Tiglath-Pileser.

Syro-Ephraimitish war, 734—3.

Hoshea, 734 —722.

In the following two years the Assyrian king invaded Syria, took Damascus, deported its inhabitants and slew Rezin.   Before his death in 727, most of the petty kingdoms of Palestine and the neighbouring countries were tributaries of Assyria.   Within a few years however (about 725), Hoshea was induced to listen to the overtures of Sabako or So, a powerful Ethiopian officer who had risen to a position of influence in Egypt, and eventually ascended the throne of Egypt as the founder of the twenty-fifth dynasty.   Sabako was uneasy at the recent expansion of the Assyrian power, and vainly hoped to form a barrier in Palestine to its further advance.   In defiance of the warnings of the prophets, Hoshea yielded to Egyptian pressure and ventured to withhold the annual tribute due to the Assyrian monarch.   Shalmaneser IV.,

[1] Isai. vii. 1—17.

who in 727 had succeeded Tiglath-Pileser, promptly marched
into Palestine to punish his rebellious vassal,
and the Assyrian army laid siege to Samaria.   Fall of
After a desperate resistance of three years—a   Samaria, 722.
fact which illustrates the great natural strength of its position—   2 Kings xvii.
the city was actually captured by Sargon, the successor of
Shalmaneser (722). Its fall involved the ruin of the northern
kingdom. The flower of the population (nearly 28,000 persons) was deported to different districts beyond the Euphrates.
Settlers from Babylonia and Assyria occupied the conquered
province, and gradually took the place of those who had been
carried into captivity. Under pressure of the perils and difficulties caused by the utter devastation of the
country, these heathen colonists took pains to   Its consequences.
enquire concerning *the manner of the god of the
land.* An Israelitish priest was sent to instruct them, and the
result was that a strange medley of cults sprang up and coexisted with a debased form of Jehovah-worship. When the
distinctive religion of Israel had thus disappeared, its separate
existence as a nation was also lost. Indeed, the Jews soon
came to regard the inhabitants of Samaria as half-heathen.
Consequently the interest of the sacred history after the fall of
Samaria is centred in the fortunes of the surviving kingdom of
Judah.

We must remember, in taking a final retrospect of the
history of the northern kingdom, that its fortunes
have been described by historians who regarded   Summary.
the house of David alone as the legitimate dynasty, and who
looked upon the ten tribes as schismatics and rebels. The
consequence is a view of Israel's career (stereotyped in the
books of Chronicles), uniformly pessimistic in tone, the fact
being that the religious judgment of later times was powerfully
influenced by abhorrence of the bull-worship, which had always
been more or less customary in the northern kingdom. It
must, however, be borne in mind that even the stern prophet

Elijah is never said to have condemned the form of worship now in question. The first prophet who openly denounces it is Hosea, who perceived the real danger and debasing influence of a cult so nearly allied to that of the heathen Canaanites. Finally, we must not forget that northern Israel gave birth to prophecy, the most distinctive and precious feature in Hebrew religion. Samuel, Elijah and Hosea belonged to the northern kingdom, and even the Judaean Amos chose Israel as the sphere of his prophetic labours. Thus in spite of the undeniable elements of weakness which undermined the stability of the kingdom of Israel, it played an important part in the development of Jewish nationality and faith.

There is however one fact which seems to justify the prophetic judgment upon Israel's career—namely, that the expatriation of the ten tribes completely arrested their religious growth. The exiled Israelites were quickly merged in the heathen population of the land whither they were carried captive. "What a difference there is," says a recent historian, "between them and the Judaean exiles, whom we shall find profiting by their deportation to Babylon, amending their lives, correcting their former errors, and so becoming capable of accomplishing a restoration, defective indeed from a political point of view, but deeply significant and pregnant with momentous consequences of a moral and religious kind, so that the exile marks at once the end of Israel's persistent idolatry, and the assured triumph of monotheism[1]."

We shall see how, during the further respite providentially granted to the southern kingdom, the teaching of the prophets, embraced by a small section of faithful Jews, prepared the way for this happy issue of an apparently irretrievable catastrophe.

---

[1] Piepenbring, *Histoire du peuple d'Israël*, p. 280.

CHAPTER IX.

THE DECLINE AND FALL OF JUDAH.

DURING the prolonged agony of Israel's decline and fall, the eyes of the prophets were turned from the apostate northern kingdom to the family and throne of David. On the comparative purity of Judah's religious worship, on the stability of its monarchy and the comparative security of its secluded capital, they based their hopes of a brighter future.

Under Uzziah and Jotham (circ. 778—736), the kingdom of Judah had been at peace with Israel, and was engaged in no more serious operations than an occasional campaign against the Philistines, the Ammonites, and the nomad hordes of the southern desert who from time to time overran its borders. Ahaz the son of Jotham was still a youth when he succeeded to the throne, and possessed neither the strength of character nor the political capacity to deal with the momentous questions of foreign policy which were raised by the hostile schemes of Pekah and Rezin, and the threatening movements of Assyria. This weak, petulant and unprincipled king was however not destitute of guidance. Beside the throne stood the commanding figure of the great patriot and prophet Isaiah, perhaps after Moses the most striking personality in Hebrew history. Without holding any official position, Isaiah was actively engaged, during a ministry of forty years, in directing and controlling the policy of his country, and indeed, the closing period of the eighth century was a critical epoch in

Ahaz: c. 736—727.

Isaiah: c. 740—700.

which such guidance was urgently needed. It is unquestionable in any case that if the existence of the kingdom of Judah was prolonged for yet another century and a half, this result was mainly due to the energy and foresight of Isaiah.

At the outset of his reign Ahaz found himself threatened by the Syro-Ephraimitish coalition. The royal house and the nation at large were alike panic-stricken by the imminent approach of danger (Isai. vii. 1, 2). Isaiah endeavoured to allay the uneasiness of the king, bidding him have no fear of *these two tails of smoking firebrands*, and offering to encourage him with a sign from Jehovah. But Ahaz would not be diverted from the course on which he was now bent, and which he ultimately adopted—that of appealing to Tiglath-Pileser. The assistance of Assyria was secured, but only at a heavy price. The temple was stripped of its treasures, and the independence of Judah was practically forfeited. Ahaz sank to the position of a mere Assyrian vassal; indeed, the embassy which the king of Judah sent to implore the help of Tiglath-Pileser described him as the *servant and* the *son* of the Assyrian monarch (2 Kings xvi. 7). The appeal of Ahaz had however an immediate effect. The Syro-Ephraimitish forces were compelled to withdraw, but not before much damage had been done to the territory of Judah; Jerusalem had been besieged and reduced to serious straits, and the army of Ahaz had suffered heavy losses. The Syrians even succeeded in capturing the seaport of Elath and probably restored it to Edom (2 Kings xvi. 6 marg.). But owing to the decisive intervention of Assyria, the ultimate failure of the expedition was complete. From that time forward Judah had nothing to fear from its northern rival.

At Damascus, which speedily fell into the hands of the Assyrian monarch, Ahaz appeared in order to do homage to his suzerain, and he thus rivetted upon his kingdom the heavy yoke of the great heathen empire. The writings of the prophets enable us to

The reign of Ahaz: 2 Kings xvi.

realize some of the consequences that flowed from the policy of
Ahaz. On the one hand the necessity of raising a heavy
annual tribute pressed very heavily upon the poorer classes in
Judah—for in the East the poor are usually the real tax-
payers[1]—and greatly aggravated the social miseries which were
already crying for redress. While Isaiah describes these evils
chiefly as they affected Jerusalem, Micah of   Activity of
Moresheth-Gath was more keenly moved by the   Isaiah and
bitter sufferings of the yeomanry class to which   Micah.
he belonged. Isaiah inveighs against the sins and follies of the
capital : the luxury and ostentation of the rich, the prevalence
of foreign fashions, the extravagance of the court, the oppression which grinds *the face of the poor*[2]. Micah, writing
somewhat later, dwells more particularly upon the condition of
the peasantry in the country districts. He denounces the
greed of those who have acquired huge estates by dispossessing
the small landowners ; the mean exactions of the trading
class ; the unscrupulousness of the judges who connive at the
wrong-doing of the rich[3]. Both prophets point the moral of
the doom already impending over Samaria, the fall of which
took place in 722. The burden of their preaching is that the
social state which is based on iniquity is doomed. 'It is
unjust ; it cannot last.'

The decay of religion in Judah was aggravated by the
childish superstition and folly of Ahaz. The   State of
king probably professed himself a zealous de-   religion in
votee of Jehovah: but *he walked*, we read, *in the*   Judah.
way of the kings of Israel, and perhaps, as the last resource of
despair, when hard pressed by the Syrians and Israelites, he
had resort to human sacrifice : *he made his son to pass through
the fire according to the abominations* of the heathen[4]. We

---

[1] Cp. Robertson Smith, *Prophets of Israel* (ed. 1) p. 287.

[2] Isai. iii. 15.

[3] Cp. Mic. ii. 1, 2, 8, iii. 5 etc.

[4] 2 Kings xvi. 3.   Cp. the conduct of Mesha, 2 Kings iii. 26, 27.

gather from the early chapters of the book of Isaiah that strange forms of heathen idolatry were widely prevalent in Judah: for instance the cult of Nehushtan[1], and probably that of Tammuz (Adonis), while other abominations flourished in secret. Ahaz himself had a taste for religious novelties. He ordered the erection of a new altar in the temple at Jerusalem, made after the pattern of one which he had observed in Damascus[2], while the ancient brazen altar was used for the king *to enquire by.* The altars which he is said to have set up on the roof of the temple were probably intended for the worship of the host of heaven[3]—a cult doubtless borrowed from Assyria.

Isaiah's principal aim, as the counsellor of a monarch like Ahaz, was to bring home clearly to the conscience of the nation the inevitable consequences of the recent compact with Assyria. He perceived that if Judah should entangle herself in the affairs and interests of a heathen empire, if she should persist in playing an active part on the stage of secular history, she would inevitably forfeit her national independence, and lose sight of her true mission. The only course of safety for Judah lay in a policy of *quietness and confidence* (Isai. xxx. 15): in trustful dependence on the guidance of Him who had been her *God from the land of Egypt* (Hos. xiii. 4). She must choose at this crisis of her fate between two alternatives. Either she must passively accept the existing situation, leaving to Jehovah the absolute control of her destinies, or she must make the futile attempt to hold her own among the kingdoms of the earth. The choice for her lay in other words between a policy of implicit trust in the holy and omnipotent God of her fathers, or of vain reliance on human resources—material wealth, munitions of war, and schemes of human statecraft. In such passages as chh. viii. 5—15 and

Teaching of Isaiah.

---

[1] Cp. 2 Kings xviii. 4.
[2] 2 Kings xvi. 10 foll.
[3] 2 Kings xxiii. 12.

xxx. 1—17, Isaiah sets before the nation and its rulers the real issues at stake when Ahaz attempted to avert the dangers which menaced him by an appeal to Assyria. He did not indeed succeed in turning the short-sighted rulers of Judah from their fatal course, but he gathered round him a band of faithful adherents who, separating themselves in thought and aim from the mass of their fellow-countrymen, resolved to *wait for Jehovah*, to leave the future in His hands, and to be guided solely by the word of His revelation (Isai. viii. 11). "The formation of this little community," it has been said, "was a new thing in the history of religion....It was the birth of a new era in the Old Testament religion, for it was the birth of the conception of the *Church*, the first step in the emancipation of spiritual religion from the forms of political life—a step not less significant that all its consequences were not seen till centuries had passed away[1]." Henceforth the religious and the political history of Israel followed different lines of development. The prophets were as a rule no longer the trusted guides, but the antagonists, of those who directed the destinies of Judah. Henceforth, with one or two notable exceptions, religious motives and principles exercised little or no controlling influence on the policy of her statesmen.

The history of Hezekiah is involved in certain chronological difficulties; but it seems on the whole probable that the moderate religious reforms which that king set on foot were carried out in the earlier period of his reign. We are not told what degree of success attended his efforts to purify the religion of Judah. He seems to have endeavoured to centralize the national worship at Jerusalem by demolition of some of the local sanctuaries, around which so many heathenish abuses had gathered[2]; but the work of suppressing the 'high places' had

The reforms of Hezekiah: 2 Kings xviii. 3 foll.

---

[1] Robertson Smith, *Prophets of Israel*, p. 274.
[2] 2 Kings xviii. 4, 22. For a discussion as to the most probable date of Hezekiah's reforms, see Hastings' *DB*, vol. ii. p. 377.

to be again undertaken nearly a century later by Josiah. It is certain that many of the *ashêrim* and *maẓẓeboth* were demolished, and among other relics of idolatry Hezekiah destroyed the brazen serpent, which had become an object of superstitious veneration. These reforms however scarcely touched the grave evils which festered beneath the surface of the national life. There was little or no response to the cry of the prophets for general amendment of life and the redress of social abuses. The results of Hezekiah's well-meant effort were at best slight and transient.

Hezekiah also carried out extensive schemes for fortifying Jerusalem and improving its water-supply, besides developing in other ways the military resources of his kingdom. He succeeded in effectually checking the inroads of the Philistines, who perpetually harassed the border towns and villages of Judah. The first years of his reign were thus on the whole a period of tranquillity for Judah. The king himself seems to have had a taste for sacred music and literature. The Chronicler ascribes to him a zealous restoration and improvement of the temple services (2 Chr. xxix. 25 foll.), and

The age of Hezekiah.

there is reason to believe that his court was a centre of great literary activity. Jewish tradition assigned to Hezekiah a song, supposed to have been written on the occasion of his recovery from a dangerous sickness (Isai. xxxviii.). He also gathered about him a band of learned men, by some of whom certain proverbs of Solomon were collected and *copied out* (Prov. xxv. 1). A curious passage in the Talmud even ascribes to 'Hezekiah and his college' the writing (*i.e.* compilation) of the books of Isaiah, Proverbs, Song of Songs, Qoheleth (Ecclesiastes)[1]—a statement which though certainly wrong in its details, may be based on reminiscences of literary work done under the auspices of the king. Certain parts of the books of Kings, especially those

---

[1] *Bâba Bathra* 14[b], quoted by Driver, *LOT*, p. vii.

which relate to the history of the temple, very probably belong to the reign of Hezekiah. In any case the age in which Isaiah and Micah wrote may fairly be described as the "classiç epoch" in Hebrew literature.

Hezekiah seems to have succeeded Ahaz in or about the year 728 or 727, but it was not till the year 722, towards the close of which Samaria fell and the northern kingdom ceased to exist, that the king and his advisers were called upon to reconsider the relations of Judah to Assyria. Hitherto Hezekiah had regularly paid the tribute promised by Ahaz, but the burden was an oppressive one, and there soon arose in Judah a 'patriotic' party, intent on forming a defensive alliance with Egypt, and throwing off the As- **Judah and Assyria.** syrian yoke. This party succeeded in gaining the ear of Hezekiah, but the king was restrained by the commanding influence of Isaiah from actually breaking faith with Assyria. Nor indeed was he encouraged to do so by the result of an attempt which the Philistine cities made in 720 to recover their independence. In that year Sargon (who succeeded Shalmaneser IV. in 722) led an expedition against the king of Gaza and his powerful ally Sabako of Egypt, and defeated their army at Raphia, near the **Battle of Raphia, 720.** Egyptian frontier. During the next seven years Sargon was busily occupied in the east, but the spirit of revolt presently revived in Palestine and was of course encouraged in his own interest by the king of Egypt[1]. In 711 however matters came to a crisis. The city of Ashdod, which ventured to withhold its accustomed tribute, was besieged and captured by Sargon, and its inhabitants were enslaved[2]. Meanwhile Hezekiah received overtures from another quarter. After the death of Shalmaneser (722) the Chaldaean Merodach-baladan,

---

[1] As Driver says in *Authority and Archaeology*, p. 103, "Egypt was at this time the evil genius of the peoples of Palestine."

[2] See Isai. xx.

prince of one of the minor states of South Babylonia[1], had seized
the throne of Babylon and thrown off his allegiance to Nineveh.
For about twelve years he succeeded in maintaining his independence (circ. 721—710), and it was apparently during this

Embassy
of Merodach-
baladan, Isai.
xxxix.

period (perhaps in 715 or 712) that he sent an
embassy to Hezekiah, nominally to congratulate
him on his recovery from sickness, but in reality
with the hope of securing the alliance of Judah,
and inducing it to revolt from Assyria. Hezekiah received the
ambassadors with undue effusiveness, and displayed to them
his accumulated stores of treasure and warlike materials, thereby drawing upon himself a severe rebuke from Isaiah, who
warned the king that all the wealth on which he prided himself
should one day be carried to Babylon, and that his descendants
should be slaves in its royal palaces. Whatever hopes or projects Hezekiah may have formed were speedily crushed by
Merodach's defeat and submission to Sargon (709). This
blow indeed amply vindicated the policy which Hezekiah,
under the guidance of Isaiah, had hitherto pursued. Those
who favoured an Egyptian alliance had been on the point of
success in 711[2]; but Isaiah restrained the king from yielding
to their pressure by publicly appearing *naked and barefoot, i.e.*
in the scanty garb of a captive, by way of visibly depicting the
inevitable issue of a revolt from Assyria (Isai. xx.). In the
year 705, however, Sargon died by the hand of an assassin, and
was succeeded by Sennacherib. Merodach-baladan seized his
opportunity and again revolted; and while Sennacherib was

Revolt of
Hezekiah.

engaged in reducing Babylonia, Hezekiah at
length yielded to the persistency of the Egyptian
party. For some time secret negotiations were
carried on with Ethiopia and with Egypt in spite of Isaiah's

---

[1] In inscriptions described as *king of the Kaldû* or *Chaldaeans*, a people
of lower Babylonia. Under Nabopolassar and Nebuchadnezzar the Kaldû
became the ruling caste in Babylonia.

[2] See the inscription of Sargon, given by Driver in *op. cit.* p. 103.

urgent warnings and predictions of the disgrace and ruin that would inevitably result from this faithless and short-sighted policy[1].   In 702 Hezekiah felt himself strong enough to precipitate a crisis by withholding the tribute due to Assyria ; his example was followed by other vassal-states of Palestine, particularly by Sidon in the north, and Ashkelon and Ekron in Philistia.

So widespread and popular indeed was the anti-Assyrian movement that Padi, the king of Ekron, who remained loyal to his suzerain, was seized by his own subjects and handed over as a hostage to Hezekiah. The nation was carried away by a frenzy of misguided patriotism.   The streets of Jerusalem were crowded by festive throngs drunken with riotous enthusiasm, and blind to the tokens of impending ruin (Isai. xxii.).   Sennacherib meanwhile advanced through Syria into Phoenicia early in 701, and the resistance of the petty kingdoms at once collapsed[2].

Sennacherib's invasion of Palestine, 701.

He first attacked Sidon, and after receiving its submission and that of other places in Phoenicia, marched southwards along the maritime plain, with the intention of reducing the Philistine cities, especially Ashkelon and Ekron, which had taken a leading part in the revolt.   At Altakû[3], not far distant from Ekron, the Assyrians found themselves confronted by a combined force of Egyptians and Arabians, who had hastened to the aid of the Ekronites.   These were speedily overthrown, and Ekron was captured.   The king Padi was surrendered to Sennacherib, and was by him restored to his throne.   A detachment of the Assyrian army was next sent to ravage the territory of Judah, and to destroy a number of its strongholds.

---

[1] See Isai. xxix.—xxxii.

[2] Sennacherib's own account of his campaign is engraved on a cylinder found at Nineveh in 1830 and now preserved at the British Museum.   For a summary see Driver, *Isaiah, his life and times*, ch. vii.; *Authority and Archaeology*, p. 104.

[3] Prob. = Eltekeh of Josh. xix. 44.

According to the account of Sennacherib himself, forty-six fenced cities and smaller towns "without number" were captured; more than 200,000 persons were carried into slavery; Jerusalem was closely invested by the Assyrians and only spared on payment of an enormous ransom, which Hezekiah paid by stripping of their gold and brass even the doors and pillars of the temple. He was forced, as we have seen, to liberate Padi, and to deliver up as hostages to the Assyrian monarch some of the women of his household. These calamities completely exposed the blindness and folly of the statesmen who had persuaded Hezekiah to conclude an alliance with Egypt[1]. The crowning vindication however of Isaiah's policy was yet to come. The Assyrian army withdrew; but Sennacherib was apparently convinced on reflection that a fortified city like Jerusalem was likely to give him trouble, especially at a time when the bulk of his army was engaged in a campaign on the borders of Egypt. He accordingly sent from Lachish[2] a body of troops, commanded by three of his principal officers, to demand the immediate surrender of the city. The historian gives a graphic account of the parley between Sennacherib's Rabshakeh (chief cup-bearer) and the citizens of Jerusalem (2 Kings xviii.). The Assyrian officer endeavoured partly to intimidate, partly to cajole the people to rise against their king, and to open the gates. To this harangue no answer was returned, but Isaiah rekindled Hezekiah's faith in the promises of Jehovah by a reassuring message. The Assy-

Isaiah's confidence, 2 Kings xix. 6 foll.

rian ambassadors withdrew, and found their master engaged in the siege of Libnah. Here tidings reached Sennacherib that Tirhakah, king of Egypt[3], was actually marching against him in person. He

---

[1] For passages of Isaiah which bear on this period, see Driver in *Authority and Archaeology*, p. 107, note.

[2] Lachish was probably one of the forty-six cities of Judah which Sennacherib boasts of having captured.

[3] Tirhakah (Tarku) is so called in the inscriptions because he belonged

again sent messengers to Hezekiah with a letter, in which he peremptorily demanded submission, but the king's only response was to take the missive to the temple and *spread it before the Lord.* His humble prayer for help was heard. Isaiah again came forward with words of encouragement. He had foretold the siege of Ariel (Jerusalem) within a year (Isai. xxix. 1); he now predicted the deliverance of the city and the triumphant overthrow of the Assyrian oppressor. *Thus saith Jehovah concerning the king of Assyria, he shall not come into this city, nor shoot an arrow there, neither shall he come before it with shield, nor cast a mount against it....For I will defend this city to save it for mine own sake, and for my servant David's sake* (2 Kings xix. 32, 34)[1]. The prophet's confidence in the inviolable security of Zion was justified at the very crisis of the peril. A sudden and unexplained catastrophe did undoubtedly overtake the Assyrian army on the borders of Egypt. Herodotus[2] gives a characteristic account of the overthrow. He ascribes it to the havoc wrought by an army of field-mice, which crippled the host by destroying their bow-strings and the leather of their equipments, but most probably the Assyrians were disabled by a sudden and violent outbreak of the pestilence, which has always haunted the southern part of the maritime plain. The Assyrian inscriptions make no mention of this disaster, but the fact is certain that Sennacherib returned discomfited to his own land, and that he never again led an expedition into Palestine. Some years later (681) a revolt against him broke out, in the

The great deliverance, Isai. xxxvii.

to the Ethiopian dynasty, founded by Sabako. The expression "king of Ethiopia" (2 Kings xix. 9) is perhaps used by anticipation. His reign lasted from 698 to 672.

[1] To the same period, roughly speaking, the passage Isai. x. 5 foll. seems to belong.

[2] Hdtus. ii. 141. Prof. G. A. Smith points out the mention in 1 Sam. vi. 4 foll. of golden mice as a symbol of plague (*HGHL*, pp. 157—159).

course of which he was assassinated by two of his sons (Isai. xxxvii. 38)[1].

Thus the faith of Isaiah and his confidence in the protecting care of Jehovah were triumphantly vindicated. It is true that Jerusalem and Judah were reduced to a condition of ruinous devastation; but for the moment the southern kingdom was saved. The deliverance was one of three events in Hebrew history[2] which manifested most signally the grace and power of Israel's God. On this memorable occasion the hand which had ever guided the fortunes of the chosen people was, as it were, laid bare. The destruction of the Assyrians was not merely a marvellous and unforeseen coincidence: it was an impressive disclosure of the Name and the glory of Jehovah[3]. In the hearts of faithful Jews the event was cherished as a sure pledge that even amid the ruin of all earthly hopes and all human resources, Jehovah would not abandon His people *which he foreknew*, would not fail to perform the mercy promised to their fathers *from the days of old* (Mic. vii. 20).

The retreat of Sennacherib's army did not bring to Judah permanent relief or security. As a matter of fact, Hezekiah seems to have quietly returned to his state of dependence, and to have duly paid his annual tribute to Assyria. Esar-haddon, who succeeded his father in 681, renewed the campaign against the cities of Phoenicia and Tirhakah of Egypt. Two campaigns served to make him master of Egypt. He set up an Assyrian vassal-king (Necho) at Memphis (671) and overran the country as far southward as Thebes. For the first time in history an Assyrian monarch was able to describe himself as 'King of the kings of

Assyrian conquests.

---

[1] This incident is corroborated by an inscription given by Driver, *op. cit.*, p. 109.

[2] The reference is to the exodus and to the restoration of the exiles in 536.

[3] Ps. lxxvi. may belong to this period.

Egypt, Paturisi (Pathros, *i.e.* Upper Egypt), and Kûsh (Ethiopia)[1].' It is most probable that the petty states of Palestine were forced to renew their allegiance, and Manasseh, the successor of Hezekiah, is mentioned in a list of twenty-two kings as having been compelled to send materials for the rebuilding of the great arsenal at Nebi-yunus[2]. Assurbanipal (the *Osnappar* of Ezr. iv. 10, Gk. *Sardanapalus*), who ascended the Assyrian throne in 668, led more than one expedition into Egypt[3], which was continually restless under the Assyrian yoke. It was possibly on one of these occasions that Manasseh was carried in chains as a hostage to Babylon[4]. The Chronicler, who relates the incident, ascribes Manasseh's misfortunes to his neglect of the warnings of the prophets (2 Chr. xxxiii. 11). His long reign, which covered a period of nearly sixty years, was marked by a violent popular reaction against the teaching of Isaiah and his adherents, a movement partly no doubt occasioned by Hezekiah's vigorous attempt to suppress the rural sanctuaries and to make the temple at Jerusalem the one centre of the national worship. To some extent also the religious reaction was the outcome of disillusionment. The glowing promises of Isaiah had been understood in a crudely literal sense; predictions of the downfall of Assyria, of the triumph of Judah and her complete liberation from heathen oppression, seemed to have been falsified by events. Accordingly the old idolatries reappeared: the *ashêrim* and the altars dedicated to the service of the local *Baalim*, were restored. Manasseh himself reintroduced from Assyria the adoration of the sun and of the stars, *made his son to pass through the fire*, and practised all the other gloomy and

Manasseh, c. 695—641, 2 Kings xxi.

[1] The record of Esar-haddon's Egyptian campaign is carved upon the rocks of the Nahr-el-kelb, a valley running westward to the sea, a short distance north of Beyrout.

[2] See *Authority and Archaeology*, p. 111.

[3] About 663 the fall of Thebes (No-Ammon) took place. The deep impression produced by its overthrow is illustrated by the allusion of Nahum iii. 8.   [4] See Driver in *op. cit.*, pp. 115, 116.

debased rites which his father had abolished.   Moreover a fierce persecution was set on foot against the disciples of the prophets, and Jerusalem was filled with the innocent blood of Hebrew martyrs and confessors.   It has been thought that Jeremiah (ii. 30) refers to this outbreak of violence in the words, *Your own sword hath devoured your prophets, like a destroying lion*[1], and it is not improbable that a fragment of prophecy incorporated in the book of Micah (chh. vi. and vii. 1—7)[2] really belongs to this period, and gives us a picture of its miseries and corruptions.   The truths however which the prophets had proclaimed were silently cherished in the hearts of the faithful, who patiently waited for the dawn of a brighter day. It may have been the stress of persecution, or the spectacle of the barbarities connected with the revived Moloch-worship, that elicited the sublime utterance contained in Micah vi. 8 respecting Jehovah's true requirement.   The God of Israel demanded of His worshippers no lavish ritualism, no holocausts, no barbarous sacrifice of human life.   *He hath shewed thee, O man, what is good ; and what doth the Lord require of thee, but to do justly, and to love mercy, and to walk humbly with thy God?* Such teaching was indeed a practical summary of the truths on which the great prophets of the eighth century had continually insisted.

During the short reign of Amon, who was murdered by conspirators two years after he came to the throne, the sufferings of the faithful Jews were unabated, but they hailed the accession of his son Josiah with new hope.   As the new king was only eight years old, the state of things remained on the whole what it had been under Manasseh.   But in his eighteenth year Josiah felt himself strong

Amon (c. 641 —639).

Josiah (c. 639 —608).

---

[1] The traditional martyrdom of Isaiah is said to have taken place under Manasseh.

[2] It is possible that the Book of Job, with its profound discussion of the problem of suffering, was composed during Manasseh's reign.

enough to inaugurate a drastic reform of religion on the lines
already laid down by the prophetical party. The
reformation needed was indeed by no means   Condition
merely of a religious character. If we may judge   of Judah.
from the testimony of the prophets Zephaniah and Jeremiah,
the social and moral condition of Judah during the early years
of Josiah's reign was terrible. It seems that faith in Jehovah
was well-nigh dead. There were many open apostates, and a
still larger number who were *settled on their lees* and were
atheists at heart, saying, *Jehovah will not do good, neither will
he do evil* (Zeph. i. 12). And this practical godlessness undermined the foundations of social order. Zephaniah denounces
the violence and fraud practised by the ruling classes; the
profanity and lawlessness of the priests; the pitiless cruelty
and corruption of the judges. *Woe*, he cries, *to her that is
rebellious and polluted, to the oppressing city* (Zeph. iii. 1). The
picture drawn by Jeremiah is equally dark. The sins of Jerusalem—the thefts, murders and adulteries, the injustice, perjury
and extortion openly practised in her midst,—had made her
ripe for judgment. And the root of all these evils, in the eyes
of the prophets, was Judah's national apostasy. She had virtually forsaken her God. *They have forsaken me, the fountain
of living waters, and hewed them out cisterns, broken cisterns,
that can hold no water* (Jer. ii. 13).

The immediate occasion of Josiah's reformation is said to
have been the discovery in the temple by Hilkiah   Events in
the high priest of the Book of the Law[1], but   Western Asia,
there is no doubt that the general course of   640—600.

---

[1] The book so discovered seems to have consisted of Deut. v.—xxvi.,
xxviii. This is proved by the fact that Josiah's reforms followed the lines
laid down in Deuteronomy, especially in regard to (1) the centralisation of
worship, 2 Kings xxiii. 8, 9; (2) the prohibition of the worship of heavenly
bodies, *ibid*. 5, 11; (3) the abolition of high places, obelisks, *ashêrim* etc.,
ibid. 4, 5, 14, 15; (4) the celebration of the passover in Jerusalem, *ibid*.
21 foll. The book may have been compiled during the troubled reign of

events in the contemporary history of Western Asia prepared the way for a revival of the prophetic spirit, and gave considerable impetus to the king's religious zeal.   The last forty years of the seventh century were a period of almost universal unsettlement, disruption, and distress of nations.

Decline of Assyria.

The power of Assyria was declining even before Assurbanipal's death in 626.   A succession of revolts gradually weakened the resources and disintegrated the fabric of the great empire[1].   Towards the close of Assurbanipal's reign Assyria was actually engaged in a life-and-death

The Scythian inroads c. 630.

struggle with Babylonia and Elam, but meanwhile another terrible foe, descending from the regions of the Caucasus, threatened its northern borders.   About the year 630, hordes of Scythians, like the Huns and Mongols of a later age, impelled perhaps by the pressure of an invasion from the north, swarmed into Media, and rapidly overran the whole of Western Asia.   When, after ravaging the Euphrates valley, they poured into Palestine itself, they left Judah unmolested, but they pillaged the cities of Philistia and penetrated by way of the sea-coast to the very borders of Egypt.   The prophets saw in these invading hosts the instruments of God's judgment upon the sins and corruptions of Judah.   The invasion of the Scythians indeed, which almost shattered the mighty power of Assyria, "shook the whole of Palestine into consternation.   Though Judah among her hills escaped them as she escaped the earlier campaigns of Assyria, they showed her the penal resources of an offended God. Once again the dark sacred North was seen to be full of the possibilities of doom[2]."   The exemption of Judah from

Manasseh, and deposited in the temple for security.   See Prof. Ryle in Hastings' *DB*, s.v. ' Deuteronomy.'

[1] Under Psammitichus I. (663—610), Egypt succeeded in throwing off the Assyrian yoke.

[2] G. A. Smith, *The Book of the Twelve Prophets*, vol. ii. p. 16.   Cp. Jer. vi. 1; Zeph. i. 14—18.

the inroads of this terrible foe was sufficiently remarkable to produce a strong though transient feeling in favour of reformation. The movement began with the thorough repair of the temple, a work which was commenced in 621 (the eighteenth year of Josiah's reign). It was at this point of time that the Book of the Law was accidentally discovered in the house of God by Hilkiah the high priest. All the available evidence points to the conclusion that this book either consisted of a portion of the present Book of Deuteronomy, or contained laws closely agreeing in tone and substance with those of Deuteronomy. The book was brought by Shaphan the scribe to the king and read before him. Josiah was greatly disturbed by the threats and warnings contained in its pages; consequently, encouraged by the prophets and their adherents, he at once undertook the work of reformation, on lines suggested by the newly-discovered code. In a formal assembly held at Jerusalem, both king and people bound themselves by a solemn covenant to obey the precepts of the Law. The temple was purged of all idolatrous emblems, and vigorous measures were taken to suppress and demolish all the local sanctuaries.

Discovery of the Book of the Law, 621.

The significance of Josiah's reformation can scarcely be overestimated. In the first place, it was based upon the express directions of a written code, the acceptance of which was a step towards the recognition of an authoritative canon of Scripture. The Law henceforth became the basis of Israel's social and religious life. Secondly, the abolition of the local sanctuaries and the limitation of the *cultus* to the temple at Jerusalem had far-reaching effects both on the character of Jewish worship and on the position of the priesthood. The influence of the hierarchy at Jerusalem was greatly augmented: the ministers of the local 'high places' were degraded to the position of inferior servitors or assistants to the priests of the temple. The heathen elements which debased the worship of Jehovah in the country

The reforms of Josiah, 2 Kings xxiii.

districts were excluded; idolatry was virtually abolished and the monotheism preached by the prophets was established as the national faith. Finally, the demolition of the popular shrines paved the way for a more spiritual type of worship; Josiah's reformation was the first stage in the substitution of the synagogue for the temple, of prayer for sacrifice[1].

The book of Deuteronomy however was not merely a manual of law and worship. It contained much of the social and moral teaching which was characteristic of the eighth century prophets and also of the earliest Mosaic legislation—the teaching embodied in the Decalogue and the primitive 'Book of the Covenant' (Exod. xxi.—xxiii.). It assigned a prominent place to laws of common humanity and brotherly kindness. It proclaimed that the service most acceptable to Jehovah consisted in humility, gratitude, and devotion of heart towards God; in justice, charity and fidelity between man and man. By adopting the principles of Deuteronomy as the law of the theocratic state, Josiah and his people bound themselves to the practice both of a purer and simpler worship, and of a higher morality than had hitherto been customary. It does not seem however that the results of the reformation were deep or permanent. The outward symbols of Judah's apostasy were destroyed or concealed; but the popular outburst of religious zeal was too readily assumed to be a sure guarantee of Jehovah's favour. The iniquities which had flourished before the reformation were still tolerated; the old delusion which prophets had so vehemently denounced was still cherished; it was still commonly believed that punctilious observance of the outward forms of religion would in some way compensate for neglect of plain duties and obligations. This is the point of the indignant protest of Jeremiah vii. 3—11,—a passage which seems to belong to a time when the effects of the recent reformation were visibly disappearing.

Teaching of Deuteronomy.

[1] Cp. Montefiore, *Hibbert Lectures*, p. 187.

So far as the external history of Judah is concerned, the period of Nineveh's decline (626—607) was comparatively uneventful. It was becoming plain that the Assyrian empire was near its dissolution. It was probably during the earlier part of Josiah's reign that the prophet Nahum of Elkosh in southern Judah predicted the imminent overthrow of Nineveh. In his tone and point of view Nahum differs remarkably from Zephaniah. He says nothing of the crying sins of Judah; on the contrary he seems rather to idealize his own country, which in comparison with Nineveh *the bloody city* (Nah. iii. 1), might appear to him relatively guiltless. His prophecy is a shout of triumph over the impending ruin of Judah's ancient oppressor, or rather it gives utterance to a cry of revenge wrung from the heart of the helpless peoples who had for ages groaned beneath the iron yoke of Assyria. Events now moved rapidly. In 625 Babylon under the Chaldaean Nabopolassar finally asserted its independence, and threw in its lot with the *umman-manda*, "hordes of the Manda" (barbarians), *i.e.* the Scythians, who after devastating Mesopotamia laid siege in 609 to Nineveh itself[1]. It was at this moment that Necho II., who had recently (610) ascended the throne of Egypt, formed the project of annexing to his dominions a portion of the moribund Assyrian empire, and accordingly in 608 he advanced with a powerful army into Palestine. Conceiving that the independence of his kingdom was threatened by this movement, Josiah resolved to resist the advance of Necho, and hastily marched northwards to meet the Egyptians. At Megiddo in the plain of Esdraelon, a spot that lay directly on the route from Egypt to the Euphrates, a bloody conflict took place, in which Josiah was defeated and slain[2]. The death of

Prophecy of Nahum: c. 625.

Siege of Nineveh.

Battle of Megiddo, and death of Josiah (608).

---

[1] See Hastings' *DB*, vol. III. pp. 311 and 554.

[2] The battle is alluded to by Herodotus ii. 159: Σύροισι πεζῇ ὁ Νεκὼς συμβαλὼν ἐν Μαγδόλῳ ἐνίκησε.

the king in the prime of life was a fatal blow to the liberties of
Judah, reducing it to a condition of helpless dependence on
Egypt.   Moreover it quenched the rising hopes of the prophetic
party and discredited its cause.   A religious reaction set in
under Jehoahaz, whom the people raised to the
throne in preference to his elder brother.   At
the end of three months, however, he was summoned by Necho to Riblah and was thence carried as a
prisoner into Egypt, where he died.   Necho
appointed Eliakim or Jehoiakim king in the
place of his brother Jehoahaz, but Judah henceforth ranked as a mere province of the Egyptian empire.   Its
internal condition was now one of pitiable weakness and
confusion.

Jehoahaz
(608): 2 Kings
xxiii. 31 foll.

Jehoiakim
(607—597).

The practical effect of Josiah's death on the nation was
to divide it into two factions : an apostate party
which openly abandoned the worship of Jehovah,
and a body of self-styled patriots who endeavoured
by means of costlier and more frequent sacrifices to win back
the lost favour of Jehovah, and to secure the inviolability of
Jerusalem.   The prophetic call to repentance and amendment
was forgotten ; the ordinances of Deuteronomy were ignored ;
the abominations of Manasseh's reign were openly revived.
The king himself was a selfish, covetous and tyrannical ruler,
who was chiefly interested in the erection for himself, by
forced labour, of a splendid palace *cieled with cedar and painted
with vermilion* (Jer. xxii. 13—19).   All that is recorded of
Jehoiakim bear witness to his hardened and reckless character:
his persecution and murder of the prophet Uriah ben Shemaiah,
who had testified against the iniquities of the land (Jer. xxvi.
22 foll.) ; the defiant insolence which caused him to destroy
with his own hands the roll containing the denunciations and
warnings of Jeremiah (Jer. xxxvi. 22 foll.) ; the selfish greed
which led him to satisfy the claims of his Egyptian over-lord
by burdensome taxation of his subjects (2 Kings xxiii. 35).

Factions in
Judah.

The suzerainty of Egypt, however, was not destined to be of long duration.

It appeared doubtful for some time to whom the supremacy of the East would ultimately belong. The siege of Nineveh by the *umman-manda* ended abruptly in 607. The precise circumstances under which Fall of Nineveh (607). the great city fell are obscure. Tradition ascribes it to an overflow of the Tigris which devastated a part of the walls and opened the city to the besiegers. At any rate the overthrow was sudden and complete, and the capture of Nineveh meant the destruction of the Assyrian empire[1]. Meanwhile Nabopolassar the Chaldaean sent his son Nebuchadnezzar to await the advance of the Egyptians who, after the battle of Megiddo, continued their march towards the Euphrates. At Carchemish, on the great river, the Chaldaean and Egyptian armies met in the year 605 (Jer. xlvi. 2). The battle, which resulted in a decisive defeat of the Battle of Carchemish (605). Egyptians and the hasty flight of Necho, sealed the fate of Palestine, and crushed the ambitious hopes of Egypt[2]. Jehoiakim in due course became the vassal of Nebuchadnezzar (601), who had now succeeded to his father's throne. For three years Jehoiakim remained loyal, and then, apparently at the instigation of Necho, revolted. The Chaldaeans, aided by bands of Syrians, Ammonites and Moabites, at once invaded and ravaged Judah (597); and in some insignificant skirmish, as it seems, Jehoiakim was slain. His son Jehoiachin or Coniah succeeded him, but within three Jehoiachin (597): 2 Kings xxiv. 8 foll. months Nebuchadnezzar with his army laid siege to Jerusalem. Resistance was hopeless, and Jehoiachin sur-

---

[1] "The whole history of the world shows no catastrophe equal to the destruction of the Assyrian empire; no nation was ever so completely destroyed as the Assyrian—a just retribution for the abominations which it had perpetrated for centuries." Cornill, *History of the People of Israel*, p. 139.

[2] 2 Kings xxiv. 7.

rendered unconditionally. The king himself was carried captive
to Babylon with the flower of the population : *all the men of*

Zedekiah
(597—586) :
2 Kings xxiv. 18
—xxv. 22.

*might, even seven thousand, and the craftsmen
and the smiths a thousand, all of them strong
and apt for war* (2 Kings xxiv. 16). Over the
remnant that remained Mattaniah, the uncle of
Jehoiachin, was appointed king, his name being changed to
Zedekiah.

The prophet Jeremiah, who had for some time remained in
comparative seclusion, now resumed his public ministry as the
counsellor of complete subjection to the supremacy of Babylon.
While prophets, like Habakkuk, whose book seems to belong to
the critical period before the decisive battle of Carchemish
(605), complained of the brutal violence and insolent pride of
the Chaldaean invader, and uttered the appealing cry, *O Lord,
how long?* Jeremiah stedfastly preached the duty of submission.   In his eyes the Chaldaean invasion was the divinely
ordained chastisement of Judah's sin ; the ruthless enemies of
his country were only fulfilling Jehovah's righteous will.   Respecting the position of affairs in Jerusalem at this time, we find
evidence not only in the writings of Jeremiah, but also in those
of Ezekiel, who was probably one of the captives carried away
after the recent siege (597).   Both prophets draw an appalling
picture of the state of Judah—the prevalence of idolatry of the
most debased type ; the iniquity of the rulers ; the fanatical
and misguided patriotism of the populace ; the delusive promises
of the false prophets, like Hananiah, who proclaimed that
Jehovah's indignation was overpast, that Judah had already
suffered enough, and that the deliverance of the captives from
the yoke of Babylon was imminent (Jer. xxviii.).   Meanwhile,
Jeremiah and Ezekiel fixed their hope on the exiles settled in
Babylon.   These were objects of contempt to their degenerate
countrymen in Judah[1]; but the true prophets perceived that on

---

[1] See Ezek. xi. 15 foll.

them depended the destinies of the Hebrew race. The book of Jeremiah contains a letter to the exiles, who in his eyes constituted the Israel of the future (Jer. xxix.). He bids them patiently submit to their hard lot, and counsels them to *seek the peace of the city* whither they have been carried captive, to turn a deaf ear to the delusive promises of false prophecy, and to wait quietly for the fulfilment of Jehovah's purpose.

In the ninth year of his reign, Zedekiah, who had long been plotting with a view to rebellion, finally broke faith with the king of Babylon, and revolted, relying on empty hopes of support held out by Hophra (or Apries), king of Egypt 588—569[1]. The vengeance inflicted by Nebuchadnezzar was swift and exemplary. With a powerful army he once more invaded Judah and besieged Jerusalem. After an eighteen months' siege, when the city was already hard-pressed by famine, a breach was made in the walls (9 July, 586). Zedekiah with his men of war attempted to escape in the direction of the Jordan valley, but they were pursued, captured, and brought to the presence of the Babylonian monarch at Riblah. The sons of Zedekiah were slain before his eyes; after which he himself was blinded and carried in fetters to Babylon, where he died miserably in prison. A month later Nebuzar-adan, the captain of Nebuchadnezzar's body-guard, arrived at Jerusalem armed with full power to inflict vengeance on the rebellious city. The temple, the palace and all the principal buildings were pillaged and burned; the walls were broken down; the chief officers, priests and notables were sent in chains to Riblah and there put to death; the sacred vessels of the sanctuary were confiscated, and the greater part of the inhabitants were carried

Revolt of Zedekiah.

Siege and fall of Jerusalem, 588—586.

---

[1] On Nebuchadnezzar's invasion of Egypt, of which scanty notices remain in the inscriptions, see Driver in *Authority and Archaeology*, p. 117.

captive to Babylon.   Only *the poorest of the land* were left *to be*

vinedressers and husbandmen.   Over this miserable remnant Gedaliah, the son of Ahikam, was
appointed governor, and established himself at
Mizpeh.   He was a friend of Jeremiah, and
shared his conviction that the only hope of safety for Judah lay
in complete submission to the Chaldaeans.   Scarcely two
months however elapsed before Gedaliah himself fell a victim
to the jealousy of Ishmael, a member of the royal family, by
whom he was treacherously slain.   Ishmael was acting partly in
his own interest, partly at the instigation of Baalis, king of
Ammon, who secretly hoped to annex part of the Judaean
territory to his dominions.   The murder of Gedaliah was
followed by the wholesale massacre of his adherents, and even
of some Chaldaeans who formed part of the governor's retinue.
Ishmael then made prisoners of the surviving inhabitants of
Mizpeh, and attempted to deport them into Ammonite territory.
In this object however he was defeated by Johanan son of
Kareah, who pursued the adventurer, compelled him to re-
linquish his captives, and forced him to seek refuge beyond

the Jordan.   The surviving leaders of the people
were panic-stricken, and fearing the king of
Babylon's vengeance, disregarded the protests of
Jeremiah, and hastily migrated with most of their countrymen
into Egypt.   The greater number of the Jews settled at
Tahpanhes, one of the frontier towns of the eastern Delta[1].
Here a curtain falls upon the life of the heroic prophet who,
in spite of bitter persecution and contumely, had never wavered
in preaching the duty of submission to the king of Babylon, as
the one hope of safety for his people.   He now felt bound to
continue his ministry among the fugitives who had sought an
asylum in Egypt, and there, according to a Jewish tradition,
'amid mournful surroundings of obstinate idolatry, his teaching

---

[1] Jer. xliii. 8.

spurned and misunderstood, his country waste and desolate[1]," he met with a martyr's death at the hands of his compatriots. All his predictions had been literally fulfilled. Jerusalem was already a heap of ruins; its inhabitants were castaways in a foreign land; Ammonites, Philistines, Edomites and other aliens spread over the deserted land. The monarchy of Judah, which had been the centre of such brilliant hopes, was extinct. Israel's career as an independent state seemed to be finally closed. The Jews who eventually returned from exile formed a religious community or church rather than a nation; in a true sense the history of the Hebrews ends with the fall of Jerusalem, and that of Judaism begins.

It should be noticed however that the second book of Kings, which describes the catastrophe and points its moral, closes with a note of hope. Israel had as it were gone down to its grave but not without the prospect of resurrection to a new life. "The flame that had consumed Jerusalem was for Judah a purifying fire; from the seed-field of the exile sown in tears was to spring up a precious and immortal harvest[2]."

---

[1] Montefiore, *Hibbert Lectures*, p. 208.

[2] Cornill, *op. cit.* p. 144.

CHAPTER X.

THE EXILE AND THE RESTORATION.

AT the time when the Hebrews of Judah were carried captive, Babylon had already become, through the exertions of Nebuchadnezzar, the most imposing and magnificent city of the East. Its famous *ziggurat*, the storied temple of Marduk or Bel, its spacious streets and enormous fortifications "mountain-high," its palaces, mansions and terraced gardens, had made it the wonder of the world[1]. The Hebrews, fresh from their little secluded capital and their vine-clad hills intersected by rushing brooks and mountain torrents, must have been well-nigh stupified by the change in their surroundings. They found themselves a forlorn handful of strangers in the midst of a teeming population; a certain number of them were sold as slaves; some were lost to sight in the mazes of the huge city; others were scattered here and there over immense plains watered by endless canals, on the willow-clad banks of which they *sat down and wept* when they *remembered Zion* (Ps. cxxxvii. 1). What hope of a brighter future, what prospect of *an appointed end*, remained to this feeble remnant? As a nation they seemed to have perished. *Our bones*, they cried, *are dried up and our hope is lost; we are clean cut off* (Ezek. xxxvii. 11).

---

[1] See passages in Is. xiii. 19; Jer. l. 38, li. 7, 13, 58, and the description by Nebuchadnezzar himself, quoted by Driver in *op. cit.* p. 120.

The Jews in Babylon.

We know but little of the condition of the exiles during the first few years of their captivity. There is, however, one book of the Old Testament which Their status and condition.
throws light on the position of some few leading
Jews at the court of Babylon, and later at the court of Persia.
The Book of Daniel in its present form belongs to a period
some centuries later than the events recorded
in it, but the hero and reputed author of the Daniel.
narrative is described as rising to high eminence in Babylon,
and as having survived to the third year of Cyrus (535). It is
impossible to determine how far the story of Daniel's career is
historical. We are told that he was one of the Jewish captives
carried away in 606, with three companions, Hananiah, Mishael
and Azariah; that he was carefully nurtured and educated at
the king's court, and became famous for his wisdom and
integrity; that in course of time he secured the good-will of
Nebuchadnezzar himself by revealing and interpreting a dream
which baffled the skill of all the 'wise men' in the kingdom;
and that consequently he was appointed ruler *over the whole
province of Babylon* and chief of the wise men, while his three
friends were also promoted to high offices (Dan. ii. 48, 49).
The fiery trial through which these three were made to pass is
related in a graphic chapter which well illustrates the fierce
and impetuous disposition of Nebuchadnezzar (Dan. iii.).
The figure of Daniel himself is prominent on two subsequent
occasions. He is summoned to interpret the fateful hand-
writing on the wall which disturbed the feast of Belshazzar
(539), and is again rewarded with high honours (Dan. v.).
Finally under "Darius the Mede[1]" he is appointed to be one
of three presidents who were set over the 120 satraps of the

---

[1] The mention of this ruler, otherwise unknown to history, may be
based on a "reflection into the past of Darius the son of Hystaspes," or he
may be identical with Gubaru (Gobryas) of Gutium, the viceroy of Cyrus
at Babylon. See Sayce, *The Higher Criticism and the Monuments*, pp. 528,
529; Driver in *Authority and Archaeology*, p. 127.

Persian empire. Accused of disobedience to a royal decree which prohibited for thirty days the offering of a petition to any god or to any man except to the king himself, Daniel is thrown into a den of lions, but his life is miraculously preserved. His accusers are consigned by Darius to the fate which Daniel escapes ; and a royal decree is issued that throughout the king's dominions, men should *tremble and fear before the God of Daniel,* who *delivereth and rescueth and worketh signs and wonders in heaven and in earth. So,* it is added, *this Daniel prospered in the reign of Darius and in the reign of Cyrus the Persian* (Dan. vi.)[1].

It is now generally acknowledged that the noble and edifying stories of the Book of Daniel are to be regarded as examples of *haggâdoth,* the Jewish name for religious narratives based indeed upon historical facts, but dealing with them freely for purposes of instruction and edification. They do not profess to record the exact incidents of Babylonian history, they merely adapt the history in such a way as may best promote the writer's immediate object, which apparently is to shew how the God of Israel controls events by His providence, how He disposes and turns the hearts of kings as seems best to His wisdom, how He protects His faithful servants in danger and brings them through affliction to honour. The writer's design was to encourage those who were suffering in the persecution of Antiochus, by depicting patterns of faith and constancy for their imitation. Incidentally it is interesting to notice how true to history is the portrait of Nebuchadnezzar, the haughty and

Character of the book of Daniel.

---

[1] In chapp. vii.—xii. Daniel is represented as the recipient of a series of apocalyptic revelations in regard to Israel's future. These chapters show clear traces of the author's acquaintance with events in the reign of Antiochus Epiphanes and his predecessors. If the story of Daniel is historical, it is strange that no mention of him occurs in any Old Testament narrative of the restoration, and that his name is omitted in the list of Israelitish worthies mentioned in Ecclus. xlix.

powerful monarch, whose chief boast it was that he had built or restored the temples of the gods and had made Babylon the most magnificent of ancient cities[1].

The position of Daniel and his friends however was clearly exceptional. We must now turn our attention to the condition of the mass of the Hebrew exiles.

The prophet Jeremiah had predicted that the period of Israel's captivity would be, in round numbers, seventy years (Jer. xxv. 12). Between the fall of Jerusalem in 586 and the actual date of Cyrus's decree for the return of the Jews to Palestine only forty-eight years elapsed. Of the circumstances of the Jews during this space of time, we find some scattered hints in the Book of Ezekiel, and in other late fragments of Hebrew prophecy. On the whole their condition was outwardly peaceful and fairly prosperous. To a great extent the exiles followed the advice of Jeremiah, who had encouraged them to pray for the land of their captivity, *for in the peace thereof* they should *have peace* (Jer. xxix.). They gradually acquired lands and houses, their sons and daughters married, they lived in separate communities, and were apparently allowed to maintain to some extent the social customs and organization of their native land[2]. That the treatment of the Jews by their captors was on the whole favourable is shown by the fact that their captive king Jehoiachin was after the lapse of some years released from prison and honoured by Evil-Merodach with special kindness (2 Kings xxv. 27).

In Babylon, the faithful remnant of those who had earnestly embraced the teachings of the prophets became the nucleus of a new people. There is reason to believe that this remnant had to undergo severe sufferings. From time to time, especially

Effects of the captivity.

---

[1] Dan. iv. 30. Of the religious devotion of Nebuchadnezzar see illustrations in Driver, *The Book of Daniel* (Camb. Bib.), pp. xxvi. foll.

[2] Ezek. viii. 1, xiv. 1, imply that the Jewish elders and judges continued to exercise their office in Babylon.

during the interval before the fall of Jerusalem, false 'nation-alistic' prophets appeared, who endeavoured by illusive pro-mises to incite the exiles to rise and throw off the Chaldaean yoke[1], and it is likely enough that such movements were sternly and perhaps cruelly repressed, without distinction between innocent and guilty. Moreover the faithful few were sorely per-plexed by the fact that though, since the beginning of Josiah's reformation, they had earnestly set themselves to *seek Jehovah* in His own appointed way[2], they were yet involved in the crushing calamity which had overtaken the guilty mass of their compatriots. Thus the exile accentuated the distinction be-tween the true Israel and the bulk of the nation. The narrow and superstitious conception of Jehovah which prevailed among the Jews before the exile could not resist the disintegrating influence of the heathenism of Chaldaea. Consequently a multitude of the Jews not only lost hope in the future of their race, but actually fell away into idolatry; others sought to enrich themselves by trade and usury; and the lukewarm and worldly-minded, who practically abandoned their ancestral faith, taunted and reviled those who who regarded the captivity as a just retribution for national sin, and clung stedfastly to the spiritual hopes and ideals of prophecy.

Thus the faith of even the devout exiles was beset by manifold trials—trials under which in too many cases it gave way altogether. To most of them, deeply imbued as they were with the teaching of Deuteronomy, the loss of the temple and its worship was in itself a crushing privation. It seemed to them to be nothing less than the severance of the tie which bound them to Jehovah. In their despair some were inclined to welcome the visions of false prophets, and to buoy them-selves up with the hope that by some means the chastisement which had descended on the nation would be reversed; others gave vent to rebellious complaints of God's dealings with them;

[1] See Jer. xxix. 21.
[2] Cp. Zeph. ii. 3.

the way of Jehovah, they cried, *is unequal.* The sins of their forefathers were being expiated by a comparatively blameless generation[1]. Others again, crushed by the weight of national and personal calamity, sank into listless apathy and despondency. *Our transgressions and our sins are upon us, and we pine away in them ; how then should we live ?* (Ezek. xxxiii. 10).

But the exiles were not left destitute of religious teaching and consolation. A prophet of strikingly powerful and resolute character was raised up by Jehovah to guide His people through this trying epoch in their history, to preach repentance and to encourage drooping faith. Ezekiel, the son of Buzi, was by office and descent a priest, who had been carried to Babylon with other captives in 597, and had taken up his abode at Tel-abib, beside the river Chebar[2], where a colony of Jews had settled. Here he exercised a kind of spiritual pastorate among his fellow-countrymen, and offered needful counsel and warning to all who cared to consult him[3]. The substance of his exhortations is contained in the first division of his book (Ezek. chh. i.— xxiv.). Like Jeremiah, he insists on the antecedent necessity of Judah's chastisement, and denounces the false prophets who fed the captives with vain hopes, or flattered the remnant in Judaea with the suggestion that the Chaldaean yoke would shortly be broken. He strives to awaken in the faithful the spirit of true penitence, and the sense of personal accountability for the misfortunes that had befallen the nation. But he also cheers them by promises of a time when they shall be restored to their own land with consciences cleansed and hearts renewed by the spirit of Jehovah[4]; when the covenant so often broken

Work of
Ezekiel,
c. 590—570.

---

[1] Ezek. xviii. 2, 25, xxxiii. 17.

[2] Perhaps to be identified with the *Kabaru*, "a large navigable canal not far from Nippur." Driver in *Authority and Archaeology*, p. 143.

[3] These were usually the elders of the Jewish community, who still administered its affairs. Cp. Ezek. viii. 1, xiv. 1, xx. 1.

[4] Ezek. xi. 16 foll.

in the past shall be faithfully observed; when Israel shall be Jehovah's people and He their God[1]. With these addresses to the nation as a whole, Ezekiel combines solemn appeals to individual souls. Let them one and all *cast away* their *transgressions, turn and live,* seeing that Jehovah has *no pleasure in the death of him that dieth,* but will judge *every one according to his ways*[2].

Apart from his pastoral work, however, Ezekiel exercised a powerful influence upon the thought and aspirations of his contemporaries. He was a man of large and comprehensive ideas[3]. He understood the real nature of the opportunity afforded by Israel's enforced sojourn in Babylon. What the nation needed at this crisis was to realize and to guard its distinctive character and vocation. Accordingly, in the latter part of his book, Ezekiel devotes himself to the task of sketching an ideal community, hallowed by the presence in its midst of Jehovah's sanctuary—its institutions based upon the principle of a theocracy, its social and religious life regulated in every detail by the fundamental idea of 'holiness.' Ezekiel's conception was destined to be more fully developed in the age of the Restoration; it seems certainly to have largely influenced the compilers of the 'priestly code.'

Meanwhile, however, religion had to adapt itself to the circumstances of the time. The loss of the temple services was supplied by meetings on the banks of rivers or canals, where common prayer was offered, and necessary acts of ceremonial purification could be performed. In course of time fixed forms of prayer came into use, and buildings were erected for worship[4]. At a later period public reading of the Law became customary,

(margin note: Religious life of the exiles.)

---

[1] Ezek. xiv. 11.

[2] xviii. 29—32.

[3] Ezekiel has been not unjustly compared to such men as Gregory VII (Hildebrand) and Calvin.

[4] *Proseuchae* or *synagogae.* Cp. Juv. iii. 296 (Mayor's note).

and since the sacrificial system was necessarily in abeyance, its place was taken by such rites as could easily be practised at a distance from Palestine, *e.g.* circumcision, fasting, and rigid observance of the sabbath. These ordinances were devoutly cherished by the exiles, and henceforth acquired peculiar importance as being distinctive marks of Jewish faith and nationality[1].

The exile also gave birth to a consciousness of the unique value of Israel's sacred writings. As we have already noticed, the foundation of a canon of Scripture was laid when the book discovered in the temple (621) was officially promulgated and accepted as the basis of a national reformation. Then came the exile, when a period of enforced inactivity and religious reflection succeeded an era of disaster and tumult. *Literary* The result was that the Jews learned to find a *activity during* new interest in the history of their nation : the *the exile.* sacred records were diligently collected and carefully studied, and more than one school of writers devoted itself to the task of compiling, revising and editing afresh the literary monuments of the past. It is indeed possible to distinguish two main groups of *literati* to whose labours the Old Testament scriptures owe to a great extent their present form. On the one hand historians of the Deuteronomic school, *i.e.* *Compilation* those whose views of history and conceptions of *of the histori-* Jehovah were moulded by the peculiar teaching of *cal books.* Deuteronomy, began to gather together into a connected historical work the extant documents that related to the earlier history of Israel. Their work seems to have been gradually brought to completion at different times and by many different hands. The result however may be seen in the narrative portions of the Pentateuch and in the books of Joshua, Judges, Samuel and Kings (the so-called 'former prophets'). The circumstances under which they were compiled explain the peculiar character

---

[1] Ezek. xx. 12, etc.

of these historical books, which may be regarded as forming collectively a kind of *theodicy*, *i.e.* a systematic attempt to justify Jehovah's dealings with His people. The calamities of the nation are uniformly regarded by this school of writers as being the due reward of its sins, especially of its frequent lapses into idolatry. To them it seemed that the religious policy of Jeroboam I. of Israel, and in a later century that of Manasseh of Judah, had brought upon the nation a retribution which the superficial reformation in the reign of Josiah had been unable to avert. The other chief school of exilic writers was sacerdotal.

The 'Priestly Code.'   We must remember that where sacrifice was impossible the occupation of the priesthood was virtually gone. Members of the priestly caste however found a new outlet for their energies in literary work. They devoted themselves to the task of codifying the ancient 'law of holiness[1]' and of compiling that elaborate exposition of Israel's laws and early history which is commonly called the 'priestly code.' These writers were apparently anxious to transmit to another generation, whose privilege it might be to restore the temple and its worship, the ancient tradition of priestly usage. The 'priestly code' was not indeed a new code of law, but rather a kind of detailed account of the immemorial practices and customs connected with the worship of the national sanctuary. "It consisted," we are told by scholars, "of a collection of laws, set in a historical framework, furnished with a brief system of genealogies and chronology which extends in unbroken continuity from beginning to end[2]." This 'priestly code' was during the course of the exile combined with the Deuteronomic work described above, and there is good reason for supposing that the Pentateuch in its present shape was completed some time before Ezra visited Jerusalem in 458.

[1] Levit. xvii.—xxvi. and other passages.
[2] W. H. Bennett, *A Primer of the Bible*, ch. viii. For a synopsis of the priestly code see Driver, *LOT*, p. 159.

The years of exile passed wearily on. The Jews had completely settled down to their life in Babylon, and there seemed no prospect of a change in their condition; but by many the hopes of a restoration to their own land were still eagerly cherished. At last, however, in the year 562 Nebuchadnezzar died. It was his successor Evil-Merodach (Amil-Marduk, 561—560) who is said to have *raised the head* of Jehoiachin, the captive Jewish king. After a reign of less than two years, Evil-Merodach was murdered, and was succeeded on the throne by his brother-in-law Neriglissar (559—556), but as yet the Babylonian empire showed no sign of dissolution. After his premature death in 556, however, a conspiracy was formed against his youthful son, which resulted in the accession of Nabonidus (Nabu-na'id), a man of simple habits and peaceful temperament, who displayed the qualities of a religious enthusiast and antiquarian rather than those of a resolute and sagacious ruler[1]. Declining to reside at Babylon, he practically handed over to his son Belshazzar the task of government. Before long his empire was threatened by a new race of conquerors. In the year 549 the famous warrior Cyrus, "King of Anshan" (a district in the south of Elam), who had raised himself to a position of supremacy in his native country (Elam), attacked and dethroned Astyages of Media, seized Ecbatana, and by the year 546 found himself, as "King of Persia," master of an empire extending from the Caspian to the Persian Gulf, and from the border of Assyria to the Indus. The rise of this formidable power was obviously a menace to the older monarchies of western Asia. In 547 Nabonidus was forced by the rapid expansion of the Medo-Persian kingdom to form a defensive alliance with Egypt, Lydia and Sparta. The same year, however, witnessed the capture of Sardis and the fall of the Lydian king Croesus.

Events in Babylon.

Rise of Cyrus, c. 560.

---

[1] According to the inscriptions he restored the ancient temples of *Sin*, the moon-god, both at Haran and Ur.

During the next seven years, Babylon neglected the opportunity of strengthening its defences, and when in 539 Cyrus turned his arms against the unwieldy empire, its power collapsed with startling suddenness.   In 538, owing it is said to the treachery of the Chaldaean priesthood, Gubaru the lieute-

Fall of Babylon 538. nant of Cyrus obtained possession of the great city without striking a serious blow.   Cyrus himself entered Babylon about 3 months later (3 Oct. 538). Nabonidus was deposed and banished; his son, the regent Belshazzar, was put to death, and Cyrus was welcomed with enthusiasm as master of Babylon.   Within the short space of twelve years the Persian warrior had subdued the whole of western Asia, and thus the hegemony over the East passed from the Semitic to the Indo-European race.

The conquests of Cyrus were undoubtedly hailed with special fervour by the Jewish community.   The exiles had watched with intense eagerness the advance of one who seemed to be marked out by Providence as the future deliverer of Jehovah's oppressed people.   It was about the time when Cyrus became king of Media (550) that the captives in Babylon first heard the thrill-

The prophet of the exile. ing voice of the great unnamed prophet whose writings are included in the last twenty-seven chapters of the book of Isaiah.   We can imagine with what emotions they hailed the word of consolation which proclaimed the near approach of Israel's restoration, the renewal of its national life, the imminent downfall of the idolatries of Chaldaea, the future glory of Israel, the world-wide expansion of the kingdom of God.   In Cyrus the prophet taught his oppressed people to see the *shepherd* of Jehovah who should perform all His pleasure; the anointed one before whom the strength of kings should melt away and the gates of iron and brass be broken in pieces[1].   The Persian conqueror did not

[1] Isai. xliv. 28, xlv. 1, etc.   In xliv. 28, where Cyrus (Koresh) is called Jehovah's 'shepherd,' there is probably an allusion to the Elamitish word *Kuraš* ('shepherd').

indeed rise to the level of these glowing anticipations. From motives of policy, as it seems, he refrained from interfering with the idols of Babylon. On the contrary, he represented himself as the favoured servant of Marduk and the vindicator of his honour and prestige, which the religious policy of Nabonidus had impaired[1]. Next, impelled by a natural desire to get rid of disaffected elements in the vast population now subject to him, rather than by any special inclination towards monotheism, he issued an edict giving permission to the Jews and to exiles from other parts of Asia to return to their own land. By this wise measure Cyrus removed a source of danger to his new empire, and at the same time dispersed into its more remote and outlying regions, populations bound to his throne and person by ties of gratitude. He recognized that in view of a possible rupture with Egypt it was important to maintain a friendly and loyal commonwealth on the Egyptian border.

Accordingly permission was given to the Jews to return to Palestine. They were not only allowed to carry with them the sacred vessels which had been taken from the temple, but were expressly encouraged by the edict of Cyrus to rebuild the ruined sanctuary at Jerusalem.

The leader of the first band of exiles who availed themselves of the king's decree was a descendant of David named Sheshbazzar, 'prince (*nâsi*) of Judah,' otherwise known as Zerubbabel, the son of Shealtiel[2];   The return.

---

[1] See inscriptions given by Driver in *Authority and Archaeology, etc.*, p. 128.

[2] Cp. Ezra i. 8, ii. 2, iii. 8, v. 14; Zech. iv. 6. The identification of Sheshbazzar with Zerubbabel is disputed, but is defended by Prof. Ryle, *Ezra and Nehemiah* (*Camb. Bible for Schools*), p. xxxi. Others think it more probable that Zerubbabel was a conspicuous Jewish noble, and Sheshbazzar a Persian or Babylonian official appointed by Cyrus to superintend the details of the migration of the exiles. (So Stade.) In any case we find Zerubbabel occupying the position of governor (*pekhah*) *in Ezra* iii. and v. See also G. A. Smith, *The Book of the Twelve Prophets*, ii. pp. 199, 200.

and the number of those who joined the expedition was 42,360. Probably this body included representatives of the different tribes and families, so that in a real sense the return might be described as a national movement. Under the direction of twelve elders, headed by Zerubbabel and the priest Jeshua, the son of Jozadak, the journey across the desert was safely accomplished and the restored exiles found themselves once more established in their ancient home. A few months elapsed during which they were engaged in rebuilding their own ruined homes in the neighbourhood of Jerusalem. In the autumn, however, they assembled for the purpose of re-erecting on its ancient site the great altar of burnt-offering. The offering of the daily sacrifice was renewed, and the feast of Tabernacles was duly observed: but the chief object with which the expedition had been undertaken remained as yet unaccomplished: *the foundation of the temple of Jehovah was not yet laid* (Ez. iii. 6),

Rebuilding of the temple begun. though preparations for the work had been set on foot. It is by no means clear when a beginning was actually made; but the most probable view is that in the second year after the return (*i.e.* in 536) the foundation-stone of the new *house of God* was laid. The historian gives a vivid description of that memorable scene; he tells how the priests and Levites sounded trumpets and cymbals, how the chant of praise was mingled with *a great shout* of exultation, how *the ancient men that had seen the first house* wept aloud, *so that the people could not discern the noise of the shout of joy from the noise of weeping* (Ez. iii. 10 foll.). But apparently the work of restoration was almost immediately suspended, owing to the opposition of the Samaritans[1], who

[1] This name included (1) the foreign colonists who were introduced by Sargon in 722 (2 Kings xvii. 24), and at a later time by Esar-haddon and Assurbanipal (Ezra iv. 2, 10), (2) the remnant of Israelites who were not carried away after the fall of Samaria, but who under the pressure of foreign immigration had fallen into idolatrous practices, though they still nominally worshipped Jehovah (Ezra iv. 1).

took offence at the decided refusal with which the Jews met their offer of cooperation, and who became thenceforward the implacable enemies of the restored community.

For 16 years this state of things continued, and meanwhile the condition of the 'children of the captivity[1]' was far from enviable. Judaea seems at this time to have suffered from prolonged famine and scarcity, and the Jews, hemmed in on every side by alien and hostile tribes, sank under the pressure of their difficulties into a state of listless apathy and despondency. Shortly however after the accession of Darius Hystaspis, who in 522 raised himself to the Persian throne, after its brief usurpation by a Magian adventurer, the venerable prophet Haggai and his youthful contemporary Zechariah roused their countrymen by their stirring appeals

Preaching of Haggai and Zechariah.

to a new effort (520). The prophets in fact understood the real gravity of this crisis in Israel's history. Henceforth, the one bond of unity for the widely-dispersed nation must necessarily be its religion, of which the temple was the visible centre and symbol. To leave the national sanctuary in ruins was "a practical denial of the truth which gave meaning to their return from exile[2]." Haggai sternly reproached the Jews for the supineness with which they had delayed for so long the reparation of the temple. He declared that the hardships and distresses from which they had suffered were the due penalty of their neglect. *Is it time,* he asks, *for you yourselves to dwell in your cieled houses while this house lieth waste? Now therefore thus saith the Lord of hosts: Consider your ways* (Hag. i. 3). The warnings of Haggai and the encouraging assurances of Zechariah had their effect. The work was resumed by permission of Tattenai the Persian governor of the province, who appealed for direction to Darius. The discovery of the original edict of Cyrus satisfied the king; the Persian officials were enjoined to give the Jews

---

[1] Heb. *benê hag-golah*, Ez. iv. 1, vi. 16, etc. A similar phrase is 'children of the province,' Ez. ii. 1.

[2] Kirkpatrick, *The Doctrine of the Prophets*, p. 427.

all needful assistance[1], and the temple was finally completed and dedicated early in the sixth year of Darius (516). The completion of the temple and the reorganization of its worship no doubt involved also the reconstitution of the priesthood. The high priest became the chief of a hierarchy which included priests, levites and temple servants (*Nethinim*)[2]. The priests were distributed in four classes or families: the sons of Jedaiah, of Immer, of Pashhur, and of Harim (Ezra ii. 36—39); as the high priesthood was an hereditary office, there arose a kind of ecclesiastical dynasty in Judah, the history of which will occupy us in a later chapter.

The course of events during the next sixty years is unknown. It has been conjectured that Zerubbabel, as the surviving representative of the house of David, was raised to royal dignity, and perhaps perished in some vain attempt to assert the independence of Judaea[3]. At any rate the death of Zerubbabel must have extinguished the last hopes of a restoration of the ancient monarchy. Accordingly a period of grievous depression and disillusionment followed. Judaea was subjected to the despotic control of a Persian satrap[4]; and although the Jews were allowed a certain degree of autonomy in domestic concerns under the rule of their high priest, into whose hands the supreme authority naturally passed after the downfall of the Davidic princedom, they probably chafed beneath an oppressive burden of taxation and other evils that were inseparable from Persian domination. Once more Israel was compelled to fix its hopes on the future. The present circumstances of the nations were not materially different from those of former days[5], and some light

The Persian domination.

---

[1] Ezra vi. 8—10.

[2] *Nethinim*, lit. 'given': slaves devoted to the service of the priests.

[3] Zech. vi. 11—13 (the account of the crowning of Zechariah) is by some supposed to favour this conjecture.

[4] Mal. i. 8.

[5] Schultz, *Old Testament Theology*, vol. i. p. 333. "It is beyond

is thrown on the condition and temper of the restored exiles at this time by the short book of Malachi. It presents us with the picture of a community "disappointed and ill at ease[1]," sullenly enduring the exactions of the Persian government and the many vexatious restraints and discomforts of life in Palestine. The faith and ardour of the first generation of exiles did not animate their successors. The old distinctions between the upper classes and the poor whom they oppressed presently reappeared; the maintenance of the priestly order and of the temple-worship was commonly looked upon as a costly burden. Enthusiasm gave way to despondency and indifference. The echo of rebellious complaints reaches us in the pages of Malachi. *Every one that doeth evil is good in the sight of Jehovah. Where is the God of judgement? It is vain to serve God: and what profit is it that we have kept his charge? And now we call the proud happy; yea, they that work wickedness are built up; yea, they tempt God, and are delivered.* Even the injunctions of the Law were evaded or disobeyed; the observance of the sabbath was neglected. What was more serious, zeal for the maintenance of Israel's distinct and separate character died down, the result being that the practice of intermarriage with the semi-pagan 'people of the land' was tolerated, while wives of Hebrew race were lightly divorced. These alliances with aliens were even encouraged by the priesthood for the sake of supposed advantages, social or political; but it is likely that in some quarters there was a genuine though perhaps premature desire to realise in fact the universalistic aspirations of the prophets, and to welcome aliens into the fold of Israel. The result however was that Judaism at this time ran a risk of losing its

Decay of faith, Mal. ii., iii.

question that the main characteristic of the Persian epoch was galling bondage and heavy burdens." Possibly the pessimism of Ecclesiastes is coloured by reminiscences of the miseries endured by the Jews in Palestine during the Persian period.

[1] Montefiore, *Hibbert Lectures*, p. 295.

distinctive character, and the growing laxity naturally led to the

Rise of a party of zealots.

formation of a party of opposition.   There were zealots—men who *feared Jehovah and thought upon his name*[1]—who energetically assisted the prevailing tendency, and who clung the more tenaciously to the precepts and hopes of their religion.   In common with their opponents, they were sensible of the apparent failure of Jehovah's promises to His people, but they recognized the real cause of their disappointment in the faithlessness and indifference of the Jews themselves.   They believed that the only hope of a future fulfilment of the prophetic visions lay in a more strenuous observance on Israel's part of the revealed conditions of Jehovah's covenant.   It was this party, small in numbers but resolute in temper, that welcomed the arrival of Ezra in 458.   At the same time the Jews who remained in Babylon, and who had been able tranquilly to develope and organize a definite system of law and theology, were occasionally disquieted by tidings which reached them from time to time concerning the religious and moral condition of the *benê hag-golah.*

Meanwhile events of grave import were happening beyond

Decline of Persian supremacy.

the horizon of Palestine.   The Ionian revolt had brought the Persians into collision with the free states of Greece.   In the year 490 the battle of Marathon had checked the advancing wave of Persian invasion ; ten years later the second great expedition under Xerxes was shattered at Salamis (480), Plataea and Mycale (479).   As the prestige of the huge empire decayed, and the old hardihood and honesty of the Persian character was gradually sapped by luxury and ease, the rule of the provincial satraps became more corrupt and oppressive; it is probable enough that during the reign of Xerxes (485—465) the property and even the lives of the Jews scattered throughout the length and breadth of the

---

[1] Mal. iii. 16.   To this party Malachi himself probably belonged.

empire lay at the mercy of a capricious and petulant tyrant[1]. In 465 however he was succeeded by Artaxerxes I., who perhaps for political reasons aimed at conciliating the Jews in Babylon, and with that object in view encouraged and supported the visit of Ezra to Judea in 458.

Ezra was a Zadokite priest and scribe (*sopher*), specially qualified for the task which he now undertook by his intimate knowledge of 'the law of Moses.'   Mission and work of Ezra. Indeed, the instrument by which he hoped to renovate the religious life of his countrymen in Judaea was that 'Book of the Law' which during the exile had been carefully revised, enlarged and finally edited in its present form. There can be no doubt that as a scribe Ezra himself had taken an active part in this important work (Ezra vii. 6). He now started from Babylon supported by the authority of the Persian monarch, who issued a commission in writing directing Ezra *to inquire concerning Judah and Jerusalem, according to the law of his God* which was in his hand (Ezra vii. 14). The rescript not only commanded the Persian officials *beyond the river* to assist Ezra liberally in his enterprize, but even granted to the Jewish priests and temple-servants the privilege of exemption from toll, tribute, and custom.   The decree ended by giving a remarkable injunction to Ezra: *Appoint* (so it ran) *magistrates and judges, which may judge all the people that are beyond the river, all such as know the laws of thy God; and teach ye him that knoweth them not.* The law of God and *the law of the king* were alike to be enforced by severe penalties (Ezra vii. 24—26).

With a caravan of nearly 1600 men, including a certain number of priests, levites and *Nethinim*, Ezra   Ezra's journey to Judaea, started from Babylon; after a brief halt at the   458. river Ahava[2] for the purpose of united fasting and

---

[1] The story of Esther may well be based upon some historical incident, arising out of the "Jew-hatred" which was a feature of the ancient as of the modern world.

[2] 'Ahava' was the name of a place where an influential colony of Jews

prayer, the caravan crossed the desert and reached Jerusalem safely (Aug. 458). Ezra brought with him rich offerings for the temple, sent by the leading Jews in Babylonia, and even by Artaxerxes himself[1]. His avowed object was to carry out a reform of the temple ceremonial on the basis of the completed Law-book, which was substantially our 'Pentateuch'; but the first task which confronted him was that of dealing with the mixed marriages—an abuse the extent of which was apparently unknown to him before his arrival in Palestine. Ezra was horror-stricken by the discovery that many of the leading Jews, and even some of the priests, had taken foreign wives. His emotion found utterance in a penitential prayer, which evidently made a profound impression on the assembled people. Ezra seized his opportunity, and imposed on the congregation an oath that the strange wives should be put away. The promise however was by no means easy to fulfil on the spur of the moment. A commission of elders was accordingly appointed to investigate the matter, but the number of offenders was so large that the process of inquiry lasted for three months. Although a considerable section of the people seems to have been roused to enthusiasm by Ezra's zeal, and to have warmly supported his action, there was from the first an influential party in Jerusalem which was hostile to reform, partly on religious, partly on social and political grounds[2]. For the moment the spirit of puritanism triumphed; many 'strange wives' with their children were expelled, but

was probably settled. The place gave its name apparently to the stream on which it stood.

    [1] Ezra viii. 25 foll.

    [2] Ezra x. 15. It has been surmised that the beautiful book of Ruth was intended to support the views of those who opposed Ezra's reforms. "Its object is to show that marriages even with foreigners of full blood need have no evil influence upon religion, seeing that the alien woman may soon learn to be as Jewish as native Jewesses themselves." Montefiore, *Hibbert Lectures*, p. 371. But see on the other side Driver, *LOT*, p. 454.

doubtless Ezra's policy sowed the seeds of bitter resentment and animosity both within and without Jerusalem.

The memoirs of Ezra are interrupted at this point[1] so that in attempting to trace the events of the next twelve years we are dependent on conjecture. It is highly probable that Ezra incurred widespread unpopularity by his drastic action in the matter of the mixed marriages, and that he, together with the party of zealots who supported him, gradually lost all influence in Jerusalem. If, as seems likely, he next undertook the task of rebuilding the walls of Jerusalem, we must suppose that owing either to some unexplained accident, or to the intrigues of Ezra's opponents, the attempt was abandoned. In the fourth chapter of the book of Ezra (which is apparently misplaced), we are told that the suspicions of Artaxerxes were aroused by the representations of the Samaritans, and that he gave orders for the immediate stoppage of the work. The Samaritans supported by the Persian officials hastened to Jerusalem, produced the king's decree, and compelled the Jews to cease from repairing the walls *by force and power* (Ezr. iv. 23). The walls which had begun to rise from the foundations were again destroyed, and Ezra himself seems to have been either banished outright or forced to retire into privacy. In any case he and his adherents remained for some years inactive.

In 445 however (the twentieth year of the reign of Artaxerxes), the party of reform was inspired with fresh hopes by the arrival of Nehemiah, a Babylonian Jew and the favoured cup-bearer of Artaxerxes, who, deeply moved by the depressing tidings that reached him from 'the province,' asked the king's permission to revisit his native city and to repair its ruined walls. Besides being armed with full powers as governor (*pekhah*), Nehemiah was provided with a body-guard of Persian troops, and also

Failure of Ezra's efforts.

Arrival of Nehemiah, 445.

---

[1] They may have been intentionally suppressed in view of the failure of Ezra's efforts.

brought with him commendatory letters to the different satraps *beyond the river*. He was thus enabled to defy the hostile schemes of the Samaritans and other enemies of Judah. Undaunted by the threats and machinations of these irreconcilable adversaries, Nehemiah resolutely set to work. He tells us how he made a circuit of the city by night, riding on his mule

State of
Jerusalem.

round the ruined walls; how he found the ravine of the Kidron so entirely choked with masses of rubbish that *there was no place for the beast that was under* him *to pass*; how he followed the course of the torrent northwards, surveying the scene of desolation, and finally returned to *the gate of the valley*[1] whence he had started. Without delay he appealed to the patriotism of the inhabitants: *Ye see the evil case that we are in, how Jerusalem lieth waste, and the gates thereof are burned with fire : come and let us build up the wall of Jerusalem, that we be no more a reproach*[2]. The

Rebuilding
of the walls.

appeal was instantly responded to, and the work of rebuilding the walls began in earnest. The whole of the able-bodied population under the direction of men belonging to the leading families took part in it. Nehemiah himself superintended the building with sleepless vigilance, stationed at a spot, where, in case of a hostile attack, he could immediately sound an alarm. The builders and the bearers of burdens, each girded with his weapon, toiled with all their might, while others, equipped with shields, spears and bows, mounted guard. In the short space of fifty-two days, during which Nehemiah and his servants neither left their posts nor even removed their clothes, the walls were completed and the gates set up (Sept. 444)[3]. A solemn service of

---

[1] Neh. ii. 13 foll. The 'gate of the valley' probably corresponded to the western or 'Jaffa' gate, 'the valley' being the 'ravine of the son of Hinnom.' See Ryle, *ad loc.*

[2] Neh. ii. 17.

[3] It is natural to compare this incident in Jewish history with a somewhat similar work carried out by the Athenians chiefly at the instigation

dedication was held amid great rejoicing (Neh. xii. 27 foll.). The courage and resolution of the new governor had frustrated the designs, both of the declared enemies of the Jews (Sanballat the Horonite, Tobiah the Ammonite, and Geshem the Arabian are particularly mentioned), and of those within the city who by means of alleged oracles treacherously sought to weaken his hands.

It was probably soon after the dedication of the walls that the memorable event described in Neh. viii. took place,—the public promulgation of the Law in the open space before the 'water gate' of Jerusalem.   Ezra relying on the support of the new governor now emerged from his retirement.   An opportunity had at last arrived for carrying out his cherished project, and reorganizing the national life on the basis of the Law-book which had been brought from Babylon, but which had hitherto been known only to the priesthood.   The completion of the walls had doubtless rekindled the national enthusiasm of the Jews, and revived their desire to maintain their distinctive character as a 'peculiar people.'   Ezra's public appearance with the book of the Law in his hands was evidently the response to a popular demand (Neh. viii. 1).   On the first day of the civil year (Tisri 1), a great assembly was held for the purpose of hearing the contents of the new code.   Standing on a pulpit of wood, Ezra read the book aloud in the audience of the people *from early morning until midday,* the lections being occasionally interrupted by parenthetic comments and explanations[1].   The effect on the audience was remarkable.   They broke forth into lamentations at hearing *the*

Reappear-ance of Ezra.

Publication of the Law-book.

of Pericles.   The 'long walls' which connected Athens with the sea were completed in 455, about ten years before Nehemiah's arrival in Jerusalem. Thuc. i. 107, 108, ii. 13.

[1] Such seems to be the meaning of Neh. viii. 8.   It is not clear whether Ezra was the only reader or whether he was relieved by a succession of Levites specially chosen for the task.   See Ryle *ad loc.*

words of the law which as a nation they had in so many particulars transgressed. But grief was unsuited to the 'holiness' of such a day. Nehemiah bade them depart in peace, and celebrate the feast with gladness. *Neither be ye grieved*, he said, *for the joy of Jehovah is your strength.* The reading was resumed on the following day, when directions were read prescribing the observance of the feast of Tabernacles, which ordinarily began on the fifteenth, and lasted till the twenty-second day of Tisri. Preparations were at once made for the due celebration of this feast. During the seven days of its continuance Ezra continued to read aloud portions of the Law,

Renewal of the covenant. and two days after its close (Tisri 24) a strict fast was proclaimed and a solemn confession was made of the past transgressions of the people[1]. The occasion seemed suitable for a renewal of the covenant between Israel and Jehovah. The covenant was formally sealed and signed by Nehemiah, and by chosen representatives of the priesthood and people. It pledged the community to strict obedience to the Law, especially in regard to two particulars : abstention from the custom of intermarriage with aliens, and careful observance of the sabbath, the sabbatical year and other stated feasts. At the same time various minor regulations for the payment of tithes, the care of the sanctuary and its services, etc., were agreed to. Perhaps the most noteworthy ordinance was that which provided that every Israelite should contribute yearly the third part of a shekel towards defraying the expenses of the temple worship (Neh. x. 32).

The movement we have briefly described marked a turning-point of deep interest in Jewish history. It laid the foundation-stone of Judaism ; it definitely transformed the nation into a congregation or church ; it made the Law not merely the basis of civic and social life, but the common possession of each individual Israelite. Hitherto familiar only to the priests, the

[1] According to the LXX. it was Ezra who uttered the noble and pathetic prayer recorded in Neh. ix. 6—38, but see Ryle's note *ad loc.*

Law became a people's book, and thus constituted the chief
bond of union between the Jews of the disper-   Social enact-
sion and the 'children of the captivity,' as the   ments of
restored exiles were usually called[1].   Meanwhile   Nehemiah.
however, other matters were pressing for immediate attention;
serious social evils had arisen at Jerusalem; the condition of
the poorer Jews especially cried for redress.   They complained
that the burden of Persian taxation had compelled them to
borrow of their wealthy neighbours at an exorbitant rate of
interest.   In default of repayment they were forced to mortgage
their scanty fields and farms, and in some cases had even been
obliged to sell their children as slaves (Neh. v.).   The governor
did not shrink from boldly rebuking the nobles for their
inhuman treatment of their 'brethren.'   As a remedy for the
prevailing distress he abolished the practice of lending on
usury, and required the rich money-lenders to restore the property which they had accepted as security from the borrowers.
By such measures and by the force of his own example Nehemiah did much to improve the social condition of the Jews.
He tells us that during the twelve years of his administration
he refrained from eating *the bread of the governor;* in other words
he defrayed the necessary expenses of his household at his own
cost.   How far he was able however to maintain the strictness
of the new *régime* which he inaugurated, we are not told.   In
the year 433 he was for some reason obliged to   Second visit
return to Persia.   When he again visited Jerusa-   of Nehemiah,
lem in 432 he found that some of the abuses,   432.
which he had formerly repressed, had already revived; for
example, laxity in the observance of the sabbath and intermarriage with aliens.   Even the priesthood had proved unfaith-
ful in this particular.   Eliashib the high priest had actually
allied himself by marriage to the Ammonite Tobiah[2], and had
assigned him a lodging within the precincts of the temple.

---

[1] Cp. Ezra iv. 1, vi. 16, 19, 20, etc.

[2] The exact relationship is not stated, but see Neh. vi. 17.

Eliashib's own grandson had married the daughter of Sanballat the Horonite, and as he refused to separate from his alien wife, he was expelled from Jerusalem (Neh. xiii. 28). This incident led to important consequences. The expulsion from Jerusalem of Sanballat's son-in-law gave the signal for the secession of many leading Jews, priests as well as laymen, who were either bitterly opposed on principle to the reforms of

Origin of the Samaritan community. Nehemiah, or had themselves contracted mixed marriages. It is probable that Eliashib's grandson is to be identified with Manasseh, the founder of the schismatic synagogue and peculiar worship of the Samaritans, who eventually, on the basis of a modified Pentateuch, formed themselves into an independent sect[1]. On the other hand, the departure of the malcontents welded the loyal Jews who remained into a compact and harmonious community.

Nothing more is known of Nehemiah's work at Jerusalem. Tradition ascribes to him the foundation of a library, and the collection of some of the sacred books[2]. It is indeed very likely that the process of collecting into a single volume the writings of the prophets began during the time of his administration. In any case Nehemiah had just cause to congratulate himself on the outcome of his *good deeds* (Neh. xiii. 14) as governor of his people. He had successfully accomplished the main objects to which he had devoted himself with high-minded zeal, unflinching courage, and shrewd worldly wisdom; namely, the separation of the Jews from idolatrous aliens, the re-organization of the temple worship, and the establishment of the Law as the basis of Israel's life and polity. It is with reason that he repeatedly prays: *Remember unto me, O my God, for good, all that I have done for this people* (Neh. v. 19).

---

[1] See Josephus, *Antiq.* xi. 7, 8.

[2] See 2 Macc. ii. 13.

CHAPTER XI.

COMPARATIVELY few facts that throw light on the condition of the Jews during the later period of the Persian domination have been recorded by secular historians. But this stage in their history was unquestionably of great importance. The nation can hardly be said indeed to have had any distinct political existence. Judaea was an insignificant province of an empire which stretched from the coasts of Asia Minor to the Indus. The Jews in Palestine formed a religious community or 'congregation' rigidly separated from aliens by their peculiar customs and traditions; but many of them were in course of time compelled to serve in the Persian armies[1], while others, as traders, slaves[2], or prisoners of war, were scattered in different parts of the empire and even beyond its borders, and thus came into contact with the culture and religious ideas of various alien races. Besides the vast number who remained in Babylonia, there were large communities of Jews in Susa and

The Jews under the Persian régime.

[1] Jewish mercenaries had served in the army of Psammitichus I. of Egypt as early as 650 B.C.

[2] Cp. Joel iii. 6, which alludes to the traffic of Phoenician slave-dealers in Judahite captives.

Ecbatana, in Mesopotamia and Syria, in the seaport towns of Asia Minor, and in the Egyptian Delta. These formed the original nucleus of the 'Dispersion,' which afterwards played so prominent a part in the early spread of Christianity.

One result of the altered circumstances in which the Jews were now placed was the gradual substitution of Aramaic for Hebrew. The adoption of this dialect was a necessity of their position, situated as they were in the midst of nations who used Aramaic, and with whom they were brought into daily contact. " In those days Aramaic was the language of business and of government in the countries between the Euphrates and the Mediterranean, just as English is in the Highlands of Scotland, and so the Jews forgot their own tongue for it, as the Scottish Celts are now forgetting Gaelic for English[1]." It is curious that while the Jews were continually becoming more exclusive in their religion they were unable to resist the influences which gradually substituted for their ancestral language the dialect of Syria. By the time of Christ, Hebrew to the mass of the people had become an unintelligible tongue.

The Aramaic dialect.

At this point may be appropriately mentioned a book of the Old Testament which, like the book of Daniel, throws some light on the position and aspirations of the more conspicuous Jews who were brought into contact with the court of Persia. The book of Esther relates how the young Jewess, Esther, rose to be the queen of Ahasuerus (Xerxes, 485 —465), and how she succeeded at an important crisis in preventing the destruction of her compatriots. The book is probably to be regarded as a religious romance, the principal aim of which is to explain the origin of

The Book of Esther.

[1] W. Robertson Smith, *OTJC*, p. 35. Prof. W. R. Smith points out that Aramaic words, idioms and modes of thought already appear in some of the later O.T. books. While Hebrew continued after the return from Babylon to be the *liturgical* and *learned* language of the Jews, the vernacular language of Palestine became to a constantly increasing extent Aramaic.

the feast of *Purim*. Like the story of Daniel, it may rest on a basis of historical fact, though the incidents recorded in it have no direct bearing on the general course of Jewish history. The book however illustrates the capacity of the Jews for making their influence felt amid their heathen surroundings; it also reflects the fierce nationalistic temper which prevailed among them at the time when the book was probably written: *i.e.* soon after the downfall of the Persian empire (332)[1]. It has often been noticed that the name of God is not mentioned in the book, but it is nevertheless the product of an unshaken faith in the providence of God, overruling the destinies of His people, and raising up fitting instruments for their deliverance[2].

During the post-exilic period, and especially after the overthrow of the Persians at Marathon and Salamis, the gradual dispersion of the Jews necessarily brought them into connection with the Greek race, and exposed them to the subtle influences of the Hellenic genius and culture. We must remember that the age of Pericles nearly coincided with the period of Ezra's activity, and in all probability Socrates was a teacher at Athens while Nehemiah was still governor of Jerusalem. Less than a century later came the conquests of Alexander (334—323) which not only gave a fresh impetus to the spread of Hellenic ideas and customs, but also prepared the way for a wider dispersion of the Jewish race. A large body of Jewish colonists settled in the newly-founded city of Alexandria[3] where they were allowed to enjoy special privileges; in wealth and culture these Jews of Alexandria gradually became pre-eminent among their

Contact of the Jews with the Greeks.

---

[1] Sayce, *The Higher Criticism* etc., p. 475. "The story of Esther is an example of Jewish *haggâdah*, which has been founded upon one of those semi-historical tales of which the Persian chronicles seem to have been full." Cp. Driver, *LOT*, p. 483.

[2] See as illustrating this point the Greek additions to Esther in the Apocrypha, esp. [Esth.] xiii. 8—18.

[3] Its foundation took place in 331 B.C.

co-religionists, and at the opening of the Christian era their numbers were estimated at a million. The process of assimilating Hellenic modes of thought naturally went on more rapidly at Alexandria than elsewhere. But everywhere the Greek influence was at work, insensibly modifying both the character and the religious ideas of the Jewish people, and preparing it in manifold ways for the advent of the Redeemer.

On the other hand we must not overlook the opposite impulse which was at work during the post-Nehemian period—the impulse towards separation and exclusiveness, which has left its traces in the later canonical literature. There were in fact two ideals present to the Jewish mind after the captivity : the ideal of the great prophet of the exile (Deutero-Isaiah), with his glowing visions of a Messianic kingdom embracing all the nations of the earth, as fellow-servants and worshippers with Israel of the one true and only God ; and the ideal of Ezra and Nehemiah— the conception of an Israel consecrated to Jehovah's service, rigidly separated from other nations by observance of the Law, and utterly eschewing as mere pollution any contact with the heathen. Doubtless the great majority of the Jews, proud of their peculiar customs and of their devotion to Jehovah, viewed with ever deepened aversion and dismay the encroachments of Hellenism. They naturally came to regard the heathen as enemies of God's people, and as therefore objects of the divine vengeance. This temper finds an almost fierce expression in certain parts of later Jewish prophecy—for instance, in the magnificent passage which is included among the writings of Isaiah (chh. xxiv.—xxvii.), in the book of Joel with its apocalyptic visions of judgment descending on Israel's foes and oppressors, in the book of Obadiah with its wail of execration against Edom, above all perhaps in the later chapters of Zechariah (ix.—xiv.), which breathe a terrible spirit of revenge against the heathen, and predict the ultimate triumph of Judaism in its narrowest sense. All these portions of the Old

Jewish feeling towards the heathen.

Testament in their present form apparently belong to the period when the supremacy of Persia was decaying, and the influence of Greece was slowly spreading eastward. One remarkable book there is, however, which perhaps represents a reaction in Israel itself against the prevailing temper of narrow exclusiveness. The book of Jonah is intended to correct the idea that the heathen lay outside the sphere of Jehovah's grace and salvation. It represents the 'larger hope' of Hebrew universalism; it teaches that God is more merciful than man, and that the infliction of vengeance on Israel's foes is not so dear an object to Him as the work of bringing all men everywhere to repentance and salvation. Jonah himself is a type of Israel in its refusal to fulfil its evangelistic mission to the Gentiles; the supposed conversion of Nineveh is intended to teach the Jews a much needed lesson[1], —that Jehovah is not only the national Deity of a single people, but the Father whose mercies are over all His works.

The book of Jonah.

The internal administration of Judaea after Nehemiah's death passed into the hands of a line of hereditary high priests, who resided at Jerusalem, and were aided in the work of administration by a kind of municipal council consisting of elders and priests of the higher rank. Of these pontiffs little is known beyond their names. Eliashib, the grandson of Joshua ben Jozadak, was high priest in Nehemiah's time; his successors were Joiada, Jonathan or Johanan, and Jaddua, the last of whom was in office at the time of Alexander's campaign against Tyre (333—332)[2]. One incident of this period is related by Josephus[3] which

The rule of the high priests.

[1] For classical references to Jewish exclusiveness and hatred of the heathen see passages quoted in Mayor's notes on Juv. xiv. 103, 104. Cp. 1 Thess. ii. 15.

[2] Cp. Neh. xii. 10, 11. Whether Alexander actually visited Jerusalem and was met by Jaddua, as Josephus relates (*Antiq.* xi. 8. 3 foll.), is very doubtful. See *Encycl. Biblica*, s.v. ' Alexander.'

[3] *Antiq.* xi. 7. 1.

proves that the high-priestly office soon became an object of unscrupulous ambition, and led to great deterioration in the character of its occupants. Johanan, the successor of Joiada, finding himself threatened by the intrigues of his brother Joshua, who, relying on Persian influence, aimed at securing the high priesthood for himself, actually murdered him within the precincts of the temple. This tragic occurrence gave the Persian officer Bagoses, the secret supporter of the murdered Joshua, a pretext for polluting the temple and imposing a heavy fine on the Jews. The fact that the high priesthood so soon became a coveted distinction significantly marks the change which had come over the prospects and aims of the Jewish community since the exile. The nation had become a church. The spirit of patriotism was by no means extinct, but the hopes which inspired it were gradually turned in a new direction. Once or twice the Jews were tempted to take part in insurrectionary movements against their Persian masters, whose rule became more disorganized and burdensome as the strength of their empire gradually declined. A widespread revolt in

Tendency to revolt among the Jews.

Syria and Egypt against Artaxerxes III. Ochus, which began about 358 B.C., was effectually suppressed in 350. The movement in Phoenicia was crushed by the siege and capture of Sidon; Judaea was ravaged; the temple was destroyed, and a fresh detachment of Jewish captives was transported to Babylonia, and even to the shores of the Caspian Sea. This disastrous revolt however was almost the only event which interrupted the tranquillity enjoyed by the Jews under Persian sway[1]. They were exposed it is true, to the many inconveniences of a demoralized and oppressive *régime*, especially those incidental to the occasional transit of Persian armies, marching through Jewish territory on their way to Egypt. They were often harassed by the recurrence of bad seasons or flights of locusts, with consequent

[1] Cp. Neh. ix. 37.

visitations of famine[1].   But on the whole the Jews enjoyed a large measure of freedom; they were able to freely organize their religious polity on the basis of Ezra's reforms, and indeed, the Persian age was the very period when the Law became the supreme factor in the development of Judaism.   The voice of prophecy was now silent, because in great measure the objects for which it had been uplifted were secured.   Israel was at last purged from the taint of idolatry; it was devoted heart and soul to the service of Jehovah, and it had separated itself with rigid exclusiveness from all contact with the pollutions of heathenism. But if the prophets had passed away, new teachers had risen, to take their place; the priests, the scribes, and the 'wise men' or moralists.   Each of these classes played an important part in the evolution of Jewish religion.   The exaltation of the priesthood naturally led to a great increase of splendour in the temple and its services.   The temple was no longer, as in the days of the monarchy, a magnificent appanage of the royal palace; it was the recognised centre of worship for a community dispersed throughout the world.   Every Israelite aged twenty and upwards was subject to a poll-tax for the maintenance of the sacrifices; the whole nation, through the attendance of chosen representatives, took part in the services of the central sanctuary.   Moreover at this time the requirements of worship gave an impulse not only to the development of stately ceremonial, but also to the composition of psalms for liturgical use. The Jewish Psalter was of gradual growth.   Probably it was arranged in its present form, and was acknowledged as a part of canonical scripture, shortly after the success of the Maccabean rising (between 161 and 141).

The temple and its worship.

The temple at Jerusalem was of course the chief outward possession and treasure of post-exilic Judaism, but its dignity

---

[1] The Book of Joel, and possibly that of Ecclesiastes, reflects the miseries of life in Palestine during this period.

was after all overshadowed by that of the Law. Consequently,
though the prestige and influence of the priest-
The Scribes.
hood was great, yet ever since the time of Ezra,
the unique importance attached to knowledge of the Law tended
to bring to the front another class of teachers, namely, the
Scribes (*sopherim*). The earliest scribes, like Ezra himself,
were priests; but in due time, when the Law became the common property of the people, a large body of lay teachers was
included in the ranks of the scribes. Knowledge of the Law
became a chief passport to fame and popularity; this was particularly the case during the so-called Hellenistic period, when
many of the priests yielded to the spell of heathen culture, and
the task of guarding and vindicating the sacred Law passed out
of their hands. From this time onwards the scribes were generally accepted as the real teachers of the people. The popular
respect for their office is attested by the titles of honour which
in later times were frequently bestowed on them, such as
"rabbi" or "father[1]." They naturally found their principal
centre of influence in the synagogue—an institution which,
dating probably from the age of the captivity, inevitably tended
to supersede the temple, as a factor in the religious life of
Judaism. The worship of the synagogue consisted mainly of
prayer, confession of faith, and the reading and exposition of
the Law. After the exile, sacrifice inevitably ceased to be
an integral part of ordinary devotion, and as the religion
of the Jews learned to become independent of the temple, it
took deeper root in the hearts of the people, and became more
energetic and successful in proselytism.

The comparative tranquillity of the period that followed the
age of Nehemiah was also favourable to the
The 'Wis-
dom' litera-   growth of what is what is called the 'Wisdom'
ture.
literature (*Khokmah*), some specimens of which
are included in the Hebrew canon, while others appear among

---

[1] See Schürer, *Hist. of the Jewish People*, § 25.

the post-canonical writings. The 'Wisdom' literature illustrates the growing receptivity of the Jewish mind, its capacity for assimilating ideas derived from the religion of Persia and the philosophy of Greece, its gradual recognition of the fact that pagan systems contained elements of truth and points of contact with the religion of Jehovah[1]. It is scarcely questionable that the pure monotheistic belief of Persia had a marked effect on the faith of Israel, and it is probable that traces of Zoroastrian influence are to be found in the Jewish ideas concerning angels, and even in the later Jewish doctrine of the resurrection and the future life. The book of Malachi already indicates a certain change of attitude towards the heathen on the part of the more spiritually-minded thinkers among the Jews. *In every place*, says the prophet, *incense is offered unto my name, and a pure offering; for my name is great among the Gentiles, saith Jehovah of hosts* (Mal. i. 11)[2]. The passage taken in its context seems to imply that greater honour is paid to Jehovah among the heathen than in Israel itself. Thus the long experience of Persian domination, in spite of all its drawbacks, appears to have taught Israel to recognize among the heathen germs of faith and goodness which proved that Jehovah had not left Himself without witness even beyond the pale of the chosen people.

The battle of Issus (333) and the overthrow of the Persian empire by Alexander involved for Israel a change of masters. Josephus tells us that Alexander actively favoured the Jews and enlarged their

The Greek period, 333.

---

[1] In this connection may be noticed the special importance of Ecclesiastes (*Qoheleth*), a book written about 200 B.C. by a Jew trained under Hellenistic influence. Though permeated by the spirit of Hellenism, the writer holds fast to his faith in the providence of God and His moral government of the world. That Judaism is not inherently hostile to the best elements in pagan culture is shown by the breadth and charity of the writer of Ecclesiasticus (composed after 200 B.C.). Cp. Cornill, *Hist. of the People of Israel* (Eng. tr.), p. 181.

[2] See G. A. Smith, *The Book of the Twelve Prophets*, vol. ii. pp. 358 foll.

privileges[1]; but the truth is that the conqueror exercised only an indirect influence on the future of Judaism. The city of Alexandria, founded by him, became, as we have seen, a new and important centre of Jewish thought and activity,—a centre in which east and west, the refined paganism of Greece, the mystic cults of Egypt and the religion of Judaea found a meeting point. The Jews of Alexandria continued to hold close intercourse with their brethren in Palestine and willingly contributed towards the regular maintenance of the temple and its services. About 150 years however after Alexander's death, the high priest Onias[2], having been deposed by Antiochus Epiphanes, fled from Judaea with a body of adherents, and was permitted to settle in the district of Heliopolis. Here he founded the fortress-city and temple of Leontopolis (*circ.* 170). The new sanctuary, modelled on the pattern of the temple at Jerusalem, and served by a priest of Aaronic descent, was regarded by the strict Palestinian Jews as the centre of a schismatic movement, but it was destroyed within a century of its foundation.

After the death of Alexander (323), his empire was partitioned among his generals, hence called the The Diadochi. *Diadochi* ('successors'). For a short time Judaea was included in the dominions of the satrap of Syria. But in 320 Ptolemy Lagi invaded and annexed Syria; by the stratagem of an assault on the Sabbath day, which the Jews refused to desecrate by any armed opposition, he obtained possession of Jerusalem, and deported a number of the inhabitants to Egypt. Ptolemy imitated the liberal policy of Alexander, and systematically encouraged the settlement of

---

[1] He may have granted them exemptions from tribute in the sabbatical year.

[2] Probably Onias III. the son of Simon II., but according to other accounts Onias IV. the grandson of Simon. Josephus, *Antiq.* xiii. 3 § 1 tells us that Onias appealed in support of his design to the prophecy of Isai. xix. 19. On this passage see Hastings' *DB*, s.v. ' Ir-Ha-Heres.'

Jews in Egypt[1]; while Seleucus Nicator, the satrap of Babylon, not only welcomed them at Antioch and other cities of Syria and Asia Minor, but even admitted them to the rights of citizenship. It was no doubt a point of importance to the rulers both of Egypt and Syria that they should be able to rely on the friendship of the thriving province which lay on the boundary of their dominions. Thus the position of the Jews under the Diadochi promised at first to be exceptionally favourable. From the time of Ptolemy's occupation of Jerusalem (320), they remained for nearly a century subject to Egyptian rule, and this was perhaps the happiest period enjoyed by Judaea since the loss of her independence.. With the exception of two brief intervals, each lasting about fourteen years, the rule of the Ptolemies was uninterrupted till the year 204. It was a point of policy with the Egyptian monarchs to promote free intercourse between their Hellenic and Asiatic subjects. Greek settlements were planted in Palestine, many of the newly-founded cities being called by Greek names (such as Paneas, Ptolemais, Scythopolis), and the practical result was that Greeks and Macedonians became a numerous and influential element in the population of Western Asia[2]. Ptolemy II. Philadelphus (285—247), a ruler of liberal and enlightened tastes, is specially worthy of mention in this connection. His interest being awakened in the history and literature of his Jewish subjects, he encouraged the work of the Seventy, whose famous version of the Old Testament scriptures was probably begun under his patronage, though it was not completed till the middle of the second century. The

The Jews under the rule of the Ptolemies. 320—204.

Greek influence in Palestine.

---

[1] Josephus tells us that Ptolemy favoured the Jews because they were the only people among his subjects on whose oath he could implicitly rely. "He knew that the people of Jerusalem were most faithful in the observation of oaths and covenants." *Antiq.* xii. 1.

[2] Cp. Grote, *The History of Greece*, vol. x. pp. 208, 209.

influence of the 'Septuagint' version can hardly be over-
The
Septuagint
version. estimated. It proves how deeply the Jews of
Alexandria were influenced by their Hellenic
surroundings. To the great majority of the Jews
of the 'Dispersion,' this Greek translation became the channel
through which the teaching of the Old Testament reached them.
On the other hand, it served to introduce to the Gentile world the
treasures of Hebrew thought and religion, while the language
employed in the new version formed a link between the faith
of Israel and the philosophy of Greece. The translation of
the Hebrew scriptures marked an important step in that gradual
and progressive 'Hellenization' of Western Asia which was the
deliberate aim of the Diadochi, though it was never successfully
accomplished.

Of the internal history of Judaea under the rule of the
Ptolemies we know little. The office of high priest became
Internal
condition of
Judaea. by degrees more influential; its holder stood by
hereditary right at the head of the Jewish community, and it is probable that before the Maccabean period (175) the council of elders (*Sanhedrim*) had
become a powerful body, aristocratic and priestly in its consti-
tution and organized more or less upon a Grecian model[1].
Among the high priests the most imposing figure is that of
Simon I., called by Josephus 'the Just' (*circ.* 300—287), the
description of whom closes the catalogue of 'famous men'
praised by the son of Sirach. Simon is said to have repaired
the temple and strengthened the fortifications of Jerusalem,
and to have discharged his functions with ideal grace and
dignity[2]. A later high priest, Onias II., described as "one of
little soul and a great lover of money," determined to withhold
the annual tribute due to the king of Egypt (225). His

[1] In the time of Antiochus III. (223—187) the name γερουσία is already
used of the council. Josephus, *Antiq.* xii. 3 § 3.

[2] Ecclus. l. This chapter gives us a picture of the most attractive
aspects of high-priestly government.

nephew, Joseph, was wise enough to cancel this rash step and thus to avert the vengeance of Ptolemy III. Euergetes. Joseph was rewarded by being appointed to the post of farmer of taxes on behalf of the king; he held this office for upwards of twenty years, and managed to effect great improvements in the financial condition of Judaea. It was apparently during his administration that a party arose in Jerusalem unfavourable to the Egyptian domination and desirous of its overthrow in the interests of Antiochus III. (the Great) who in 223 succeeded to the throne of Syria. In 219 war broke out between Antiochus and Ptolemy IV. Philopator, the degenerate successor of Euergetes (221), in the course of which Jerusalem suffered severely and the temple was again outraged by the Egyptian king. In 204 Egypt finally lost the control of Palestine. The confusion in Egypt which followed Ptolemy IV.'s sudden death (205) and the accession of his son, a child of five years, gave Antiochus his long-desired opportunity of advancing into Judaea. He was apparently welcomed by a considerable section of the Jews, and after various chances of war Jerusalem fell into his hands without a struggle (198). Henceforward until the outbreak of the Maccabean struggle, Judaea remained a province of Syria. An effort on the part of Egypt to regain its former supremacy was speedily defeated. Thus Antiochus at last secured the object for which he and his predecessors had so long been striving, and Palestine was incorporated in the kingdom of the Seleucidae.

> Judaea a province of Syria.

The founder of this dynasty, Seleucus, shortly after the death of Alexander became satrap of Babylonia; but under his successors the seat of government was transferred to Antioch in Syria. The collapse in 301 of the formidable power of Antigonus, to whom had been allotted the satrapy of Phrygia, but who aspired to become master of the whole Alexandrine empire, left Seleucus without any rival except the kingdom of the Ptolemies. His

> The rule of the Seleucidae : 203—167.

dominions embraced a somewhat ill-defined area of territory, which varied considerably in extent at different times. For a few years (294—280) Judaea was nominally a province of his empire, till on the death of Seleucus it was again annexed by Ptolemy II. The treatment of the Jews by Seleucus was uniformly favourable. He induced many of them to settle in Antioch, his new metropolis, "and gave them privileges," Josephus tells us, "equal to those of the Macedonians and Greeks[1]." It is probable that from this time onwards there was always a party in Judaea favourable to the hegemony of Syria; and in proportion as the rule of the Ptolemies degenerated, the desire of the Jews to attach themselves more closely to Syria doubtless increased. This circumstance seems to explain the alacrity with which Antiochus was welcomed by the citizens of Jerusalem in 203, but subsequent events made it evident that the Jews had gained nothing by their change of masters. Antiochus indeed showed marked favour to the Jews, but before long he was engaged in a life and death struggle with Rome. An expedition into Asia Minor ended in the crushing defeat of the Syrian army by Scipio Africanus near Magnesia (190), and three years later Antiochus died, his successor being Seleucus Philopator (187—176). The internal history of Judaea till the close of his reign was marked by only one incident of importance. The arrangement by which the collection of the revenues had passed out of the hands of the high priest, and had been placed under the control of a civil official appointed by the Egyptian king, led to dissensions in Judaea, finally culminating in a deplorable dispute between a certain Simon, the commander of the temple guard, and Onias III., the reigning high priest. Simon, failing to gain his ends, revenged himself by secretly drawing the attention of Apollonius, the viceroy of Seleucus, to the vast treasure accumulated

Seleucus Philopator: 187—176.

---

[1] Josephus, *Antiq.* xii. 3 § 1.

in the temple coffers. Seleucus, who had inherited the heavy burden of debt which Antiochus had incurred during his disastrous war with Rome, eagerly welcomed the information of Simon, and resolved to act upon it. An envoy called Heliodorus was sent to plunder the temple, and Jewish tradition related that the impious attempt was only frustrated by a miracle[1]. The event was significant as indicating the antagonism that was destined to become so acute between the two chief factions in Judaea. Onias was the leader of the religious and patriotic party which favoured the hegemony of Egypt. Simon, and his brother Menelaus, were the representatives of a Seleucid faction which included the 'Hellenizing' portion of the community, *i.e.* those who were anxious to break down the barriers which separated Judaism from the Gentile world, and to introduce among the Jews the language, manners and dress of the Greeks.

Parties in Judaea.

The successive steps by which this party acquired influence cannot be traced with certainty. Doubtless the foundation of new towns in Palestine, bearing Greek names, and the gradual Hellenization of such old-established cities as Gaza, Joppa and Samaria, had gradually familiarized the Jews with Hellenic culture and modes of thought. At the beginning of the second century B.C., indeed, they were already "compassed and penetrated by influences as subtle as the atmosphere: not as of old uprooted from their fatherland, but with their fatherland itself infected and altered beyond all power of resistance[2]." We must, moreover, bear in mind that the spread of Hellenism, which lacked any true religious or ethical foundation, carried with it the seeds of social corruption. "The Greeks," it has been truly said, "became for the Orient the bearers of civilization indeed, but also the bearers of moral degeneration[3]." A spirit of frivolity and of

[1] 2 Macc. iii. 23 foll.
[2] G. A. Smith, *The Book of the Twelve Prophets,* ii. p. 445.
[3] Cornill, *Hist. of the People of Israel,* p. 179.

O. H.   17

scepticism seemed to haunt the Greek culture of that age; and it was inevitable that this spirit should eventually come into collision with the austere puritanism and deep religious serious-

Antiochus Epiphanes, 175. ness of the Jew. The accession of Antiochus IV. Epiphanes (175) brought matters to a head, and demonstrated the real strength of the Hellenizing faction in Jerusalem. Owing probably to its intrigues, Antiochus deprived the patriotic and faithful Onias of the high priesthood, and conferred the office, in return for a large bribe,

Strife of Jason and Menelaus. upon the high priest's younger brother Jason (a Grecized form of 'Joshua'). The new pontiff at the same time sought and obtained permission to establish a Greek *gymnasium* at Jerusalem, and to enrol its inhabitants as citizens of Antioch. The result was an outbreak of Greek fashions in Jerusalem. Even the priests neglected their duties in the temple courts, and indulged themselves in the amusements of the gymnasium[1]. Jason himself went so far as to send a sum of money to Tyre to be expended on sacrifices to Hercules. These proceedings naturally led to fierce dissensions between the Hellenizers and the loyalists (*Chasidim*, Gk. Ἀσιδαῖοι, 'pious' or 'devoted ones') who clung tenaciously to their national customs. After a tenure of three years Jason was himself ousted from the priesthood by Menelaus (Menahem), a man of savage and unscrupulous temper, and the strife which ensued between the two rival claimants forced Antiochus to intervene. As he was returning from a fruitless campaign in Egypt he visited Jerusalem, resolved to suppress the disorders in the city, which he regarded as a defiance of his own authority. The temple was profaned, and its treasure confiscated. Thousands of Jews were put to death. Menelaus, who had in the meantime secretly procured the murder of the late high priest Onias, was forcibly reinstated as high priest, and a body of Syrian soldiery took possession of the citadel (Acra).

[1] 2 Macc. iv. 14.

Antiochus, however, meditated a more sweeping measure.
He aimed at nothing less than the total eradi-
cation of Judaism. The attempt at coercion
had indeed no fair prospect of success, for the
majority of the Jews headed by the Scribes and the *Chasidim*
adhered stubbornly to the faith and practice of their fathers.
But the Syrian monarch was encouraged by the overtures of
the Hellenizing party, and he may have been genuinely anxious
for political reasons to reduce to religious uniformity the different
races of his heterogeneous empire[1]. Accordingly, in 168, he
sent Apollonius with an army of 20,000 men to Jerusalem.
The city fell into his hands on the sabbath day, and the
forcible conversion of the inhabitants to heathenism was at once
attempted. All that was distinctive of Judaism was ordered
by a royal decree (Oct. 168) to be removed; the observance
of the sabbath, the practice of circumcision, and the sacrificial
worship of the sanctuary were prohibited; all copies of the
Law that could be found were rent in pieces and burned; an
altar to Zeus Olympios was erected in the temple courts[2];
pagan ceremonies were introduced, and the Jews were compelled on pain of death to take part in heathen worship and to
eat swine's flesh. Of the agonies suffered by the faithful in the
persecution which followed, we catch some echoes in such
psalms as the forty-fourth and seventy-ninth. A considerable
number of Jews outwardly submitted to the king's demands;
but many chose to die rather than *profane the holy covenant*[3].
To the number of these *Chasidim* who offered a stedfast but
passive resistance, belonged the noble scribe Eleazar, and
the mother with her seven sons, whose heroic martyrdom is

The perse-
cution of Anti-
ochus, 168 B.C.

---

[1] Cp. 1 Macc. i. 41 foll.

[2] This altar, erected upon the altar of Burnt-offering, is called 'the
abomination of desolation' in 1 Macc. i. 54. Cp. Dan. ix. 27, xi. 33,
xii. 11; 2 Macc. vi. 2. The event took place on 15 Chisleu (Dec. 25),
168.

[3] 1 Macc. i. 63.

recorded in the second book of the Maccabees (chh. vi. and vii.).

'Meanwhile there were others who meditated more active measures of resistance. Towards the close of 167 a rising took place at Modin, a small town westward of Jerusalem. An attempt was here made by the Syrian officers to compel certain Jews to sacrifice to heathen deities. Matta-

The Macca-baean rising. thias, the priest, belonging to the Hasmonaean family, was required as a leading personage, to set the example. He not only refused, but with his own hands slew one of his countrymen who was about to sacrifice, and also struck down the Syrian officer who was presiding at the function. *Whosoever,* he cried, *is zealous of the law and maintaineth the covenant, let him follow me* (1 Macc. ii. 27). Mattathias then fled, accompanied by his five sons and a resolute body of adherents, to the hill-country. He now found himself at the head of a desperate band pledged to defend their ancestral religion to the last gasp. They boldly traversed the country, destroying heathen altars, and enforcing the circumcision of Jewish children[1]. In 166 however, Mattathias died, giving with his last breath a solemn and stirring charge to his sons, and nominating Judas, one of their number, as

Judas Maccabeus. his successor in the leadership. Under Judas the guerilla mode of warfare hitherto pursued was exchanged for a systematic campaign. The Jews were trained and organized so effectively by their new leader that the Syrian army was defeated with heavy loss at Bethhoron in 166, at Emmaus, and finally at Bethzur (165), where Lysias himself, the regent of Syria, was in command. In December 165, during the breathing-space afforded by the enforced retreat of Lysias to Antioch, Judas accomplished his long-cherished design of re-consecrating the polluted sanctuary, and restoring the daily sacrifice. This event took place on 25 Chisleu, 165, exactly three years after the profanation of

[1] 1 Macc. ii. 45.

the temple by Apollonius[1].   During the next eighteen months Judas was practically master of Judaea, and devoted his energies to the task of aiding the hard-pressed Jewish garrisons in Gilead and Galilee, and transferring the inhabitants of the various towns to Judaea.   Meanwhile Antiochus IV. died (164); and two years later Judas felt himself strong enough to attempt the expulsion of the Syrian garrison from Acra (162). At this juncture the regent Lysias resolved to take fresh measures towards restoring order in Judaea.   With an immense host, consisting of 100,000 foot-soldiers, 20,000 cavalry and 32 elephants, he besieged Bethzur, which fell into his hands, after a conflict in which the relieving force under Judas suffered a crushing defeat.   Advancing to Jeru- **Successes of Lysias.** salem, Lysias laid siege to the temple; but being compelled by private affairs to return once more to Antioch, he made a treaty with the Jewish garrison restoring to them their religious liberties.   But the nomination as high priest of Alcimus (Jakim or Eliakim), a leader of the **Alcimus,** Hellenistic party, provoked the resentment of the **high priest.** Maccabaeans.   Alcimus appealed for assistance to the new ruler of Syria, Demetrius I., who at the close of the year 162 had usurped the throne, and caused the reigning king Antiochus V., together with his chief supporter Lysias, to be put to death.   Demetrius sent an army under Nicanor to support Alcimus, but it was defeated by Judas in a battle at Adasar near Bethhoron, Nicanor himself being slain (March 161). Within a month however, a fresh host of Syrians under Bacchides marched into Judaea and encountered the Jewish army at Elasa.   Dismayed by the overwhelming forces of the Syrians, many of the Jews abandoned their cause in despair, and the army of Judas dwindled to less than **Defeat and** a thousand men.   In spite of their scanty **death of Judas,** numbers the Jews held their ground, but towards **161.**

---

[1] 1 Macc. iv. 36 foll.   From this period dates the feast of the Dedication. Cp. Ps. xxx., title ; St John x. 22.

evening Judas himself fell, and his troops were instantly scattered in panic-stricken flight (April 161). They succeeded in safely carrying off the body of their leader, which was afterwards buried with due honour in the tomb of his fathers at Modin.

A noteworthy incident of Judas' later career is the fact that he had already made secret overtures to Rome. The senate, anxious to weaken the power of Syria, had even agreed to form a defensive alliance with the Jews, and had sent a message to the Syrian monarch warning him not to oppress *the friends and confederates* of the Republic[1]; but as Demetrius had already despatched his army into Judaea, the treaty with Rome was practically inoperative. The conflict of the Jews with the mighty power of Syria was not ended by the fall of the brave and high-souled Judas, but its character was somewhat altered. Henceforth the Maccabaeans, under the leadership of Jonathan the brother of Judas, carried on a desultory struggle mainly in the interests of their own house. The religious war, properly so-called, had been brought to a conclusion by the treaty of Lysias, which conceded to the Jews full liberty *to live after their own laws as they did before* (1 Macc. vi. 59). Judas is without question the greatest warrior that Israel ever produced. He had to revive the warlike spirit among a people who for four hundred years had seen little or nothing of warfare. In his sacred fervour, his idealism, his courage, he stands without a rival among the worthies of the Hebrew race.

The distresses and fears of the faithful Jews, during their life and death struggle with Hellenism, find

The book of Daniel.

utterance, as we have noticed, in some of the Psalms. The apocalypse of Daniel seems to have been written (probably early in the year 164) with the design of encouraging and sustaining the heroes and martyrs of the Maccabaean persecution under the pressure of their sufferings.

---

[1] 1 Macc. viii. 31.

The book is remarkable in many respects, chiefly perhaps for
its comparative freedom from the fierce passions that were
excited by the conflict.   The book of Daniel is not classed by
the Jews among 'the prophets,' but it reflects some of the
noblest characteristics of Hebrew prophecy; its sense of the
divine Providence ruling in history, and its invincible confidence
in the final victory of the cause of God.

CHAPTER XII.

FROM JUDAS MACCABAEUS TO HEROD THE GREAT.

ALTHOUGH the high priest Alcimus belonged to the Hellenizing faction among the Jews, and was supported by the political
influence and armed force of Syria, he was apparently accepted
by the mass of the Jewish people and even by the Assidaeans,
who were satisfied with the liberty which they now enjoyed
under the convention of Lysias. But the Hasmonaean[1] family
regarded Alcimus as an obstacle to their own advancement.
Jonathan, who succeeded his brother Judas as the leader of the
Maccabaeans, aimed at the high priesthood, but while Alcimus
lived it was beyond his reach. In 159, however, Alcimus

Jonathan,
the brother of
Judas.

suddenly died, and during the interregnum of
seven years which ensued, Jonathan came to the
front. He took a prominent part in operations
against the Syrians, and inflicted a defeat on Bacchides which
compelled him to consent to an armistice, and to evacuate
Judaea (153). Jonathan now established himself at Michmash
as governor of the Jewish nation, until the internal troubles of
Syria placed the great object of his ambition within his reach.
The rival claimants for the throne of Syria (Demetrius who
since 162 had actually held the sovereignty, and the low-born

---

[1] The 'Hasmonaeans,' the family name of the Maccabees. Josephus
mentions a certain Ἀσαμωναῖος (Hashmon) as the ancestor of Mattathias.
Antiq. xii. 6. 1.

pretender Alexander Balas, who called himself a son of Antiochus IV.) vied with each other in making overtures for the friendship of Jonathan. By Alexander he was appointed *high priest of the nation*, and saluted as *the king's friend* (1 Macc. x. 20). Further honours were heaped on him when Demetrius was slain in 150; and his position was undisturbed even by the fall of Alexander himself, who was defeated by Ptolemy Philometor, and afterwards killed in Arabia (145). The new king of Syria, Demetrius II., confirmed Jonathan in the high priesthood, and his position might have been one of independent sovereignty, had he not needlessly involved himself in the dynastic troubles by which Syria was distracted. In the war of succession between Demetrius II. and Antiochus, the son of Alexander Balas, Jonathan actively supported the latter. But Trypho, the ambitious general of Alexander Balas, having put forward Antiochus as a claimant for the Syrian throne, was now secretly plotting against him, and viewed the rising power of Jonathan with jealousy and alarm. Accordingly he found an opportunity of treacherously seizing the person of the high priest, and ultimately put him to death (142).

The power of the Maccabees nevertheless remained unbroken. Simon, the last surviving son of Mattathias, assumed the leadership, and owing **Simon the Maccabaean, 142.** to the internal weakness of Syria was enabled actually to effect what had been the ambitious design of Jonathan—namely the complete emancipation of the Jewish nation from Syrian control. He induced Demetrius to release Judaea from tribute, and by this concession *the yoke of the heathen was taken away from Israel* (1 Macc. xiii. 41). The year 142 was indeed a memorable epoch in Jewish history. In official documents it was described as *the first year of Simon the high priest, the governor and leader of the Jews* (1 Macc. xiii. 42). **The rule of Simon Maccabaeus, 142— 135.** But the crowning success of Simon was the capture of Acra, the garrison of which was at length forced by famine to surrender. The power and prestige of the Hasmonaeans had now reached its height. Once more Judaea, though nominally subject to the suzerainty of Syria, enjoyed a real independence. The nation signified its gratitude in a formal decree (Sept. 141) confirming Simon in his authority as *high priest and captain and governor of the Jews,* and making his position hereditary in the Maccabaean family *until there should arise a faithful prophet* (1 Macc. xiv. 41, 47). So well-established was Simon's power that when, three years later, new demands were put forward by Syria, the Jewish ruler refused to comply, and an attempt on the part of the Syrians to enforce submission by arms was defeated. Till Simon's death, Judaea enjoyed a period of peace and prosperity which the Jewish historian describes in glowing terms (1 Macc. xiv. 4 foll.).

The high priest spared no pains to improve and further develope the resources of his realm. He managed to obtain possession of the port of Joppa, and thus secured for Jewish commerce an outlet to the west. His rule, we are told, brought peace and plenty to the land, but his chief title to honour was held to be that he firmly established the supremacy of the Law. *The law he searched out, and every contemner of the law and wicked person he took away* (1 Macc. xiv. 14).

Simon's end was tragical. At the fortress of Dok, near Jericho, he was treacherously murdered by his brutal son-in-law Ptolemy (Feb. 135). Two of his sons shared his fate.

John Hyrca-
nus, 135—105.

The third, John surnamed Hyrcanus, thus succeeded to a position which had practically become one of independent sovereignty. The tranquillity of Judaea however was soon threatened by the Syrian king Antiochus VII. (Sidetes, 139—128) who, having secured his throne, renewed after Simon's death the demands which the late high priest had successfully repelled [1]. The Syrian army invaded

---

[1] These included the surrender of the citadel of Jerusalem (Acra) which Antiochus, as suzerain of Judaea, insisted on occupying with a Syrian garrison.

and devastated Judaea and even laid siege to Jerusalem itself. Hyrcanus was at last compelled by the severe straits to which his country was reduced to come to terms with Antiochus. By the offer of a large indemnity and the promise of paying tribute, he purchased the withdrawal of the Syrian army and the immunity of his capital. But this condition of dependence on Syria only lasted till the death of Antiochus, who lost his life in an expedition against Parthia (128). As had happened so frequently before, Syria was crippled by intestine conflicts, and its state of weakness was Israel's opportunity. Hyrcanus boldly asserted his independence by annexing new districts to his kingdom. He seems indeed to have actually contemplated a restoration of the original borders of the ancient Hebrew monarchy. He carried on successful campaigns eastward of the Jordan, and the capture of Shechem enabled him to destroy the schismatic temple on Mount Gerizim. He attacked the Edomites and forced them to submit to the rite of circumcision. Finally he took Samaria after an arduous siege and razed the city to the ground.

Josephus speaks in high terms of the internal administration of Hyrcanus, and even ascribes to him the gift of prophecy[1]. He must however be regarded as a brilliant secular prince rather than as a religious pontiff. It is noteworthy in this connection that Hyrcanus withdrew himself from the party of the Pharisees, *i.e.* the successors of the *Chasidim*, with whom the Maccabaeans had always hitherto allied themselves, and associated with the Sadducees, whose interests were much more secular and political than religious.

When Hyrcanus died (105), the Jewish commonwealth had attained to dimensions which recalled the grandeur of the monarchy in the days of Solomon. But his inheritance fell into unworthy hands when it passed to his sons, Aristobulus, Antigonus and Alexander Jannaeus. Aristobulus having imprisoned his

Aristobulus I. 'king' of Judaea.

[1] *Antiq.* xiii. 10, § 7.

mother, who disputed his claims, succeeded to the high priest-hood. He at first allowed Antigonus to share his power, but the latter speedily fell a victim to his brother's jealousy, nor did Aristobulus himself long survive. He was the first to assume and to transmit to his successors the title and state of a king[1]. He also conquered and annexed a large portion of Ituraea in Northern Palestine. On his death, after a reign of only a year's duration, his brother, Alexander Jannaeus, suc-ceeded him (104—78).

It is needless to give any detailed account of the ad-ministration and military enterprizes of Jannaeus,
Alexander one of the most contemptible figures in Jewish
Jannaeus, history. As regards his administration it may
104-78. suffice to say that in spite of serious reverses and disturbances he managed to further extend the limits of his dominions by annexing several of the Greek cities on the coast, and con-siderable districts in the trans-Jordanic region. The real interest of Jannaeus' long and troubled reign lies in the cleavage which it introduced between the adherents of the Maccabees, and that part of the community, including the Scribes and Pharisees, which cherished the original ideals and principles of Judaism, and viewed with intense repugnance the gradual secularization of the high priesthood, and the con-version of a sacred theocracy into a kingdom of this world. In the view of these persons "God and the Law could not but be forced into the background if a warlike kingdom, retain-ing indeed the forms of a hierocracy, but really violating its spirit at every point, should ever grow out of a mere pious com-munity," if "temple and priesthood were cast into the shade by politics and the clash of arms[2]." Alexander himself was a man of dissolute life, whose habits stood in the sharpest contrast to the sanctity of his office.

The growing dissatisfaction at length found a vent on the

---

[1] Josephus, *Antiq.* xiii. 11, § 1.

[2] Wellhausen, *Sketch of the History of Israel and Judah*, p. 157.

occasion of the feast of Tabernacles. When Alexander was standing at the altar ready to offer sacrifice, the assembled worshippers rose upon him and pelted him with the citrons which the custom of the feast required them to carry. They also upbraided him with his servile origin, and his scandalous unworthiness to hold the priesthood. Alexander repressed this outbreak with such merciless and wholesale severity that a general rebellion broke out. For six years the high priest was forced to fight against his own people with mercenary troops. In the conflicts

Civil war in Judaea.

which ensued, not less than 50,000 Jews are said to have perished. Ultimately, the Pharisees called in the aid of Syria, and forced Alexander to flee from Jerusalem: but by an appeal to the patriotic feelings of the nation, which again rallied to the side of the heir of the Maccabees, he succeeded in recovering his throne, and inflicted a bloody vengeance on the party of the Pharisees[1]. It is said that eight hundred crosses were set up on which the chief men of the party were crucified, while by Alexander's orders their wives and children were butchered before their eyes. But the days of the tyrant were already numbered. Worn out by an almost unbroken series of campaigns, he died in 79 at the age of only 40, while occupied in besieging a city in Peraea.

Alexandra, the widow of Jannaeus, was prudent enough to come to terms with the Pharisees and so entirely submitted herself to their guidance that they became the real rulers of Judaea[2]. Relying on the aid of a powerful body of mercenaries, she overawed the neighbouring kings

Alexandra, 78.

[1] The 'Pharisees' ('separated ones') were apparently so called by their opponents because of their scrupulous avoidance of ceremonial pollution through contact with persons or things that might cause defilement. They became in an increasing measure the popular party among the Jews. The name perhaps came into vogue during the latter half of the second century, B.C. Cp. Schürer, *The Jewish People in the time of Christ*, § 26.

[2] Josephus, *Antiq.* xiii. 16, § 2.

and secured the internal tranquillity of her dominions. Meanwhile her eldest son Hyrcanus held the office of high priest, and would have succeeded peaceably to his mother's throne at her death in 69, had not his brother Aristobulus resolved to wrest from him the sovereignty. The conflict between the brothers was short. Hyrcanus II., a man of feeble character, resigned his royal and priestly dignity in favour of Aristobulus, who had long been preparing in secret for insurrection. He was powerfully supported by the Sadducees, who chafed under the domination of the Pharisees, but his successful usurpation of the throne speedily revived the old antagonism between the Hasmonaeans and the Pharisaic party. The prestige and ascendency of the Maccabaean family began to decline, and already a new aspirant for power was about to appear upon the scene.

Aristobulus II., 69.

Antipater or Antipas was an Idumaean by descent, and at this time held, in succession to his father, the post of governor ($\sigma\tau\rho\alpha\tau\eta\gamma\acute{o}s$) of Idumaea. As the intimate friend of Hyrcanus he took his side in the dispute between him and Aristobulus. He succeeded at length by persistent intrigues in undermining the position of the usurper, and Hyrcanus himself was finally induced to openly attempt the recovery of his throne. The Arabian king Aretas, with whom Hyrcanus had taken refuge on the advice of Antipater, espoused his cause and led an army into Judaea. Aristobulus was defeated in battle, and was subsequently deserted by most of his adherents; but he took refuge with a small force on the temple mount, to which Hyrcanus and Aretas promptly laid siege. The attempt to restore Hyrcanus might have succeeded, since the Pharisees and the masses of the people ranged themselves on his side against Aristobulus. But at this juncture the Romans intervened. Scaurus, the lieutenant of Pompey in the East, arrived in Syria (65). Each of the rival Jewish princes offered a heavy price for his support. Scaurus took the part of Aristobulus

Antipater.

The Romans in Syria.

and ordered Aretas to withdraw from Jerusalem. For the first time in the history of the Jews, their internal disputes were left to the arbitration of Rome. Aristobulus now endeavoured to further strengthen his position by courting the favour of Pompey, who himself reached Damascus in the following year (64), and at once proceeded to settle the affairs of Syria and Palestine. Syria and Phoenicia were formed into a Roman province; Antiochus XIII., the last of the Seleucid kings, was deposed, and relegated to a petty throne in the district of Commagene.

Pompey was now about to give his attention to the claims of the two rival princes in Judaea, when an appeal reached him from the Pharisaic party and their adherents, complaining of the tyranny of the Hasmonaeans and demanding the entire abolition of the monarchy and the restitution of the high priesthood on its ancient basis[1]. Pompey for the moment deferred his decision, and Aristobulus, suspecting that it would in any case be adverse to himself, rashly prepared to resist the further advance of the Roman army. Pompey at once marched southward and issued an order to Aristobulus to deliver up the fortresses held by his troops. Aristobulus hastily yielded and even promised to surrender Jerusalem; but his fanatical adherents were determined to resist the Roman advance into Judaea. They were quickly driven by the Romans from the open country, and took refuge in the citadel and temple mount. It was only after an arduous siege of three months that Pompey succeeded in forcing an entry through a breach in the walls; the final assault took place on the sabbath day, when the defenders had neglected to man the walls (June 63)[2]. A frightful massacre followed, in which 12,000 Jews perished, including the priests who were engaged in offering sacrifice. The conqueror himself, in spite of the remonstrances of the priests, insisted upon entering the Holy of Holies, but left the

---

[1] Josephus, *Antiq.* xiv. 3, § 2.

[2] According to one account the final assault took place on the Day of Atonement.

treasures of the temple untouched. The vanquished Jews were severely dealt with; the promoters of the war were beheaded; of the rest, large numbers, including Aristobulus himself with two of his sons, were carried as captives to Rome and ultimately graced the great triumph of Pompey in 61; the Jewish monarchy was abolished, though Hyrcanus was suffered to retain the title and office of high priest, his jurisdiction being restricted to Judaea proper, which was now made tributary to Rome. Other districts which had formerly submitted to the sway of the Hasmonaeans were provisionally included in the newly-formed Roman province of Syria. Thus the independence of the Jewish nation, which had lasted for nearly eighty years, was brought to an end. Seventy years more passed, however, before Judaea was formally annexed to the Roman province of Syria (6 A.D.).

Hyrcanus was now the nominal governor of the Jews, but he was in fact completely under the control of Antipater, whose object in attaching himself to Hyrcanus had been solely the gratification of his own ambition, and who now exercised whatever vestige of authority the Romans had left in Jewish hands. The removal of Aristobulus left him practically the most powerful person in Judaea, and it was his consistent policy to attach himself closely to the Romans, and to serve them by every means in his power. He aided Scaurus in an expedition against Aretas, and gave valuable assistance in other minor campaigns. In 49 the Roman civil war broke out. After the battle of Pharsalia (48), Antipater rendered valuable services to Julius Caesar, who rewarded him in 47 by making him a Roman citizen, and appointing him 'procurator' (ἐπίτροπος) of Judaea, while Hyrcanus was allowed to assume the title of 'ethnarch.' Caesar also sanctioned the restoration of the walls of Jerusalem (destroyed by Pompey), and in general showed marked favour to the Jews, a fact which explains the sincerity of the regret with which they are said to have lamented the dictator's murder. In the year 43 (the year

after the assassination of Julius Caesar), Antipater himself was murdered, but the position of his family was already secure. His eldest son Phasael was governor of Jerusalem; his second son Herod **His death, 43.**
—a man of brilliant gifts and forcible but unscrupulous character—was governor of Galilee. But the advancement of Herod was hindered by the intrigues of the surviving Hasmonaeans, who during the latter part of Antipater's career had been allowed by the Romans to persistently disturb the peace of Judaea.

In the year 40 the Parthians invaded Syria, and Antigonus, the son of Aristobulus II., persuaded them to aid him in an attempt to seize the throne of Judaea. The masses of the people, who hated the domination of an Idumaean family, rallied to the side of Antigonus. He succeeded in getting possession of the persons of Hyrcanus and Phasael, the former of whom he cruelly **Attempt of Antigonus.** mutilated, while the latter committed suicide in prison. Herod meanwhile escaped, and for three years Antigonus, who resumed the kingly title, enjoyed a precarious term of sovereignty. Herod, who took refuge at Rome, used his opportunity to secure the favour and support of Antony and Octavian, and through their influence was declared by the senate 'king of the Jews' (40 B.C.)[1]. The Parthian invaders however being still in possession of Palestine, three more years passed before Herod could make good his formal claim to the Jewish throne. In the spring of 37, Herod for the third time renewed his campaign against Antigonus, and laid siege to Jerusalem. Here he was presently reinforced by the army of Sosius, the procurator of Syria; the city was ultimately taken by assault on a sabbath day; the temple was stormed and the defenders put to the sword. Antigonus fell into the hands of the Romans and was afterwards beheaded at

---

[1] Josephus, *Antiq.* xiv. 14 § 4.

Antioch[1]. Josephus relates the anecdote that when the craven Antigonus fell at the feet of Sosius, the stern Roman scornfully called him 'Antigone,' thus giving him the title of a woman while spurning him as a slave.

Such was the ignominious end of the Hasmonaeans after a supremacy which had lasted 126 years. "This family," observes Josephus, "was a splendid and illustrious one, both on account of the nobility of their stock and of the dignity of the high priesthood, as also for the glorious actions which their ancestors achieved for our nation; but these men lost the government through their dissensions one with another, and so it came to Herod, the son of Antipater, who was of no more than a vulgar family and of no eminent extraction, but one that was subject to other kings[2]."

With a brief outline of the reign of Herod (37—4 B.C.) our short history finds its appropriate close. Early in the year 37, while actually engaged in the siege of Jerusalem, Herod allied himself to the Hasmonaean family by marrying Mariamne, the grand-daughter both of Hyrcanus and Aristobulus; he thus contrived to unite in his own person the claims of both the brothers. This was obviously a politic step, and was calculated to disarm the jealousy with which the Jews regarded the rise of an alien family. The cause of Antigonus had been ardently embraced by the mass of the nation, and they could never forget that Herod owed his advancement to the overthrow of the old dynasty by the legions of Rome. When however he became the actual ruler of the Jews, Herod, having once got rid of his most zealous opponents, who belonged chiefly to the Sadducean party, tried to conciliate the people by showing marked favour to the Pharisees, and treating the national customs, social and religious, with respect. By the display of a studied

The career of Herod.

---

[1] Josephus, *Antiq.* xv. 1 § 2, notes that this was the first time the Romans had executed such a sentence on a king.

[2] *Antiq.* xiv. 16 § 4 s. fin.

munificence and by bestowing great pains on the embellishment of Jerusalem, he succeeded in effacing to some extent the memory of the unscrupulous cruelties by which he had gained his throne. Thus in the year 20 B.C. he undertook the reconstruction of the temple on an imposing scale—a work which was only completed seven years before the fall of Jerusalem (63 A.D.). At the same time he displayed his Hellenizing tastes by celebrating games in honour of Augustus and by erecting a theatre, an amphitheatre and a hippodrome at Jerusalem. He also dedicated temples to the honour of the Roman emperor in many of the Greek cities of Palestine. Samaria, and Straton's Tower on the coast, were magnificently rebuilt under the new names of Sebaste and Caesarea. Further, Herod invited Greek writers and teachers to his court, one of whom, Nicolaus of Damascus, subsequently became his biographer. But in spite of the success of his administration and the splendour of his projects, Herod's reign was darkened and embittered by domestic troubles. Furious jealousies disturbed the peace of his own household. First the youthful Aristobulus, Mariamne's brother, who had been allowed to hold for a brief space the office of high priest, and next the aged Hyrcanus, the nominal head of the Hasmonaean house, were put to death in order to gratify the spite of Salome, Herod's sister. Mariamne herself fell a victim to Herod's jealousy in the year 29 B.C., and her mother Alexandra in 28. Towards the close of his life, the king's suspicious fears were roused by the popularity of the two sons of Mariamne, Alexander and the younger Aristobulus; accordingly they too were put to death (7 B.C.). Finally, Herod's eldest son Antipater, by whose intrigues his resentment against the sons of Mariamne had been inflamed, was executed by his father's orders a few days before his own death (B.C. 4).

Throughout his reign, Herod retained the warm friendship of the Romans. After the defeat of Antony at the battle of Actium (31), he had hastened to secure the favour of Augustus, which he retained to the close of his life. He was shrewd enough to perceive that the good will of Rome not only gave material support to his own dynasty but lent a certain prestige to the Jewish nation. The rise of the Herodian party among the Jews is a proof that by some of them at least the practical benefits of Herod's policy were appreciated; but to the mass of the Jews he was simply an alien, an Idumaean, a friend of the Romans, and a heathen at heart. The hatred of ruler and subjects was mutual, and nothing that Herod could devise rendered the rule of Rome tolerable. At the same time it must be acknowledged that the condition of Judaea was peaceful and prosperous under his sway, and the Jews really derived advantage from the prestige of their able and ambitious monarch.

On Herod's death, his surviving sons were allowed after some delay to divide his inheritance. To Arche-

The sons of Herod. laus as 'ethnarch' was assigned the government of Samaria, Judaea and Idumaea. The shameful misgovernment of Archelaus provoked the Jews to appeal to Rome in the year 6 A.D., with the result that the ethnarch was deposed and banished by Augustus. From that time forward, except for a brief interval (41—44 A.D.)[1] Judaea was placed under the control of a Roman procurator. The disastrous insurrectionary movements which henceforth continually disturbed the peace of Palestine culminated in the fearful war of 66—70 A.D., in which the Jews, maddened by the misrule and tyranny of successive procurators[2], made a final and

---

[1] From 41–44 A.D., by the favour of the Emperor Claudius, Agrippa reigned over Judaea and the former tetrarchies of Antipas and Philip, with the title of king.

[2] Of Antonius Felix, procurator from 52–60 A.D., Tacitus says 'ius regium servili ingenio exercuit,' *Hist.* v. 9 ; of Albinus (62–64) and Gessius Florus (64–66) see the account in Josephus, *Wars,* ii. 14 §§ 1, 2, *Antiq.* xx. 11 § 1. 'It was this Florus,' says Josephus, 'who made it necessary for us to take up arms against the Romans, since we thought it better to be destroyed at once than by little and little.'

desperate effort to throw off the yoke of Rome. But the fall of Jerusalem and the destruction of the temple are events which lie beyond the scope of this history.

To render our sketch of Jewish history to the Roman period complete, it is necessary to describe briefly the internal condition of Judaea at the opening of the Christian era,—its mode of government, the condition of religious parties, and the popular hopes and ideals which the coming of Christ either satisfied or disappointed.

The condition of Judaea was somewhat altered by its annexation to the Roman province of Syria (A.D. 6). It was henceforth governed by a procurator who was to a certain extent subordinate to the imperial legate of Syria. The official residence of the procurator was at Caesarea, but on special occasions, such as the chief feasts, when a large concourse of Jews was gathered together at Jerusalem, he visited the capital and resided in the palace which had belonged to Herod, and which was henceforth called the *praetorium*. The procurator exercised supreme military and financial control of the province; and capital sentences pronounced by the *Sanhedrim* required confirmation from him before they could be carried into execution. We must recollect that Roman rule was necessarily odious to the Jews. The Herods had understood Jewish sentiment and had to a large extent humoured it. The Roman rule on the other hand was harsh and unsympathetic. The procurator could neither appreciate nor respect the peculiar customs and traditions of the Jew, who for his part regarded a pagan government as hopelessly irreconcileable with the essential principles of the theocracy. Indeed, he saw "in the simplest rules of administration, such as the proposal of a census made at the very beginning, an encroachment upon the most sacred rights of the people[1]." Yet for sixty years the Jews patiently endured

Status of Judaea after 6 A.D.

[1] See Schürer, *The Jewish People in the time of Christ*, § 17.

these hard conditions, which wise and careful administration might have rendered tolerable. The great war of 66—70 was the inevitable result of the perverse misgovernment of two successive procurators, Albinus and Gessius Florus, whose contempt for Jewish feeling goaded the oppressed and irritated nation into wild and desperate revolt.

Other parts of Palestine were still subject to the rule of the sons of Herod. Antipas, who put John the Baptist to death, was tetrarch of Galilee and Peraea (4 B.C.—39 A.D.), and founded the city of Tiberias. Philip was for nearly forty years tetrarch of Ituraea and Trachonitis ; he proved himself to be a just and popular ruler of a district which for the most part was populated by heathen. In Judaea the abolition of the king-ship restored some political importance to the high priest, the priestly college over which he presided, and the *Sanhedrim* to which was left in great measure the administration of justice. Its jurisdiction was nominally restricted to Judaea, but its de-cisions were naturally received as authoritative in all parts of the Jewish world. The most influential party in the *Sanhedrim* was that of the Sadducees (Zadokite priests), whose main interest lay in the jealous conservation of their aristocratic privileges, and who had always been disposed to welcome the spread of Hellenic culture in Israel. The Pharisees, whose almost exclusive aim was the care-ful fulfilment of the Law, displayed little direct interest in politics, but they naturally sympathized with the patriotic and anti-foreign sentiment of the masses, among whom, since hatred of the Roman power was their dominant tendency, the rising sect of Zealots easily found adherents. The care of the Pharisees for the maintenance of Israel's traditional customs naturally made them the popular party in Judaea. Their numbers were large, and were constantly augmented by diligent proselytism. The Zealots were the party of action, prepared to go all lengths in resisting and subverting the rule of the alien Romans.

There was another Jewish sect which played even a less conspicuous part in public affairs than the Pharisees. This was the community of the Essenes, which from one point of view represented an extreme side of the Pharisaic movement:—its reverence for the authority of Moses, its rigid observance of the sabbath, its exaggerated regard for ceremonial purity[1]. But many of the beliefs and peculiar practices of this sect seem to have been derived from a non-Jewish source, and point to Egyptian or possibly Persian influence. Their seclusion, asceticism, and indifference to the worship of the temple did not however entirely debar them from occasionally visiting Jerusalem and other cities. Some of them indeed seem to have taken part in the great struggle against Rome. Of the scribes, it is sufficient to say that they had already become, before the Christian era, a numerous and powerful body. Many of them belonged to the party of the Pharisees, but their political influence was only indirect. It was their function to inculcate in all parts of the Jewish world, but especially in Judaea, the principles of the Law. By their untiring efforts was kindled that fierce enthusiasm for Judaism, that zeal for "the full triumph of the Law and the Law's religion[2]" which mainly brought about the collision with Rome, and the ultimate ruin of the nation.

On a survey of the confused and bewildering period which we have traversed in this final chapter, one fact stands out clearly, namely that the rash attempt of Antiochus Epiphanes to suppress Judaism and to Hellenize the Jewish race really saved the religion of Israel. It woke into new and vigorous life feelings and ideals which under the depressing *régime* of Persia and Egypt had well-nigh become extinct. The 'Apocalyptic' literature of the two centuries preceding the Christian era was the product of Israel's newly-kindled hopes. It pointed beyond the heathen oppression of the present to a future

The Apocalyptic literature.

---

[1] Cp. Josephus, *Wars of the Jews*, ii. 8 § 9.

[2] Montefiore, *Hibbert Lectures*, p. 438.

triumph of that divine kingdom which the prophets had proclaimed. It rekindled interest in Messianic prediction; it revived the spirit of patriotism and self-sacrifice; it encouraged drooping faith by the promise of a final vindication of God's righteousness, and by the offer of rewards beyond the confines of this life; resurrection from death for the individual Israelite, a reign of the saints in glory, and the annihilation of Israel's heathen foes. It is impossible to overrate the influence of this strange literature in educating the faith and patriotism of Israel "in preparing the most religious and ardent minds of Judaea either to pass over into Christianity or else to hurl themselves in fruitless efforts against the invincible might of Rome[1]." It is indisputable that the hopes to which the Maccabaean rising gave birth lived long in the national consciousness of the Jews, producing at one time the fruit of a pure and noble enthusiasm, at another wild outbreaks of fanaticism. In its crudest form the object of the Messianic expectation was the sudden advent of a warlike prince, an 'anointed' Son of Man, who should overthrow, and inflict a fearful vengeance on, Israel's foreign oppressors, and thus establish the visible earthly supremacy of Judaism. This was the dream of the Zealots, and more than once it excited them to rise in futile revolt. The Pharisees doubtless shared to a great extent the popular hopes, even though they looked down with lofty contempt on the common people (the *'am ha-aretz*); but the triumph for which they waited was religious rather than purely national. Their sole ideal was the observance of the Law in all its details. *Fiat lex ruat coelum* might have been their motto. Under the Syrian domination they had been the soul of the movement which resisted the Hellenization of the Jewish people. They had followed the Maccabaean leaders with dauntless and devoted enthusiasm, till it became apparent that the degenerate successors of Judas aimed at the establishment of a powerful

[1] See *Encyclopaedia Biblica*, vol. i. p. 215.

dynasty rather than the vindication of the Law and its principles. It is only just to admit that the Pharisees did not look for a mere kingdom of this world. The Sadducees, on the other hand, had no special interest in Messianic prediction, and held aloof from the popular expectation. Their policy was that of opportunists who waited on events, neither sharing the religious ideals of the common people, nor sympathizing with the hopes that stirred their hearts. They had no pre-judice against heathen culture, and they were only anxious to avoid needless collision with the power of Rome. But the influence of neither party, Pharisees nor Sadducees, availed to restrain the outbreak of those elements of disorder and de-fiance which rallied round the sect of the Zealots: and Jewish history, so far as it is traced in this book, ends with the desperate and ruinous venture of an enthusiasm which had once been enlisted in a worthy cause and had produced glorious and heroic deeds, but which now in its degeneracy brought upon the Jewish nation a catastrophe tersely described in the memorable sentence of Josephus. "I shall speak my mind here at once briefly:—That neither did any city ever suffer such miseries, nor did any age ever breed a generation more fruitful in wickedness than this was, from•the beginning of the world[1]."

The fall of Jerusalem was not the last act in 'the Hebrew tragedy[2].' A complete history of Judaism would have to tell of all that the Jews were made to suffer during the middle ages, of all that to the shame of Christianity they endure in certain parts of Europe to this day. Rabbi Ben Ezra's 'Song of

[1] *Wars of the Jews*, v. 11 § 5.
[2] A suggestive little sketch of Jewish history under this title has been recently published by Col. C. R. Conder (Blackwood and Sons).

death' gives voice to the age-long cry of his people to the
God of their fathers:

> "By the torture, prolonged from age to age,
> By the infamy, Israel's heritage,
> By the Ghetto's plague, by the garb's disgrace,
> By the badge of shame, by the felon's place,
> By the branding-tool, the bloody whip,
> And the summons to Christian fellowship,"

by these untold woes and sufferings Israel still mutely appeals
to the compassion of Him whose purpose of grace stands sure:

*I will have mercy upon her that had not obtained mercy;
and I will say to them which were not my people, Thou art my
people; and they shall say, Thou art my God*[1].

[1] Hos. ii. 23.   Cp. Rom. ix. 25, xi. 31 folL

APPENDIX I.

Chapters I.—IV. *The Hexateuch*.

Until the ninth or eighth century B.C., the only records of Israel's history were those contained in song or saga. A few such national lyrics, or fragments of them, are still preserved in the Pentateuch and the Historical books of the Old Testament. Perhaps the oldest of these is the *Song of Deborah* (Judg. v.) which was apparently composed shortly after the victory described in it. The *Song of the Bow* (2 Sam. i. 17 foll.) may well be an authentic work of David himself, as also perhaps the short elegy on the death of Abner (2 Sam. iii. 33 foll.). Other lyrical fragments containing historical allusions are the excerpts from the *Book of the Wars of Jehovah* (Num. xxi. 14, 15), the *Song of the Well* (ibid. 17, 18), and the *Song of triumph over Sihon* (ibid. 27 foll.). Certain passages are borrowed from the *Book of Jashar*, which was probably a collection of ballads celebrating the exploits of national heroes (Josh. x. 12, 13), and possibly a passage in Solomon's prayer of dedication, 1 Kings viii. 12 foll. = viii. 53 LXX. with the addition οὐκ ἰδοὺ αὕτη γέγραπται ἐν βιβλίῳ τῆς ᾠδῆς. See Driver, *LOT*, p. 192). Probably other collections of the same kind existed and were recited at religious festivals. Some longer lyrics, which seem to belong to the time of the monarchy, are also included in the Pentateuch : the *Blessing of Jacob* (Gen. xlix.), the *Song of Moses at the Red Sea* (Exod. xv.), the *Prophecies of Balaam* (Num. xxiii., xxiv.) the *Song* and *Blessing of Moses* (Deut. xxxii., xxxiii.).

The earliest attempts however to form a continuous historical narrative probably originated in the so-called 'Schools of the Prophets.' Two such versions of the history were gradually formed during the century before 750 B.C., and are incorporated in the Hexateuch. The Jehovistic document (J) so-called because it habitually uses the divine Name *Jehovah*, bears traces of having originated in Judah; the Elohistic document (E), employing the divine Name *'Elôhim*, was apparently composed in the Northern kingdom. There are well-marked differences between these two documents which may be studied in well-known books on the literature of Israel, but both are alike in their religious purpose and standpoint. Both are rightly called *prophetical narratives* in the sense that they embody some of those religious ideas of which the great Hebrew prophets afterwards became the exponents; but strictly speaking they give a picture of the higher elements in the religion of the *pre-prophetic* period. From a historical point of view the importance of these two narratives lies in the fact (i) that they are based on ancient traditional narratives and written sources, (ii) that they reflect the religious and moral ideas current in the age of the early monarchy.

About the middle of the seventh century as it seems (*c.* 650), these two "Prophetic" sources were skilfully combined in a single narrative (JE), the result of the unknown editor's work being a mosaic constructed by the piecing together of sections taken from both documents. Somewhat later (in 621), the code which forms the kernel of the Book of Deuteronomy (D) was promulgated, and accepted as the basis of Josiah's reformation. In course of time this code was provided with a historic setting, and combined with JE, by the school of writers under whose influence the original code had already been compiled. They carefully revised the earlier history from the religious standpoint of Deuteronomy, and in particular made numerous additions to the last section of JE—that which relates the history of the conquest of Canaan. The result of their work is generally described by the formula JED.

During the exile a new code of ritual law was compiled, possibly under the actual direction of the prophet Ezekiel (*c.* 590—570). This is known as the *Priestly Code* (P). It did not actually contain much new matter. It was rather a codification and exposition of ancient priestly usages and traditions. Probably at a somewhat later time P was enlarged by the incorporation of the ancient *Law of Holiness* (Levit. xvii.—xxvi.). This in turn was followed by a new version of the history, intended to be a kind of framework for the legislation. The aim of the writer, or school of writers, to whom we owe the composition of the Priestly narrative, was "to give a systematic view, from a priestly standpoint, of the origin and chief institutions of the Israelitish theocracy. For this purpose an *abstract* of the history is sufficient; it only becomes detailed at important epochs, or where the origin of some existing institution has to be explained; the intervals are bridged frequently by genealogical lists, and are always measured by exact chronological standards[1]." At some period between the death of Ezekiel (*c.* 570) and the first visit of Nehemiah to Jerusalem (444), the Priestly narrative and code were combined with the Deuteronomic work above-mentioned (JED) and the main portion of it was promulgated at Jerusalem in the assembly described in Neh. viii., ix.[2]. It is important however to bear in mind that the Law must have been enlarged by minor additions and expansions during the period that follows the death of Nehemiah.

The historical value of the Hexateuch.

The materials available for the reconstruction of the earliest period of Israel's history are thus seen to belong to various dates, and are drawn from various sources—not all of equal value and importance. The most detailed and statistical narrative—that of P —is the furthest removed from the actual events, and therefore the least to be depended upon. It gives an ideal sketch of institutions and incidents the exact details of which were lost in remote antiquity. "It is only in *form* an historical document; in substance it is a body of laws and precedents having the value of law, strung on a thread of history so meagre that it often consists of nothing more than a chronological scheme and a sequence of bare names... It follows with certainty that the priestly re-casting of the origins of Israel is not history (save in so far as it merely summarises and reproduces the old traditions in the other parts of the Hexateuch) but *Haggada, i.e.* that it uses old names and old stories, not for the

[1] Driver, *LOT,* p. 126.
[2] The part so promulgated was probably the *Pentateuch* without the narrative contained in the Book of Joshua.

purpose of conveying historical facts but solely for purposes of legal and ethical instruction[1]."

Another point to be noticed is the tendency of the " Prophetic." narratives to project back into the past the ideas and customs of their own age. They only incidentally give indications of the beliefs and customs current in the primitive age which they describe. In fact the Hexateuch supplies us merely with a bare general outline of the origin and early migrations of the Hebrew tribes. We are left to correct or supplement the biblical narrative by evidence derived from other sources. We have to conjecture from the ideas and beliefs of a later age the probable course of events in a period of which we possess no contemporary account. Archaeological discoveries give us many valuable illustrations of the patriarchal history, especially perhaps of those portions which relate to the sojourn of the Hebrews in Egypt, but hitherto they have not supplied any direct *proofs* of the patriarchal story as described in the book of Genesis, or of the incidents related in Exodus and Numbers[2].

Chapter IV. *The Book of Joshua.*

This book forms, as we have seen, the supplement and completion of the five books of the Pentateuch. The conquest of Canaan under Joshua is narrated in chh. i.—xii. Chh. xiii.—xxi. record the details of the allotment of the land to the different tribes. Chh. xxii.—xxiv. are an appendix, describing the closing scenes of Joshua's life and his final exhortations. The chief documents of the Pentateuch are present in Joshua: the bulk of the narrative is from JE and P, interspersed with Deuteronomic passages. In the Heb. canon however Joshua is separated from the five books of the Law, and is placed first in the series of 'former prophets.' The final redaction of the book belongs to a late period in Israel's history, possibly the fourth or third century, B.C. There are various historical difficulties in the narrative—the chief of which perhaps is the discrepancy between the different accounts of the conquest, D and P representing it as thorough and complete, and effected by all the tribes acting in concert, while JE depicts it as the work of

[1] W. R. Smith, *OTJC*, lect. xiii., p. 420.
[2] Cp. *Authority and Archaeology, sacred and profane*, p. 149.

separate tribes acting at different times, and as being only partial in its total result. There are good reasons for accepting the narrative of JE as the earlier and more trustworthy account. That the invasion of particular districts however by separate tribes was the outcome of a previous understanding among them, that it was directed from a single centre, and that the basis of a real national unity had already been established when the Hebrews crossed the Jordan—these facts are clearly attested by later tradition.

Chapter V. *The Book of Judges.*

The basis of this book seems to consist of (1) various fragments of an ancient account of the conquest of Canaan, in which the conquest is represented as due to the efforts of individual tribes; (2) a series of older narratives fitted into a somewhat artificial framework by a Deuteronomic redactor; (3) two traditional narratives relating certain incidents of ancient Israelitish life (chh. xvii.—xxi.).

There may have existed a book containing accounts of the exploits of the 'Greater Judges' (Ehud, Deborah, Barak, Gideon, Jephthah, and Samson). The work of the Deuteronomic editor is most apparent in the middle division of the book (chh. ii. 6—xvi.). He uses the ancient narratives chiefly as a means of illustrating his theory of the history of the period. In each section of the narrative we find the same features "the same succession of apostasy, subjugation, the cry for help, deliverance, described often in the same, always in similar phraseology"(Driver, *LOT*, p. 164). The account may be regarded as a "religious philosophy" of the history, rather than as history in the strict sense. Nevertheless the book gives a picture of the age of the Judges which in its leading features seems to be correct. The redaction of the book by the "Deuteronomic editor" probably took place during the captivity.

Chapters VI.—IX.

The Books of Samuel, Kings, and Chronicles.

The two books of Samuel originally formed a single work. These, with the two books of Kings, were regarded by the Septuagint translators as a complete history of the Hebrew monarchy, and the four books together were called βίβλοι βασιλειῶν.

The books of Samuel apparently existed, very much in their

present form, before the beginning of the seventh century B.C. *i.e.* shortly after the fall of the northern kingdom. The additions made by the Deuteronomic editors of the exilic period are comparatively few. The ancient sources on which the books of Samuel are based may have been (1) contemporary chronicles compiled by early prophets, *e.g.* by Samuel, Nathan, and Gad (cp. 1 Chron. xxix 29), and preserved in the 'Schools of the Prophets' at Ramah or elsewhere ; (2) *The Chronicles of king David* (1 Chron. xxvii. 24) *i.e.* probably state documents, lists of officials, brief records of warlike expeditions, etc. ; (3) In 1 Sam. x. 25 a book or charter describing *the manner of the kingdom* is mentioned. Possibly this charter "was added to *the Book of the Law* kept by the side of the ark *before the Lord*" (Kirkpatrick, note *ad loc.* in Camb. Bible); (4) Collections of national poetry, the *Book of Jashar* etc. The *Song of Hannah* (1 Sam. ii. 1—10) seems to be a later composition put into the mouth of Hannah by the redactor of the book. The section 2 Sam. xxii. 1—xxiii. 7 seems also to be a later insertion. There are thus many indications that the work is for the most part based on contemporary testimony. The frequent occurrence of *double narratives*, inconsistent in their minor details, tends to confirm the general impression of trustworthiness, since it shows that "the compiler faithfully embodied the authorities he consulted, instead of harmonizing them into what might have seemed a more consistent whole" (Kirkpatrick on *The first book of Samuel*, Camb. Bible, p. 14). Whether the Pentateuchal sources J and E extend into the historical books, is at present a disputed question.

The Books of Kings have had a similar history. In this case also a collection of older narratives has been fitted by a compiler into a framework supplied by himself. Certain original sources are expressly named, *e.g. The Book of the acts of Solomon* (1 Kings xi. 41), the *Book of the annals of the kings of Israel* and *Judah* (1 Kings xiv. 19 and 29). The book incorporates some prophetical narratives, *e.g.* those relating to Elijah and Elisha, which are probably borrowed from a document compiled early in the eighth century in northern Palestine (*c.* 800—750). The writer may also have had access to the temple archives, and to various state documents and official registers ; an official 'recorder,' lit. *he who brings to remembrance*, is mentioned among the ministers of the court in various passages (*e.g.* 1 Kings iv. 3 ; 2 Kings xviii. 18, 37; cp. 2 Sam. viii. 16, xx. 25 ; 2 Chron. xxxiv. 18). One passage seems to be borrowed from the *Book of Jashar* (1 Kings viii. 12 foll.). Certain features of the work indicate that it was substantially complete in its present form before the exile (*c.* 600 B.C.). The original compiler was probably "a man like-minded with Jeremiah and almost certainly a contemporary who lived and wrote under the same influences" (Driver, *LOT*, p. 199). Certain additions were evidently made, and didactic comments added by a later editor of the exilic period, himself imbued with the "Deuteronomic" mode of thought.

The writings of various prophets shed an important light upon the period between 750 and the fall of the southern kingdom (586): especially those of *Amos, Hosea, Isaiah, Micah, Zephaniah, Jeremiah.* The Assyrian inscriptions of the period between the ninth and sixth century are also of great interest and importance. These are occasionally alluded to or quoted in the notes.

The Books of Chronicles (which originally formed part of a single work, including the Books of Ezra and Nehemiah) are of little value as an independent source of information. They contain a narrative of the history of Judah and of the temple compiled from the standpoint of an ecclesiastic, writing late in the post-exilic period. "Chronicles represents the late post-exilic theory of the Jewish monarchy, according to which the good kings scrupulously observed the laws of the Pentateuch" (Bennett, *A Primer of the Bible*, p. 110). The author may have been a levitical chorister or porter.

The question of importance in regard to Chronicles is the nature and value of the sources to which the author constantly refers. To some extent, of course, he employed the *canonical* books (esp. Samuel and Kings) as the basis of his narrative. He refers also to a work called *The Book of the kings of Judah and Israel,* which is supposed by scholars to be an expanded edition or *midrash* of the canonical Book of Kings, produced some time between the exile and the third century, B.C. "The midrash may be defined as an imaginative development of a thought or theme suggested by scripture, especially a didactic or homiletic exposition or an edifying religious story. To judge from the title [*midrash of the Book of Kings,* 2 Chron. xxiv. 27], the book here referred to will have been a work on the book of Kings, developing such incidents as were adapted to illustrate the didactic import of the history" (Driver, *LOT*, p. 529). The Chronicler also refers frequently to the *Words* or the *Vision* or the *Midrash* of certain prophets ; but it is most likely that these were sections incorporated in the historical work already mentioned, a work which embraced not only the acts of the kings but also passages from the lives of particular prophets.

The Books of Chronicles cannot be used without corroboration as an independent source of information. They throw a valuable light on the ecclesiastical Judaism of the post-exilic period : but though some of the incidents related in them may be regarded as *probable* (*e.g.* Uzziah's buildings and campaigns, Manasseh's captivity in Babylon), they cannot be accepted as certain in the absence of other information.

Chapter X. *The Books of Ezra and Nehemiah.*

The original basis of these books (which originally formed one work with the Books of Chronicles, and were apparently compiled by the same hand) was a collection of 'memoirs' relating to the work of Ezra and Nehemiah. Certain sections of Ezra (iv. 8—vi. 18 and vii. 12—26) are written in the Aramaic dialect. These sections seem to be borrowed from a historical work written in Aramaic, narrating either the complete history of the restored community, or the troubles which arose between the restored exiles and their neighbours until the reign of Artaxerxes. Besides using certain memoirs of Ezra and Nehemiah, the compiler evidently had access to official edicts, lists and genealogies. The main drawback to the historical value of the books is a certain disregard of chronological sequence. But the documents contained in them, though not all of equal historical value, supply us with the only materials available for reconstructing the history of an important epoch. They describe "the foundation of the system of Judaism at a time when the influence of the Aryan races first made itself felt upon the life and culture of the Israelite people" (Ryle, *Ezra and Nehemiah, Camb. Bib.*, p. lxix).

Other authorities bearing upon the period of the Exile and the Return in 536 are the writings of the Prophets, especially *Ezekiel, Isaiah*, chh. xl.—lxvi., *Haggai, Zechariah*, chh. i.—viii., *Malachi.*

There are three inscriptions of special interest bearing on the accession and policy of Cyrus. These are mentioned in the notes.

Chapters XI. and XII.

Of the various authorities for the period between 432 and 4 B.C. may be specially mentioned (1) the writings of *Josephus*, (2) the two *Books of the Maccabees*.

(1) Josephus was born at Jerusalem, at the beginning of Caligula's reign (37—38 A.D.). He was descended from a priestly family and received a careful rabbinical education. At the age of 19 he joined the party of the Pharisees. In the year 64 he was sent to Rome to negotiate the release of certain Jewish prisoners. In the war of 66 he was entrusted with the post of Jewish commander-in-chief in Galilee. In 67 he was captured by the Romans and brought to Vespasian, to whom he foretold his future elevation. To this fortunate prediction Josephus owed his later success in life. In 69 he was released by Vespasian and assumed the family name of the new emperor, "Flavius." He returned to Palestine and was employed by Titus as an agent in negotiating with the Jews. At the close of the war he settled in Rome, enjoyed the favour of three successive emperors, and died early in the second century. His years of literary leisure at Rome enabled him to produce four important works : (1) The history of his own life, especially of his military career in the war of 66—67, (2) *The Treatise against Apion*, a kind of apology for the Jewish people and their religion, (3) *The Wars of the Jews* (περὶ τοῦ Ἰουδαϊκοῦ πολέμου) in seven books, covering the period between 175 and 4 B.C. This work was originally composed by Josephus in Aramaic, and re-written at a later period in Greek ; (4) *The Antiquities of the Jews* (Ἰουδαϊκὴ Ἀρχαιολογία), 20 books embracing the history from the earliest times to the outbreak of the war of 66 A.D. Books 1—10 relate the history of the Jews to the close of the exile, books 11—20 from the return to the year 66. His main authorities seem to have been the canonical books (especially the LXX. version). He also makes free use of the Jewish *Haggadah* and *Halachah*, and other (Hellenistic) reproductions of the biblical story. The chief extra-biblical writings to which he occasionally refers are the first book of the Maccabees, and the works of Polybius, Strabo, Nicolas of Damascus (especially for the life of Herod), and other less trustworthy authors.

(2) *The first Book of the Maccabees* is the main source for the period 175—135 B.C.   The book is a document of primary importance.   It was probably compiled early in the first century, B.C. Originally written in Hebrew or Aramaic, it was translated into Greek before the time of Josephus.   As regards the general character of the narrative, it is so complete and circumstantial that the writer must be supposed to have had access to written notices of the Maccabaean struggle and of the three chief figures in it, Judas and his brothers Jonathan and Simon.   Some minor errors have been detected in the narrative, and in particular there is a tendency to exaggerate numbers, but this is a fault characteristic of the age in which the writer lived.

The second Book of the Maccabees covers the period 175—161 B.C. It is ostensibly a mere rhetorical abridgement of a work in five books by Jason of Cyrene (2 Macc. ii. 23), a Hellenistic Jew of whose original history no remains are extant.   The epitome may have been compiled at about 35 or 40 A.D.   Apart from some serious discrepancies between 1 Macc. and 2 Macc., there is a broad contrast in the style and purpose of the two books.   The writer of 2 Macc. clearly aims at religious edification ; he "selects and modifies his historical material with a view to homiletic ends" (Fairweather in Hastings' *DB*, s. v. 'Maccabees, Books of').   The chief object of the book is perhaps to exalt the temple and its worship in the eyes of the Jews of the Dispersion.   It has been conjectured that the author belonged to the Pharisaic party, and bore no good will to the Hasmonaean dynasty.

The canonical Books of *Daniel* and *Esther* belong to the period covered by chh. xi.—xii., and both have a certain historical importance.   A brief notice of each is given in the narrative and in the notes.

Of the copious Jewish and Hellenistic literature that illustrates the history and theology of Judaism during the last two centuries, B.C. a full account is given by Schürer, *History of the Jewish People*, §§ 32—34.

APPENDIX II.

I. The earliest stage of Hebrew legislation is that described in Exod. xviii. 15 foll., where Moses is represented as giving decisions on matters of dispute between man and man. These decisions were called *torôth* (plur. of *torah*, 'direction' or 'instruction' on matters of law and conduct). Tradition points to Moses as the author of this system. In Exod. *l.c.* we read of his delegating to others a portion of his judicial and administrative work. Within a short period however the duty of declaring *torah* was assigned to the priests. Judicial decisions were given at the sanctuary, in Jehovah's name, and probably use was made of the sacred lot in determining the divine will (Exod. xviii. 19, xxi. 6). These decisions (*torôth*) would gradually acquire the force of consuetudinary law, and an elementary code of justice would thus be founded.

In process of time however the word *torah* acquired two senses. (1) In its broader sense as used by the *prophets* the word *torah* included a moral element. It came to mean teaching given in Jehovah's name on points of moral and social duty. This teaching was embodied in the living 'Word of Jehovah' declared by the mouth of His prophets (cp. Isai. i. 10; Amos ii. 4; Hos. iv. 6 viii. 12). This prophetic *torah* seems to have been traced also to Moses, who was regarded as the first prophet of Israel, and whose teaching was primarily, if not exclusively, *moral.* The prophets imply that the *torah* of Moses was not concerned with matters of ritual (cp. Jer. vii. 22, 23). "Worship by sacrifice, and all that belongs to it, is no part of the divine *torah* to Israel. It forms, if you will, part of natural religion which other nations share with Israel, and which is no feature in the *distinctive precepts* given at the Exodus " (W. R. Smith, *OTJC*, p. 303). (2) *Torah* in the narrower sense signified *oral direction* on points of ritual or ceremonial observance, *e.g.* the ritual of sacrifice, distinctions between clean and unclean, etc. (cp. Deut. xxiv. 8; Hag. ii. 11). What the prophets occasionally censure in the priests is their neglect of the true principles which ought to guide them in giving 'direction (cp. Jer. ii. 8; Zeph. iii. 4; Hab. i. 4, etc.). In process of time *torah* was naturally extended to mean a body of technical directions on ceremonial points. Thus we read of 'The *torah* of the Burnt-offering,' etc. (Lev. vi. 9; cp. 14, 25, etc.). This expression is frequently found in the Priestly Code, and of course refers to a custom or law, which having been originally a matter of oral tradition had ultimately been codified in written form. After Ezra's time, when the Pentateuch had virtually assumed its present shape, the *torah* came to signify the Pentateuch as a whole (so 1 Chron. xvi. 40), and particularly its legal portions (so often in the Psalms). As the prophetic *torah* was traced to Moses, so the foundation of priestly *torah* was ascribed to him. From the first, Hebrew law was placed under the sanction of Jehovah; His sanctuary was the seat of justice, the priests were His spokesmen; and the system instituted by Moses was in fact the foundation of the complete *torah*, which was afterwards embodied in the Pentateuchal codes.

II. In the Pentateuch we find several distinct collections of laws, clearly belonging to different epochs in the history. At an early period the original 'decisions' of the priests must have been tabulated. These would be revised or expanded from time to time to suit the changing requirements of the nation. It is clear from such a passage as Hos. viii. 12 that some *written* code existed before the prophetic period.

The following codes can be distinguished.

A. *The Decalogue.*

It has been assumed in the text of Chapter III. that the traditional account of the decalogue is correct: that it was actually delivered to the Hebrews by Moses speaking in the name of

Jehovah, and that it was originally engraved on tables of stone in a short and primitive form (without the parenetic additions given in Exod. xx. and Deut. v.). It has been supposed that the original decalogue ran somewhat as follows:

1. Thou shalt have no other gods beside me.
2. Thou shalt not make unto thee any graven image.
3. Thou shalt not take the name of Jehovah thy God for a vain end.
4. Remember the sabbath day to hallow it.
5. Honour thy father and thy mother.
6. Thou shalt do no murder.
7. Thou shalt not commit adultery.
8. Thou shalt not steal.
9. Thou shalt not bear false witness against thy neighbour.
10. Thou shalt not covet thy neighbour's house.

The Mosaic origin of the decalogue is questioned by critics mainly on the ground (1) that such purely *moral* precepts are out of harmony with the essentially *ritualistic* tendency of early religion; (2) that the prohibition of images seems to have been unknown, or at least a dead letter, till the time of Hosea; (3) that we find distinct traces of another and older decalogue in Exod. xxxiv. 10—28; the precepts there given are described as 'the words of the covenant, the ten words,' and are said to have been written upon two tables (Exod. xxxiv. 28). This decalogue (if it be one) is found in the Jehovistic narrative, whereas Exod. xx. 2 foll. belongs to E. According to Wellhausen, its precepts may have run somewhat as follows:

1. Thou shalt worship no other god.
2. Thou shalt make thee no molten gods.
3. The feast of unleavened bread shalt thou keep.
4. Every firstling is mine.
5. Thou shalt keep the feast of weeks.
6. Thou shalt keep the feast of ingathering at the end of the year.
7. Thou shalt not offer the blood of my sacrifice with leaven.
8. The fat of my feast shall not be left over until the morning.
9. Thou shalt bring the best of the firstfruits of thy land to the house of Jehovah thy God.
10. Thou shalt not seethe a kid in his mother's milk.

It may suffice to say that at present we have not the necessary *data* for solving with certainty the question whether there were two conflicting traditions among the Hebrews as to the original charter of the covenant. In the absence of such data we are justified in arguing that the traditional view of the decalogue is intrinsically credible. It is consistent with the admitted fact that the religion taught by Moses was peculiarly *ethical*: that it taught higher conceptions of God and of moral duty than were current among other Semitic peoples. It also explains satisfactorily the vitality and vigour which gave to the Hebrews their physical superiority over the inhabitants of Canaan. At the same time it must be admitted that in its present form the decalogue may possibly show traces of prophetic expansion. The second commandment may in fact be "a development by the prophetic school of a consequence originally only latent in the Mosaic prohibition of the worship of other gods" (Hastings' *DB*, s. v. 'Decalogue'). With regard to the 'decalogue' in Exod. xxxiv. it may be observed (*a*) that critics are not agreed as to the precise precepts included in it; (*b*) that in any case it is not attributed to Moses but to a somewhat later stage in the history; (*c*) that the account in the Pentateuch of the Sinaitic legislation shows traces of dislocation and confusion which are probably due to the circumstances under which it was compiled (cp. W. R. Smith, *OTJC*, pp. 336 foll.).

B. *The Book of the Covenant* (Exod. xx. 20—xxiii. 33. Cp. xxxiv. 10—28). This original code contains laws adapted to the needs and conditions of a simple agricultural community. It evidently embodies the different 'decisions' which had accumulated during the early stages of Israel's history. If it belongs to the Sinaitic period, it has evidently been expanded and revised to meet the needs of a settled community. The details of the system may be illustrated by parallel usages in the codes of other nations (*e.g.* Solon's code at Athens). Some of the enactments relate to *civil and criminal* law: *e.g.* the rights of slaves (Exod. xxi. 2—11), the penalties to be inflicted for crimes of violence, and the compensations due for injury done to life and limb or property of a neighbour (xxi. 12—xxii. 16). Other precepts are moral, religious and ceremonial. The main points worthy of notice in the code are:

(1) The simplicity of the religious arrangements and duties contemplated in the code, *e.g.* the law as to altars (xx. 24—26),

firstfruits (xxii. 29 foll.), observance of the sabbath, the sabbatical year, the three annual festivals (xxiii. 10—17), and the mode of sacrifice (xxiii. 18—19).

(2) The regard paid to the claims of humanity and justice. "Jehovah is behind the law and He will vindicate the right. He requires of Israel humanity as well as justice. The *gêr*, or stranger, living under the protection of a family or community, has no legal status, but he must not be oppressed" (*OTJC*, p. 341). The widow and the orphan, the poor and the slave, are all taken as it were under the protection of Jehovah (xxii. 21—27); even an enemy is not to be wronged (xxiii. 4 foll.). In a word "the ordinances are not abstractly perfect...but they are fit to make Israel a righteous, humane and God-fearing people, and to facilitate ahealthy growth towards better things" (*OTJC*, p. 343).

C. *The Law of Deuteronomy* (chh. v.—xxviii.) consists of a code of laws, ethical, social and religious, mostly repeated or expanded from those contained in the *Book of the Covenant*. It is obvious that the Deuteronomic law contemplates a community living under more complex social conditions. The early laws are accordingly adapted to later requirements; new definitions are added, and hortatory introductions and comments are inserted.

The following points are worthy of special notice:

(1) The main feature of Deuteronomy is the fundamental law restricting the worship of Jehovah to the sanctuary at Jerusalem (Deut. xii.). This regulation cut at the roots of the popular religion of the pre-prophetic period. Its aim was to purge the worship of Jehovah from the contaminations of Canaanitish heathenism. It was this law that constituted the guiding principle of Josiah's reformation (620), and indeed it was the necessary practical outcome of the strict monotheism preached by the prophets. A marked feature of the Deuteronomic code is its denunciation of every symbol of idolatry (see xii. 2 foll., xvi. 21 foll., xviii. 9 foll.), every trace of heathen superstitions or practices. Israel was to separate itself rigidly from alliance or intermarriage with the heathen (vii. 3 foll., xiii. 6 foll.). It was to adhere with perfect fidelity and devotion to the God who had loved and redeemed His people from the beginning. The love of Jehovah is proclaimed as the first principle of religion (vi. 5, x. 12, xi. 1, 13, 22, xxx. 6, 16, 20, etc.).

(2)   Another distinctive feature of the Deuteronomic legislation is its regard for charity and humanity.   " Regard not only for the rights, but also for the needs of the widow, the orphan, the landless Levite, the foreign denizen, is urged at every turn.   The interests of debtors, slaves, and hired labourers, are carefully guarded. Various provisions protect the rights of the wife or the female slave. Nor are the animals forgotten.   The spirit of the legislation is seen not least clearly in the laws which appear to us altogether utopian, such as xx.; cp. xxiv. 5, xvii. 14—20, xv. 1—6 " (Moore in *Encyc. Bibl.* s.v. ' Deuteronomy ').

(3)   The civil laws of Deuteronomy clearly belong to a later stage of the history than the first legislation: *e.g.* there is some restriction of the law of retaliation (cp. Deut. xix. 16 foll. with Ex. xxi. 23 foll.); in the administration of justice a civil judge is associated with the priest (Deut. xvii. 9, 12); the rights of a Hebrew woman are extended (cp. Deut. xv. 12—17 with Exod. xxi. 7 foll., which treats the female slave as absolute property).   There are other minor regulations in Deut. which mark a growth in morality and refinement.   "The growth of custom and usage is on the whole upward, and ancient social usages, which survived for many centuries after the age of Josiah among the heathen of Arabia and Syria, already lie behind the Deuteronomic code." (*OTJC*, p. 370.)

The Deuteronomic code in fact illustrates the way in which the teaching of the great eighth-century prophets had leavened the better part of the nation, and had elevated their ideas of Jehovah's character and their conceptions of His moral requirement.

D.   The *Law of Holiness* is the title given by modern scholars to a short code of moral and religious precepts contained in Levit chh. xvii.—xxvi.   The nucleus of this code is much more ancient than the form in which it now appears.   It was probably compiled in or near the time of Ezekiel, *i.e.* between *c.* 595—570 B.C.   The editor's hand appears in the parenetic passages with which the code is interspersed.   The code derives its modern title from the fact that its regulating idea is that of *holiness*, moral and ceremonial, this being the special quality demanded of Israel by Jehovah.

Characteristic of this short code is:

(i) The prominence of duties connected with agriculture (see Lev. xix. 9 foll., 23 foll., xxiii. 9 foll., xxv. 1—7).

(ii) The conception of sin as impurity, by which Jehovah's land and community are defiled (see Lev. xviii. 25 foll., xx. 3, 7). Hence the frequent warnings against the immoral customs and superstitions of the heathen (*e.g.* in chh. xviii. 3, 24, 30, xx. 23 etc.).

(iii) The care for duties of humanity and justice. See ch. xix. *passim*, esp. v. 18 where the passage culminates in the injunction *Thou shalt love thy neighbour as thyself.* In this respect, and in its appeal to religious motives, the 'Law of Holiness' is akin to the teaching of Deuteronomy. (Note the characteristic refrain *I am Jehovah* in ch. xix. and elsewhere.)

E. The Law of Holiness was ultimately incorporated in the *Priestly Code* (P), compiled in Babylon during and after the age of Ezekiel. "Its object was to present a picture of Israel's sacred institutions as they should be, and as the author doubtless hoped that by means of his book they would become. On the precedent of older models, this desired ideal is represented as having been originally prescribed by God through Moses and realized in the distant past. It is cast in the form of a history extending from the creation of the world to the Israelite settlement in Canaan" (Montefiore, *Hibbert Lectures*, p. 317). The historical framework, sometimes very slight and meagre, in which the laws are set, only concerns us in so far as it illustrates the manner and aims of the compiler. Thus the Creation is described as inaugurating the observance of the Sabbath; the Flood leads to a primitive declaration of the sacredness of life and the consequent prohibition of eating flesh with the blood; the custom of circumcision is connected with the birth of Isaac. Historical incidents are mentioned as the original basis of certain enactments, *e.g.* Num. ix. 6 foll., xxvii. 1 foll. Regarded merely as a code of laws, P is distinguished by its fulness and elaboration, and by its limitation for the most part to ceremonial ordinances connected with the sacrificial worship of the tabernacle, the rites of purification and atonement, the duties, revenues and perquisites of the priesthood.

A rough outline of the legal code is all that can be attempted here:

1.   The Law of Circumcision (Gen. xvii.).

2.   The Law of the Passover (Ex. xii.).

3.   The description of the Tabernacle and its furniture, the dress and consecration of the priests, the law of the daily burnt-offering, etc. (Ex. xxv.—xxxi., xxxv.—xl.).

4.   The ritual of the sacrifices (*a*) the Burnt-offering (Lev. i.); (*b*) the Meal-offering (ii.); (*c*) the Peace- (or thank-) offering (iii.); (*d*) the Sin- and guilt-offerings (iv. 1—vi. 7).

5.   Regulations relating to the Priests, their dress, perquisites, etc. (vi. 8—x.)

6.   Laws of Purification and Atonement, culminating in the description of the ritual of the Day of Atonement (xi.—xvi.; Num. v. 1—4, xix.).

7.   The commutation of tithes and vows (Lev. xxvii.; Num. xxx.).

8.   The Law of the Nazirite (Num. vi.).

9.   Duties, revenues, and distribution of tithes appointed for the priests and Levites (Num. xviii.). The Levitical cities (xxxv. 1—8).

10.   Miscellaneous laws, some supplementary, some intended to harmonize various passages in the completed code, others dealing with civil matters, *e.g.* the law of inheritance for daughters (xxvii. 1—11), the distribution of spoil captured in war (xxxi. 21—30), the law relating to homicide, and appointment of cities of refuge (xxxv. 9—34).

For a full description and examination of P the reader is referred to such works as Driver, *LOT*, esp. pp. 126 foll., Montefiore, *Hibbert Lectures*, no. vi.

Regarded as a code, it is distinguished by its leading idea, viz. that Israel is called to be a holy community, sanctified by the presence of Jehovah dwelling in its midst. The nation is treated as a Church living only for the service of God. Hence the number of rites connected with the removal of all possible sins and defilements which are inconsistent with the presence of God in His earthly sanctuary. P (and especially the *Law of Holiness*) in this respect shows clear traces of the influence of Ezekiel xl.—xlviii.—a kind of programme of the rites and laws to be observed by Israel after its restoration to its own land.

In spite of its idealistic character, however, it is important to remember that the Priestly Code is based upon ancient and traditional ordinances. Indeed the ceremonial system of the Hebrews was doubtless closely akin to that of other Semitic nations ; it contained elements probably borrowed from the Canaanites. This point is amply illustrated in such a book as W. Robertson Smith's *Religion of the Semites.* The peculiar feature of the *Hebrew* system in its developed form is that it gives concrete expression to certain spiritual ideas. There lies behind it the prophetic conception of a holy people sanctified by the indwelling presence of the God of holiness (cp. Ezek. xlviii. 35).

The general effect of this elaborate and formal code was twofold. On the one hand it played a real part in the religious education of Israel. It tended to develope and deepen the sense of sin, and it awakened in devout souls religious affections : trust, devotion, self-surrender, thankful love, the longing for divine grace. But the dangers that might beset the observance of so detailed a code are obvious enough ; the spirit of formalism, the confusion of technical holiness with moral purity, the readiness to acquiesce in a merely external standard of religion.

We should remember however that the very book which included the priestly legislation also contained the deeper spiritual teaching of Deuteronomy. "The prophets moreover remained the eloquent and moving exponents of spiritual religion, and of the paramount claims of the moral law above all ritual observances. The correction for the ceremonialism of P was thus close at hand in writings acknowledged by the Jews themselves as authoritative....The ceremonial legislation never had a separate existence of its own ; and the Jewish 'law,' if it is to be judged properly, must be judged as a whole, and not with exclusive reference to one of its parts" (Driver in Hastings' *DB.* s.v. 'Law (in O.T.)': vol. iii. p. 72).

We may indicate in conclusion certain lines of thought and study in regard to the law :

(1) Its religious and moral symbolism. See esp. Willis, *Worship of the Old Covenant.* (Parker & Co., 1880.)

(2) The effect of the Law in the post-exilic age as a safeguard against the disintegrating influences of Hellenism. See esp. Montefiore, *Hibbert Lectures,* lectt. vii.—ix.

(3) The place of the Law in the N.T. and in post-biblical Judaism.

APPENDIX III.

I. Connected with the Sabbath.

(1) The weekly Sabbath.

(2) The New Moon (Num. x. 10, xxviii. 11—15).

(3) *The Feast of Trumpets* on the first day of the seventh month (Tisri). This day marking the commencement of the civil year was observed with special solemnity. Additional sacrifices were offered, and the silver trumpets used on the occasion of each New Moon were blown more frequently. See Num. xxix. 1—6; Lev. xxiii. 24 fol.

(4) *The Sabbatical Year:* during which the land was to *rest and lie still* (Exod. xxiii. 11), debts were to be remitted, and Hebrew slaves set free (Deut. xv. 1—3, 12—15).

(5) *The Year of Jubilee* (mentioned only in P) closed a cycle of 7 × 7 years. In the fiftieth year, which was proclaimed by the sound of a trumpet on the Day of Atonement, alienated property was to revert to its original owners. This ideal arrangement was intended to assert the principle that all the land occupied by Israel belonged to God. Another feature of the Jubilee was the liberation of all bondmen of Hebrew race (Lev. xxv. 8—16, 23—35, xxvii. 16—25).

II. The three great national festivals (Heb. *Chaggîm, i.e.* occasions of 'pilgrimage' [Arab. *ḥaj*] to Jehovah's sanctuary): the *Passover, Pentecost,* the feast of *Tabernacles.*

These three feasts were annual occasions of rejoicing connected with different stages of the harvest. The Hebrews however assigned to them a certain historical significance as well. They were associated with memories and incidents of the Exodus and the period of the wanderings.

1. *The Passover* (פֶסַח, πάσχα) was closely followed by the Feast of *Mazzoth* or 'unleavened bread' (ἑορτὴ τῶν ἀζύμων). As a matter of fact the origin of the two feasts seems to have been distinct: but in Exod. xii., xiii. they are closely combined, and in the N.T. they are practically identified. The Passover falling on Nisan 14 served as a preparation for the Feast of *Mazzoth* (Nisan 15—21) just as the great Day of Atonement (Tisri 10) heralded the Feast of Tabernacles (Tisri 15). The two feasts together (*Passover* and *Mazzoth*) marked the beginning of harvest. On Nisan 16 the first ripe sheaf of barley was to be brought into the Sanctuary and waved before Jehovah. Before this ceremony took place no produce of the new harvest might be eaten (Lev. xxiii. 9—14).

The *Passover* was a memorial of the nation's redemption from Egypt. Its distinctive feature, in virtue of which it is spoken of as Jehovah's 'sacrifice' (Exod. xii. 27, xxxiv. 25), was the slaughter of a lamb. The victim was selected on the 10th day and slain on the 14th. It was then roasted whole with fire and eaten with unleavened bread and bitter herbs by the assembled household. Anything left was consumed with fire. Later ceremonies, *e.g.* the introduction of four cups of wine, the first of which was solemnly blessed by the head of the company, the singing of the Hallel, etc. are implied in the N.T. See St Luke xxii. 17 foll. (Cp. Hastings' *DB*, art. 'Passover'; Edersheim, *Life and Times of Jesus the Messiah*, vol. ii. pp. 496 foll.)

Throughout the Feast of *Mazzoth* special sacrifices were offered daily. The first and last days, Nisan 15 and 21, were days of 'holy convocation.' See Num. xxviii. 19 foll. ; Lev. xxiii. 7.

2. The Feast of *Pentecost* or *Weeks* (חַג שָׁבֻעוֹת, ἑορτὴ ἑβδομάδων) took place at the close of seven weeks from Nisan 16. Other titles imply its connection with the operations of harvest, 'The Feast of Harvest' (Exod. xxiii. 16), 'The day of Firstfruits' (Num. xxviii. 26). The feast marked the completion of the corn-harvest. Its most characteristic feature was the waving before Jehovah of two loaves of wheaten flour (Lev. xxiii. 15—17). Special sacrifices were also

prescribed. In post-biblical times Pentecost was regarded as a commemoration of the giving of the Law on Sinai, which was supposed to have occurred on the fiftieth day after the Exodus (see Hastings' *DB*, art. 'Pentecost'). The festive joy of the Pentecostal feast was to be shared by all classes of the community, the slave, the stranger, the fatherless and the widow (Deut. xvi. 11).

3. The Feast of *Tabernacles* or *Booths* (חג הסכות, ἑορτὴ σκηνῶν) also called the 'feast of ingathering' (Exod. xxiii. 16, xxxiv. 22), was observed from Tisri 15 to 22. It marked the completion of the harvest, when the corn, wine and oil were all gathered in. It was the Hebrew 'harvest-home,' and was the most joyous and largely frequented feast of the year. Its special feature was the custom of living in tents or booths made of boughs gathered from the trees. See Exod. xxiii. 16; Lev. xxiii. 34 foll.; Num. xxix. 12—40; Deut. xvi. 13 foll., and cp. Neh. viii. This custom was intended to commemorate the wanderings of the Israelites in the wilderness. In post-exilic times, portions of the Law were publicly read on each day of the feast, and the sacrifices were more numerous than at any other festival. Other picturesque customs were introduced at a later time, two of which (the procession to Siloam to fetch water which was solemnly poured out at the foot of the altar, and the illumination of the 'court of the women' in the temple) are probably alluded to in St John vii. 37, and viii. 12. See Westcott, *ad loc.*

III. *Minor Historical Festivals.*

1. *The Feast of Purim*, or 'lots,' is said to have been instituted in commemoration of Haman's overthrow and the failure of his plot for the destruction of the Jews (Esth. iii. 7, ix. 15—32). Hence also the title 'day of Mordecai' in 2 Macc. xv. 36. It was celebrated on Adar 14 and 15. The 13th Adar was at a later time observed as a fast in preparation for the Feast. On the evening of the 13th the book of Esther was publicly read at the synagogue service amid the execrations of the congregation. Some scholars ascribe to this feast a Persian origin.

2. *The Feast of Dedication* was instituted to commemorate the re-dedication of the temple after its desecration by Antiochus

Epiphanes (25 Chisleu, 165 B.C.). It lasted for eight days, and was the occasion of extensive illuminations.

Other minor feasts are mentioned by Josephus and in 1 Macc., but they seem never to have been generally observed.

IV. *Fasts.*

1. *The Day of Atonement* (יום הכפרים, ἡμέρα ἐξιλασμοῦ) was observed on Tisri 10, five days before the joyous feast of Tabernacles. It was the only fast appointed by the Law. The observances of the day are fully prescribed in Lev. xvi. As there is no mention of its observance in biblical times, it has been inferred that the Day of Atonement was not instituted before the time of Nehemiah (see Hastings' *DB*, art. 'Atonement, Day of'). In any case the developed ritual must have gradually assumed the form described in Lev. xvi.

The leading features of the day were three:

    1. The entry of the high priest into the Holy of Holies.
    2. The sending away of the scape-goat.
    3. The observance of a rigorous fast.

The day was in fact the culminating institution of the sacrificial system. It "summed up and interpreted the whole conception of sacrifices which were designed by divine appointment to gain for man access to God" (Westcott, *Hebrews*, p. 279). It related to *all* the sins of the people, thus completing the series of piacular sacrifices. Once a year took place an atoning rite, which included not only the people but the sanctuary itself, in so far as it had contracted defilement from its presence in the midst of a sinful people (Lev. xvi. 16).

See *inter alia* Schultz, *Old Test. Theology* [Eng. Tr.], vol. i. pp. 367 foll., 402 foll.; Robertson Smith, *Religion of the Semites*, pp. 388 foll.; Delitzsch's and Westcott's commentaries on the *Ep. to the Hebrews*.

2. From Zech. vii. 3—5 it may be inferred that two fasts were observed after 586, one in memory of the destruction of Jerusalem (5th month), the other in memory of the murder of Gedaliah and the extinction of the Jewish state (7th month). Two other fasts are mentioned in Zech. viii. 19, both connected with the fall of the city, but it is uncertain whether these were publicly observed. The

teaching of Zechariah seems to be directed against the continued observance of these fasts in the literal sense. He recalls to the memory of the restored exiles Jehovah's true requirement. "Let them drop their fasts, and practise the virtues the neglect of which had made their fasts a necessity" (G. A. Smith, *The Book of the Twelve Prophets*, vol. ii. p. 321).

Subjoined is a calendar of the Jewish year.

| Year | | Month | English months (roughly) | Festivals and Fasts | Season |
Sacred	Civil				
i.	7	Abib or Nisan	Apr.	14. The PASSOVER and F. of *Mazzoth*	The *latter* or Spring rains
ii.	8	Zif	May		Barley and Wheat Harvest
iii.	9	Sivan	June	6. PENTECOST or F. of Weeks	
iv.	10	Thammuz	July		Hot and Dry Season. Grape Harvest
v.	11	Ab	Aug.		
vi.	12	Elul	Sept.		
vii.	1	Tisri or Ethanim	Oct.	1. F. of TRUMPETS 10. Day of ATONEMENT 15. F. of TABERNACLES	The *former* rains. Ploughing and seed time
viii.	2	Bul	Nov.		
ix.	3	Chisleu	Dec.	25. F. of DEDICATION	Winter
x.	4	Thebeth	Jan.		
xi.	5	Shebat	Feb.		
xii.	6	Adar	Mar.	14, 15. F. of PURIM	Approach of Spring

CHRONOLOGICAL TABLES.

TABLE I.

Primitive History to accession of Solomon.

[The following dates are for the most part extremely uncertain. In particular there are wide differences of opinion respecting the date of Khammurabi's reign, which is variously assigned to B.C. 2376 (Sayce), 2285 (King), and 1772 (Hommel).]

  c. 4000 Semitic kingdom of Uruk (Erech in South Babylonia).

  c. 3800 Semitic kingdom in North Babylonia.
      SARGON of Agade.

  c. 3750 NARÂM SIN ruler of North Syria, Mesopotamia, Elam and North Arabia.

  c. 2800 Semitic kingdom of Ur.

  c. 2400 Kings of Babylon.

  c. 2376 KHAMMURABI king of Babylon.

  c. 2350 *The age of Abraham.*

  c. 2098–1587 Period of HYKSOS' rule in Egypt.

  c. 1700–1650 *Descent of the Hebrews into Egypt.*

   1503 THOTHMES III.

   1414 AMENOPHIS III. Correspondence preserved in Tel-el-Amarna tablets.

   1327 SETI I. (Nineteenth dynasty).

   1275 RAMSES II.

   1208 MERENPTAH.

  c. 1200 *Exodus of the Hebrews from Egypt.*

   1181 RAMSES III. (Twentieth dynasty).

  c. 1020 *Saul king of Israel.*

  c. 1010 *David king of Israel.*

  c. 970 *Solomon king of Israel.*

TABLE II.

The divided Kingdom. c. 970—722.

Date	Judah	Israel	Internal History	Syria, etc.	Egypt	Assyria	Date
c. 930	Rehoboam	*Jeroboam I.*	....	REZON founds kingdom at Damascus	Shishak (960–939)	....	c. 930
c. 920	Abijam	....	....				c. 920
c. 917	Asa	Nadab *Baasha* Elah *Zimri*	....	BENHADAD I.	Osorkon II. ? Zerah of 2 Chr. xiv. 9	....	c. 917
c. 890	....	*Omri*	....	⎱	....	....	c. 890
885	....		....		....	ASSUR-NAZIR-PÂL (885–860)	885
c. 875	....	Ahab	⎱	....	....	....	c. 875
c. 874	Jehoshaphat	....		....	....	....	c. 874
c. 860	....	....	⎬Elijah	? Revolt of Mesha of Moab	....	SHALMAN-ESER II. (860–825)	c. 860
854	....	Israelites Ahaziah	and Syrians	defeated at battle of Ka rkar			854
c. 853	....	Jehoram	⎰	....	....	....	c. 853
c. 852	Jehoram		⎱	HAZAEL	....	....	c. 852
c. 849	Jehoram	....		Constant	war between	....	c. 849
c. 844	Ahaziah	....		Syria and	Israel. Syria	....	c. 844
c. 843	....	*Jehu*		weakened	by aggres-	....	c. 843
c. 842	*Athaliah*	Jehu pays tribute to Assyria		sion of	Assyria	....	c. 842
c. 836	Joash	....	⎬Elisha	....	....	....	c. 836
c. 815	....	Jehoahaz		....	....	....	c. 815
812	....			BENHA-DAD III.	....	RAMMAN-NIRÂRI III.	812
c. 802	....	Jehoash	⎰	....	....	....	c. 802
c. 797	Amaziah	....	....	....	....	....	c. 797
c. 782	....	*Jeroboam II.*	....		....	SHALMAN-ESER III.	c. 782
c. 778	Uzziah	....	....	....	....	....	c. 778
c. 760	....	....	Amos	....	....	....	c. 760
754	....	....	....	....	....	ASSUR-NIRÂRI	754
745	....	....	....	....	....	TIGLATH PILESER III. (745–727)	745
c. 741	....	Zechariah	⎰	....	....	....	c. 741
c. 740	Jotham	*Shallum*	⎬	REZIN	....	....	c. 740
738	....	*Menahem*	⎬	....	....	....	738
c. 737	....	Pekahiah	⎬Hosea	....	....	....	c. 737
c. 736	Ahaz	Pekah	⎬	....	....	....	c. 736
c. 735	....	....	Syro-Ep hraimitish w ar			....	c. 735
c. 734	....	*Hoshea*	⎬Isaiah			....	c. 734
733	....	....	⎬	Damascus	taken by As syrians		733
c. 727	Hezekiah	....	⎬	....	....	SHALMAN-ESER IV.	c. 727
722	....	Fall of Sa-maria	⎭	Micah	....	....	722

TABLE III. *From the fall of Samaria* (722) *to the fall of Jerusalem.*

Date	Judah	Internal History	Syria, etc.	Assyria	Babylon	Egypt	Date
722	....	....	....	SARGON (722–705)	....	....	722
721	....	....	....	....	Merodach-baladan seizes Babylon	....	721
720	....	Isaiah and Micah	....	Battle of Raphia	....	....	720
715	....	....	....	....	....	Sabako king of Egypt	715
711	....	....	Ashdod	captured by	Sargon	....	711
705	....	....	....	SENNACHERIB	....	....	705
701	....	Revolt of Judah, Phoenicia and Philistia	....	Assyrian campaign in Palestine	....	.....	701
c. 695	Manasseh	....	....	....	....	....	c. 695
690	....	....	....	....	....	Tirhakah k. of Egypt	690
681	....	....	....	ESARHADDON	....	....	681
668	....	....	....	ASSURBANIPÂL	....	....	668
664	....	....	....	Assyrian campaigns in Egypt	....	Fall of Thebes	664
663	....	....	....	....	....	Psammitichus	663
c. 641	Amon	....	....	....	....	....	c. 641
c. 639	Josiah	....	....	....	....	....	c. 639
c. 630	....	....	Scythian invasion of Western Asia	....	....	....	c. 630
626	....	....	....	....	....	....	626
c. 625	....	? Zephaniah ? Nahum	....	....	NABOPOLASSAR founds the new Babylonian empire	....	c. 625
621	....	'Book of the Law' discovered	....	....	....	....	621
610	....	....	....	....	....	Necho II.	610
608	....	Josiah falls at battle of Megiddo	....	....	....	Battle of Megiddo	608
—	Jehoahaz	? Habakkuk Jeremiah	....	....	....	....	—
607	Jehoiakim	....	....	Fall of Nineveh	....	....	607
606	....	First deportation of Jews to Babylon	....	....	....	....	606
605	....	....	....	....	Egyptians defeated at Carchemish	....	605
604	....	....	....	....	Nebuchadnezzar (604–561)	....	604
597	Jehoiachin Zedekiah	....	....	....	....	....	597
586	....	Fall of Jerusalem. Ezekiel in Babylon	....	....	....	....	586

TABLE IV.

From destruction of Jerusalem to the second visit of Nehemiah.

Date	History of Jews	Babylon	Media and Persia	Greece	Date
586	Fall of Jeru-salem *Ezekiel* in Babylon	....	....	....	586
570 561	....	EVIL-MERODACH	....	Peisistratus at Athens	570 561
559 555	....	NERIGLISSAR NABONIDUS (555–538) and his son	Cyrus dethrones Astyages and conquers Media	....	559 555
550 549 547	*The 'second Isaiah'*	Belshazzar	....	Sardis captured by Cyrus	550 549 547
538	....	....	CYRUS enters Babylon	....	538
536	Return of Jews under Zerubba-bel and Joshua	....	....	....	536
529	....	....	CAMBYSES	....	529
521	....	....	DARIUS HYSTASPIS	Aeschylus b. 525	521
520	Building of Temple renewed. *Haggai* and *Zechariah* i.–viii.	....	....	....	520
516	Dedication of Temple	....	....	....	516
500	....	....	....	Ionian Revolt Sophocles b. 495	500
490	....	....	....	Battle of Marathon	490
485 480	....	....	XERXES Campaign of Xerxes against Greece	Battles of Thermopylae and Salamis Euripides b. 480	485 480
464 458 445	Ezra	....	ARTAXERXES I.	Pericles in power at Athens	464 458 445
444	Nehemiah Publication of Law-book. Re-building of walls ? *Malachi*	....	....	....	444
432	Nehemiah's second visit	....	....	Peloponnesian War (431)	432

TABLE V. *From Nehemiah to the Maccabaean rising.*

Date	Jewish History	Persia	Egypt	Syria	Greece	Date
424	....	Darius II.	....	....	....	424
413	Joiada High Priest	....	....	....	....	413
404	....	Artaxerxes Mnemon	....	....	....	404
373	Johanan H. P.	....	....	....	....	373
358	....	Darius Ochus	....	....	Philip king of Macedon (359)	358
c. 350	? *Book of Joel*	....	....	....	....	c. 350
341	Jaddua H. P.	....	....	....	....	341
336	....	Darius III. (Codomannus)	....	....	....	336
333	? *Isaiah* 24–27	Darius defeated at battle of Issus	....	....	....	333
332	? *Zechar.* 9–14 ?*Jonah* (between 333–300)	....	....	....	Alexander in Syria and Egypt	332
323	....	....	Ptolemy Lagides obtains Egypt	....	Death of Alexander	323
321	Onias I. H. P.	....	....	....	....	321
320	Jerusalem captured by Ptolemy	....	....	....	....	320
314	....	....	....	....	....	314
312	Palestine a *Syrian* province	....	....	Seleucus Nicator	....	312
302	Palestine retaken by Ptolemy	....	....	....	....	302
301	....	....	Battle of Ipsus	....	....	301
300	Simon the Just H. P.	....	....	....	....	300
284	....	....	Ptolemy Philadelphus	....	....	284
250	Onias II. H. P.	....	*LXX.* version of *O.T. begun*	....	....	250
246	....	....	Ptolemy Euergetes	....	....	246
223	....	....	....	Antiochus III. (the Great)	....	223
221	....	....	Ptolemy Philopator	....	....	221
217	Simon II. H. P.	....	....	....	....	217
204	....	....	Ptolemy Epiphanes	....	....	204
198	....	....	....	Antiochus annexes Palestine	....	198
195	Onias III.H.P.	....	....	....	....	195
187	....	....	....	Seleucus Philopator	....	187
176	Heliodorus attempts to plunder the Temple	....	....	....	....	176
175	Onias deposed Jason H. P. Palestine again a *Syrian* province	....	....	Antiochus IV. (Epiphanes)	....	175
170	....	....	....	Antiochus in Egypt	....	170
169	Jerusalem attacked by Antiochus	....	....	....	....	169
168	Daily sacrifice suspended	....	....	....	....	168
167	Maccabaean rising	....	....	....	....	167
166	Victory of Judas Maccabaeus at Emmaus	....	....	....	....	166

TABLE VI.

From Judas Maccabaeus to the death of Herod.

Date	Jewish History	Egypt	Syria	Rome	Date
166	*The Book of Daniel*	....	....	....	166
165	Syrians defeated by Judas at Beth-sur	....	....	....	165
—	Re-dedication of the Temple	....	....	....	—
164	....	....	Antiochus Eupator	....	164
162	Alcimus High Priest	....	Demetrius Soter	....	162
161	Nicanor defeated at Beth-horon	....	....	....	161
—	Defeat and death of Judas at Beth-sur	....	....	....	—
159	Death of Alcimus	....	....	....	159
153	Jonathan made H.P. by Balas	....	Alexander Balas set up against Demetrius	....	153
143	Simon (bro. of Jonathan) H. P.	....	....	....	143
142	Maccabaean commonwealth under Simon	....	....	....	142
135	John Hyrcanus	....	....	....	135
106	Aristobulus I. assumes title 'King of the Jews'	....	....	....	106
105	Alexander Jannaeus	....	....	....	105
78	Alexandra. Hyrcanus II. H. P.	....	....	....	78
69	Aristobulus II.	....	....	....	69
66	....	....	....	Pompey in Syria	66
63	Jerusalem taken by Pompey	....	....	....	63
57	....	....	....	Gabinius proconsul of Syria	57
51	....	Cleopatra	....	....	51
48	Antipater procurator of Judaea, Samaria and Galilee	....	....	Battle of Pharsalia	48
44	....	....	....	Caesar assassinated	44
43	Antipater murdered	....	....	....	43
42	....	....	....	Battle of Philippi	42
41	Herod and Phasael tetrarchs of Judaea	....	....	....	41
40	Herod at Rome: declared by senate 'King of the Jews'	....	....	....	40
37	Herod takes Jerusalem	....	....	....	37
31	....	....	....	Battle of Actium. Augustus supreme (31 B.C.—14 A.D.)	31
30	....	Death of Cleopatra. Egypt a Roman Province	....	....	30
4	Death of Herod	....	....	....	4
6 A.D.	Judaea annexed to province of Syria	....	....	....	6 A.D.

LIST OF CHIEF WORKS CONSULTED.

BENNETT, Prof. W. H. *A primer of the Bible* (Methuen, 1897).

CORNILL, Prof. Carl H. *History of the people of Israel.* 2nd edition (Kegan, Paul, Trench, 1899).

DILLMANN, Dr A. *Genesis critically and exegetically expounded.* Eng. Translation by Stevenson (T. and T. Clark, 1897).

DRIVER, Prof. S. R. *Introduction to the literature of the O.T.* [*LOT*]. 6th edition (T. and T. Clark, 1897).

    „   „   *Isaiah, his life and times* (Nisbet and Co.).

    „   „   Essay on 'Hebrew Authority' in *Authority and Archaeology, sacred and profane* (Murray, 1899).

Encyclopaedia Biblica, edited by T. K. Cheyne and J. Sutherland Black, vols. I. and II. (A. and C. Black, 1899).

HASTINGS, J. (edited by). *A Dictionary of the Bible* [*DB*], vols. I., II., and III. (T. and T. Clark, 1898).

Hexateuch, the, according to the revised version, edited by J. Estlin Carpenter and G. Harford Battersby (Longmans, Green and Co., 1900).

HOMMEL, Prof. F. *The ancient Hebrew tradition as illustrated by the monuments.* Eng. translation (S.P.C.K., 1897).

KITTEL, Prof. R. *A History of the Hebrews.* Eng. translation by Taylor (Williams and Norgate, 1895).

KIRKPATRICK, Prof. A. F. *The Divine Library of the O.T.* (Macmillan, 1891).

    „   „   *The first and second books of Samuel* (Camb. Bib. for Schools).

MONTEFIORE, C. G., *Lectures on the origin and growth of religion as illustrated by the religion of the ancient Hebrews* (Hibbert Lectures, 1892). 2nd edition (Williams and Norgate, 1893).

MOORE, Prof. G. H. *The Book of Judges* (Polychrome Bible. J. Clarke and Co., 1898).

PIEPENBRING, C. *Histoire du peuple d'Israel* (Librairie Grassart, Paris, 1898).

RYLE, Bp H. E. *The early narratives of Genesis* (Macmillan and Co., 1892).

    ,,   ,,   *The books of Ezra and Nehemiah* (Camb. Bib. for Schools, 1893).

SANDAY, Prof. W. *The oracles of God* (Longmans, Green and Co., 1891).

SAYCE, Prof. A. H. *The early history of the Hebrews* [*EHH*] (Rivingtons, 1897).

    ,,   ,,   *Fresh light from the ancient monuments* (Religious Tract Society, 1893).

    ,,   ,,   *The Higher Criticism and the monuments.* 5th edition (S.P.C.K., 1895).

SCHULTZ, Dr Hermann. *The theology of the O.T.* 2nd English edition (T. and T. Clark, 1895).

SCHÜRER, Dr Emil. *A history of the Jewish people in the time of Jesus Christ.* Eng. trans. by J. Macpherson (T. and T. Clark, 1896).

SMITH, Prof. G. A. *The historical geography of the Holy Land* [*HGHL*] (Hodder and Stoughton, 1897).

    ,,   ,,   *The Book of the Twelve Prophets* in *The Expositor's Bible* (Hodder and Stoughton, 1898).

SMITH, Prof. H. P. *A critical and exegetical commentary on the books of Samuel* in *International Critical Commentary* (T. and T. Clark, 1899).

SMITH, Prof. W. Robertson. *The Old Testament in the Jewish Church* [*OTJC*]. 2nd edition (A. and C. Black, 1892).

    ,,   ,,   *The Prophets of Israel* (A. and C. Black, 1882.)

WELLHAUSEN, Prof. J. *Sketch of the history of Israel and Judah.* 3rd edition (A. and C. Black, 1891).

INDEX I.

GENERAL.

INDEX II.

HEBREW AND OTHER SEMITIC WORDS.

Cambridge Uni

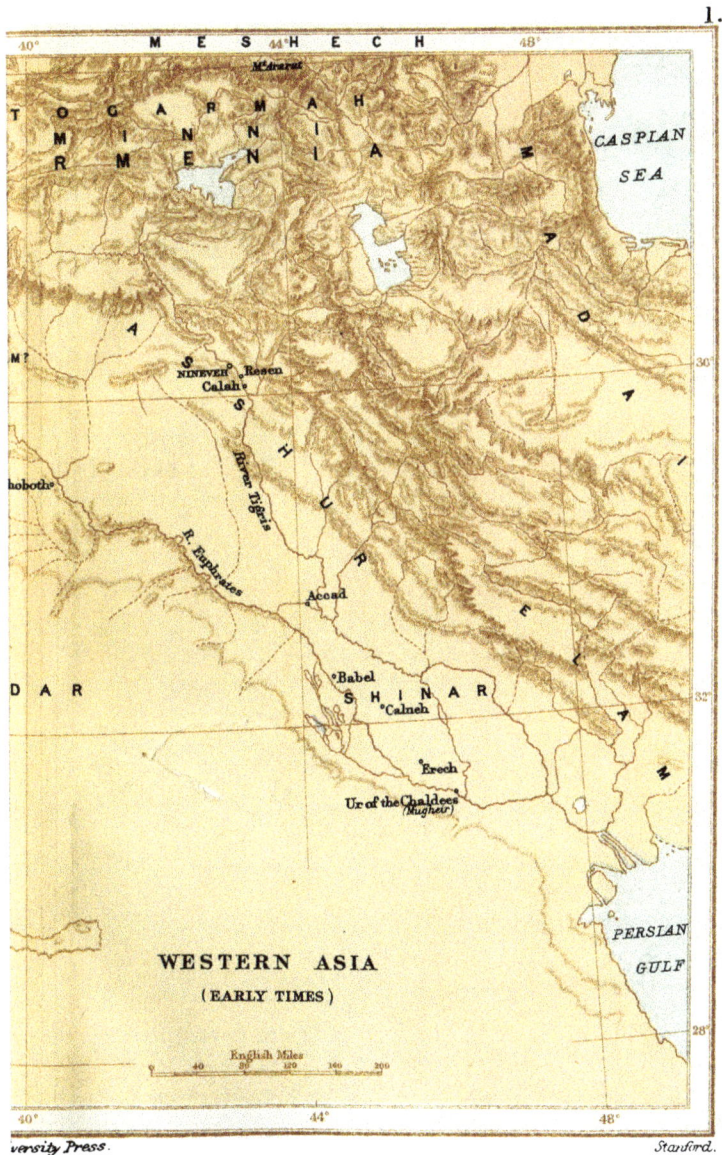

MES H E CH

M.t Ararat

TOGARMAH

A R M E N I A

M
R
M
A

CASPIAN
SEA

M?

A

NINEVEH Resen
Calah

M A D I A

Rehoboths

S
S
H
U
R

River Tigris

R. Euphrates

Accad

DAR

Babel

S
SHINAR
Calneh

E
L
A
M

Erech

Ur of the Chaldees
(Mugheir)

PERSIAN
GULF

WESTERN ASIA

(EARLY TIMES)

English Miles

40   80   120   160   200

EGYPT, SINAI
AND CANAAN

Scale of English Miles.

Probable Route of the Israelites

MEDITERRA

LUD

EGYPT

Zoan
Tahpanhes

GOSHEN

Pithom

On

Memphis

River Nile

28

30

32

32

30

28

Cambridge Un

34

36

32

N E A N   S E A

Sidon

Tyre

Dan

Bethel

Ai

Jericho

Gaza

Ephrath

Arba

At Nebo

Kirjath Arba

Gerar

Beersheba

J. Sinah

Rehoboth

Desert of

Kadesh

J. el Magrah

30

Wilderness of Paran

or of

The Wanderings

Ezion Geber

Elath

28

ARABIA

Gulf of Akabah

J. Serbal

J. Katerin

Jebel Musa

Um Shomer

S I N A I

R E D   S E A

34

36

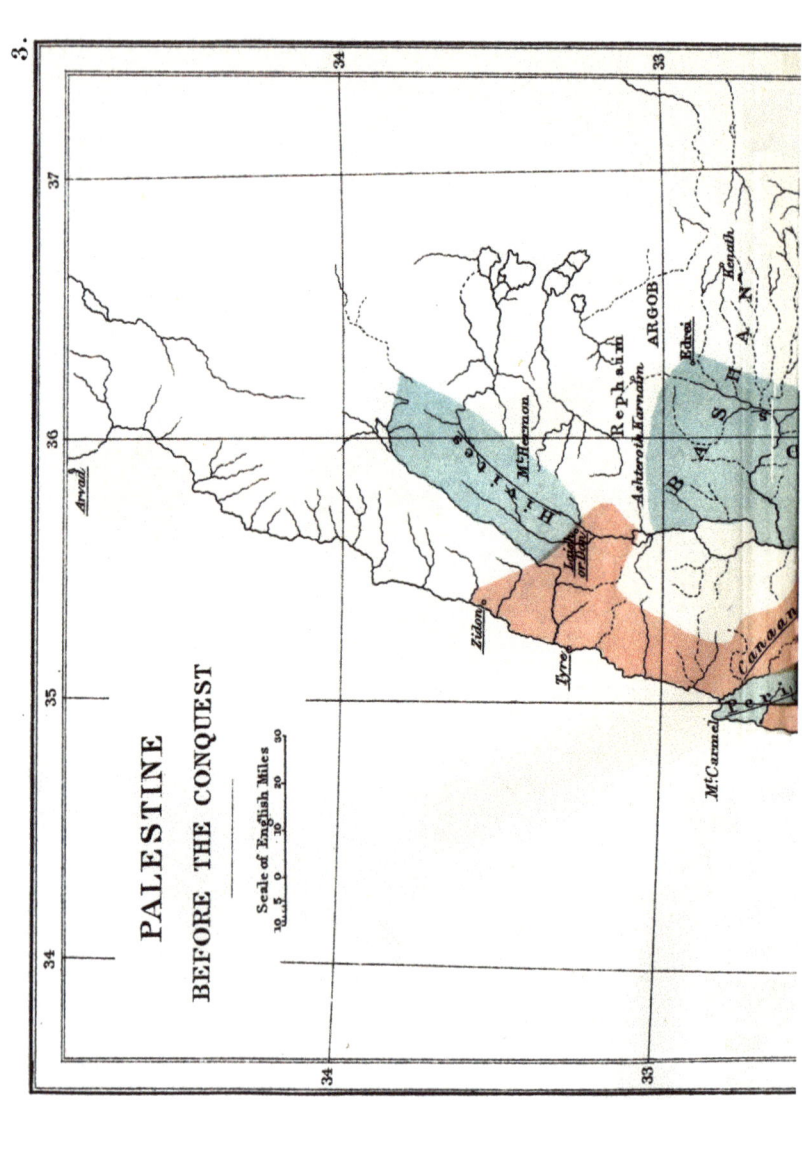

PALESTINE
BEFORE THE CONQUEST

Scale of English Miles

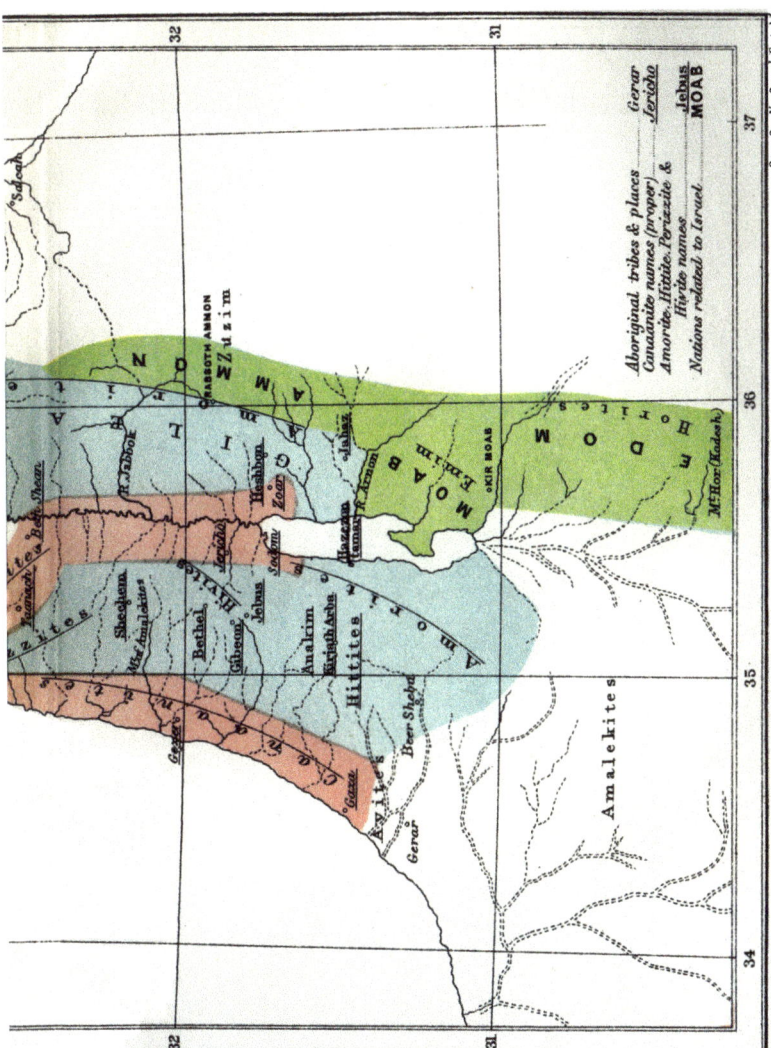

Aboriginal tribes & places .... Gerar
Canaanite names (proper) .... Jericho
Amorite. Hittite. Perizzite &
    Hivite names .... Jebus
Nations related to Israel .... MOAB

Stanford's Geog.¹ Estab.ᵗ

Cambridge University Press.

PHYSICAL MAP
OF
PALESTINE

Cambridge University Press.

PALESTINE
(OLD TESTAMENT)

Scale of Statute Miles

Roman Miles

The cities of refuge are underlined

GREAT SEA

ARAM · SYRIA

DAMASCUS

Mt. Hermon

B A S H A N

Havoth Jair

MANASSEH HALF TRIBE

Golan

GILEAD

Mahanaim

Ramoth

R. Jabbok

R. Jordan

Zidon

Tyre

Accho

Dor

Joppa

Zarephath

Kedesh Naphtali

Hazor

N A P H T A L I

A S H E R

Z E B U L O N

Waters of Merom

S. of Gennesaret

I S S A C H A R

MANASSEH HALF-TRIBE

E P H R A I M

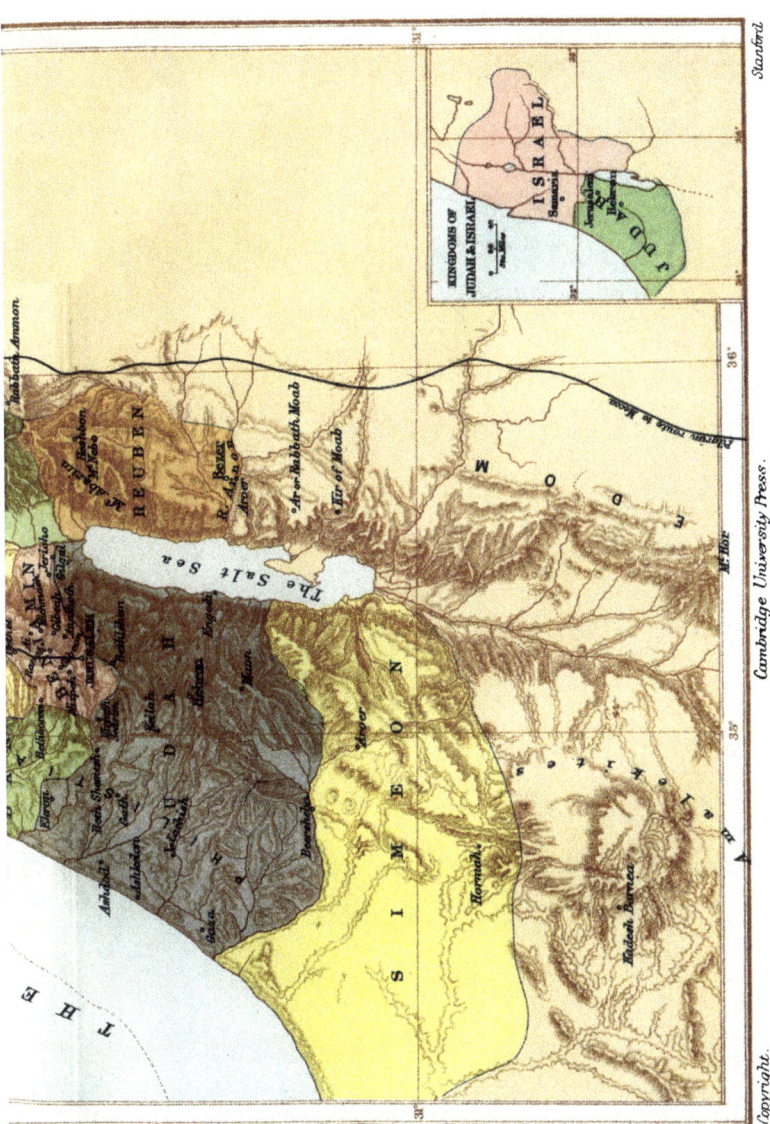

Cambridge University Press.

KINGDOMS OF
JUDAH & ISRAEL

ISRAEL

Samaria

JUDAH

Jerusalem
Hebron

REUBEN

Nahr Ammon

Rabbath Ammon

Bezer

Ar

Ir or Rabbath Moab

Dir of Moab

The Salt Sea

BENJAMIN

Jericho

JUDAH

Hebron

SIMEON

Hormah

Kadesh Barnea

THE

Pilgrim route to Mecca

M' Hor

EDOM

Amalekites

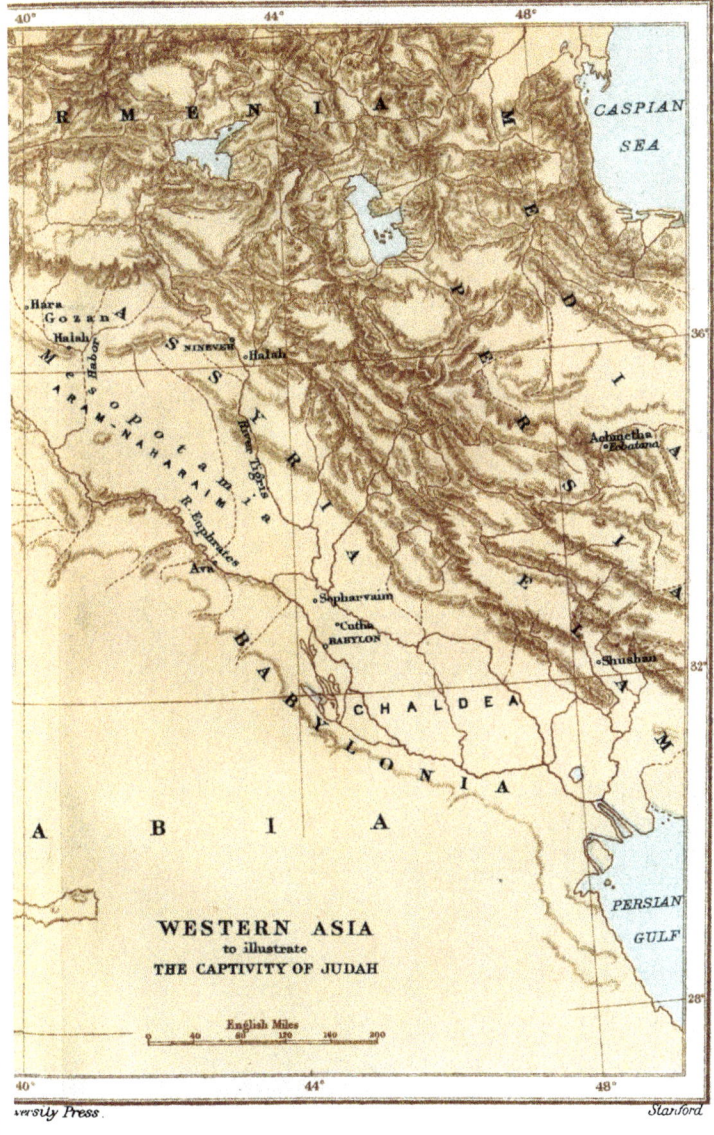

WESTERN ASIA
to illustrate
THE CAPTIVITY OF JUDAH

English Miles

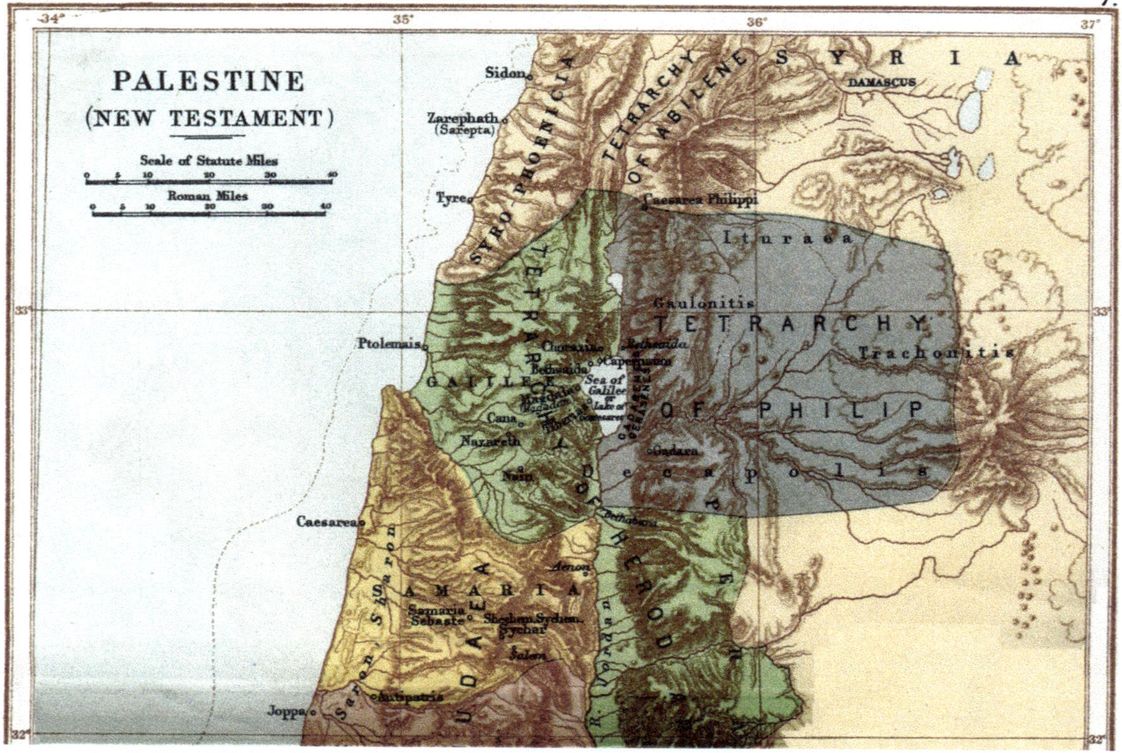

PALESTINE
(NEW TESTAMENT)

Scale of Statute Miles

Roman Miles

S Y R I A

DAMASCUS

T E T R A R C H Y   OF   ABILENE

Ituraea

TETRARCHY

Trachonitis

OF   PHILIP

Gaulonitis

D E C A P O L I S

Caesarea Philippi

SYRO PHOENICIA

Sidon

Zarephath o
(Sarepta)

Tyre

Ptolemais

GALILEE   TETRARCHY   OF   HEROD

Sea of
Galilee
Lake

Cana

Nazareth

SAMARIA

Samaria
Sebaste

Sychar
Sychem
Jacob's

Sharon's

Caesarea

Joppa

JUDAEA

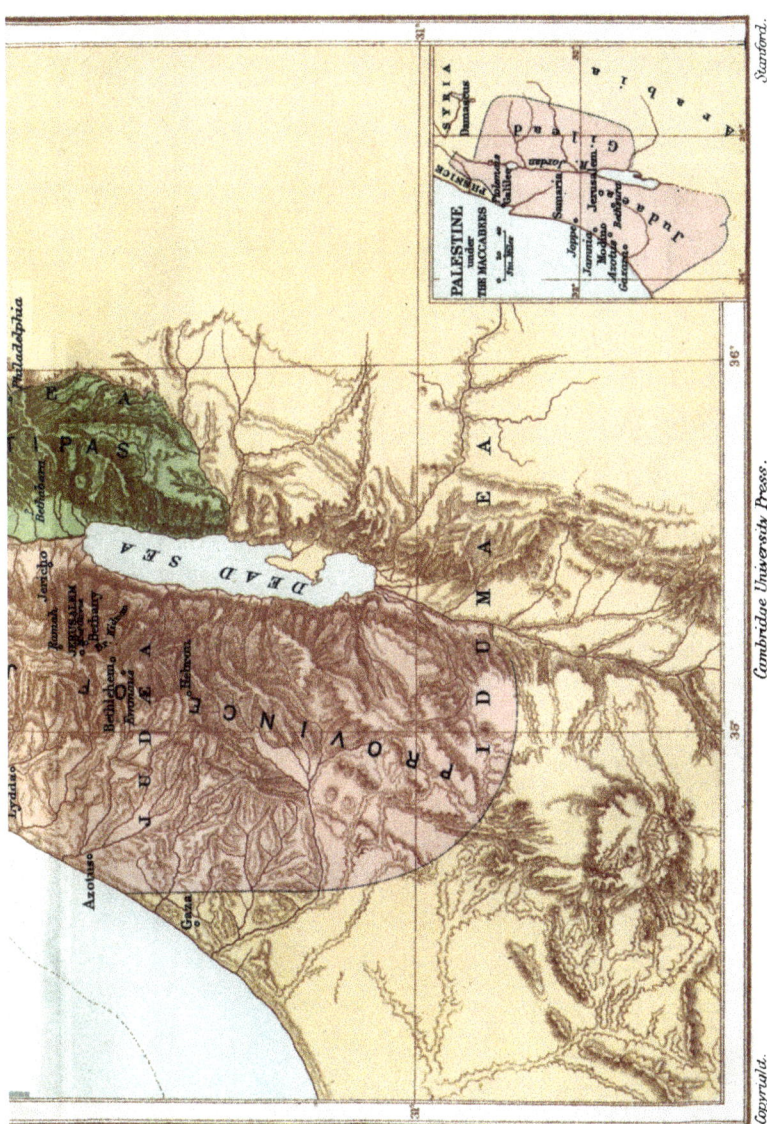

Cambridge University Press.

For EU product safety concerns, contact us at Calle de José Abascal, 56–1°,
28003 Madrid, Spain or eugpsr@cambridge.org.

www.ingramcontent.com/pod-product-compliance
Ingram Content Group UK Ltd.
Pitfield, Milton Keynes, MK11 3LW, UK
UKHW020507240426
470322UK00012B/252